Chess

FOR

DUMMIES®

3RD EDITION

by James Eade

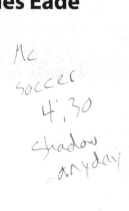

WILEY

John Wiley & Sons, Inc.

Chess For Dummies®, 3rd Edition

Published by
John Wiley & Sons, Inc.
111 River St.
Hoboken, NJ 07030-5774
www.wiley.com

Copyright © 2011 by John Wiley & Sons, Inc., Hoboken, New Jersey

Published simultaneously in Canada

For general information on our other products and services, please contact our Customer Care Department within the U.S. at 877-762-2974, outside the U.S. at 317-572-3993, or fax 317-572-4002.

For technical support, please visit www.wiley.com/techsupport.

Wiley also publishes its books in a variety of electronic formats and by print-on-demand. Some content that appears in standard print versions of this book may not be available in other formats. For more information about Wiley products, visit us at www.wiley.com.

Library of Congress Control Number: 2011936927

ISBN 978-1-118-01695-4 (pbk); ISBN 978-1-118-16235-4 (ebk); ISBN 978-1-118-16236-1 (ebk); ISBN 978-1-118-16237-8 (ebk)

Manufactured in the United States of America

10 9 8 7 6 5 4 3 2 1

About the Author

James Eade began taking chess seriously in 1972, when Bobby Fischer was taking the chess world by storm. He competed on his high school and college teams and became a United States Chess Federation (USCF) chess master in 1981. In 1984 he became a USCF correspondence chess master as well. International organizations awarded him the master title in 1990 (for correspondence) and in 1993 (for regular tournament play), but his chess-playing career has gradually given way to chess writing, organizing, and teaching.

James has written three other books on chess: *Remember the MacCutcheon* (Chess Enterprises), *San Francisco, 1995* (Hypermodern Press), and *The Chess Player's Bible* (Barron's). He has written numerous articles for a variety of magazines and has edited both the *Golden Gate Chess News* and the *California Chess Journal.*

In 1991 James began taking an interest in chess political organizations and was elected vice president of CalChess, the Northern California Chess Association, later that year. In 1995 he became CalChess president and was also elected to be president of the Chess Journalists of America. In 1996 he was elected to the USCF's policy board, the executive committee charged with oversight of the multi-million-dollar corporation. He was appointed zone president for the United States for the Fédération Internationale des Échecs (FIDE) from 2000 to 2002 and has served on the U.S. Charitable Chess Trust board of trustees since 2000. He was elected president of the Trust in 2010.

James holds a master's degree in organization development from the University of San Francisco and still bristles at being called a chess nerd.

Dedication

To Sheri — for suffering chess fools gladly.

Author's Acknowledgments

I would like to thank Sheri Anderson for all her encouragement and support throughout this writing project. I really appreciated the feedback I got from the first edition of *Chess For Dummies,* especially the input I received from George Mirijanian, Frisco Del Rosario, and Wayne Praeder.

My editors for the first edition, Bill Helling and Bill Barton, deserve a special thanks for drilling it into my head that not everyone knows Ruy Lopez from Nancy Lopez, and for keeping me on the straight and narrow. My thanks also go to the first edition's technical editor, John Peterson, who is a better friend than chess player — and he happens to be a very good chess player. I also wish to thank my editors for the second edition, Sherri Pfouts, Kristin DeMint, and Jon Edwards, for their help. I would like to thank my editors for the third edition, Georgette Beatty and Christy Pingleton, as well as my technical editor, Al Lawrence. Al is the former Executive Director of the USCF and made a number of first-rate contributions to this latest edition. M.L. Rantala was more than helpful with the glossary of terms, which I couldn't have done without her most able assistance.

I wish to thank my father, Arthur Eade, for teaching me chess, and my mother, Marilyn, for her touching advance order for the first edition. Lastly, a special thank-you to Lore McGovern, who was the wind at my back from start to finish.

Publisher's Acknowledgments

We're proud of this book; please send us your comments at http://dummies.custhelp.com. For other comments, please contact our Customer Care Department within the U.S. at 877-762-2974, outside the U.S. at 317-572-3993, or fax 317-572-4002.

Some of the people who helped bring this book to market include the following:

Acquisitions, Editorial, and Media Development

Senior Project Editor: Georgette Beatty

    (Previous Edition: Sherri Cullison Pfouts, Kristin DeMint)

Acquisitions Editor: Stacy Kennedy

Copy Editor: Christine Pingleton

    (Previous Edition: Kristin DeMint)

Assistant Editor: David Lutton

Editorial Program Coordinator: Joe Niesen

Technical Editor: Al Lawrence

Editorial Manager: Michelle Hacker

Editorial Assistants: Rachelle Amick, Alexa Koschier

Cover Photo: © iStockphoto.com/Floortje

Cartoons: Rich Tennant (www.the5thwave.com)

Composition Services

Project Coordinator: Patrick Redmond

Layout and Graphics: Corrie Socolovitch

Proofreaders: Rebecca Denoncour, Toni Settle

Indexer: BIM Indexing & Proofreading Services

Publishing and Editorial for Consumer Dummies

    Kathleen Nebenhaus, Vice President and Executive Publisher

    Kristin Ferguson-Wagstaffe, Product Development Director

    Ensley Eikenburg, Associate Publisher, Travel

    Kelly Regan, Editorial Director, Travel

Publishing for Technology Dummies

    Andy Cummings, Vice President and Publisher

Composition Services

    Debbie Stailey, Director of Composition Services

Contents at a Glance

Table of Contents

Introduction

• •

Some chess players hate to hear someone call chess a game. They think that doing so trivializes what is actually a profound intellectual activity. Try as they may, however, chess enthusiasts seem incapable of convincingly placing chess solely in the context of art, science, or sport. Uncannily, chess contains elements of all three — and yet chess remains a game.

Actually, I prefer to think of chess as a game — the best game ever invented. Chess is a game loved by engineers and free-verse poets alike. It imposes a set of rules and has finite limits, but just as you start to think that you're finally solving its mysteries, it thwarts you. As a result, sometimes the game is frustrating, but far more often, chess proves to be both surprising and delightful. The deeper you dig into chess, the more of its secrets you unearth — but interestingly enough, the game has never been tapped out. Even today's monster computers are far from playing the theoretically perfect chess game.

To master chess, you must combine a kind of discipline normally associated with the hard sciences and a creative freedom akin to the inspiration of artists. Few people develop both aspects equally well, and few activities can help you do so. Chess, however, is one such activity. The methodical scientist is forced to tap into his creative energies to play well. The fanciful artist must, in turn, conform to certain specific principles or face the harsh reality of a lost game. Not only is chess an excellent educational tool that helps strengthen both sides of your brain, but the game is also an endless source of pleasure.

After most people discover that I play chess, they usually say, "You must be very smart." They should instead say, "You must have a lot of spare time." Chess has been played throughout history by people with above-average leisure time, not necessarily by people with far-above-average intelligence — so if you don't consider yourself in the "I-aced-the-MCAT" crowd, fear no more.

As a matter of fact, chess tutors can teach preschoolers the rules of the game. (So maybe they can't get the tots to stop chewing on the pieces, but they *can* teach the youngsters how to play.) In fact, anyone can learn how to play chess with a bit of spare time. And you don't even need too much of that to learn the rules.

About This Book

This book is designed to help you become a better chess player in several ways:

- First, it contains a great deal of information and advice on how to play chess. You can read the book from cover to cover, or you can read only the sections or chapters that interest you — it's completely your call.

- You also find in these pages information about how to talk about chess, which, to many players, is at least as important as knowing how to play. (Part of the fun of chess is the social element involved in discussing other people's games — called *kibitzing.*)

- Finally, this book offers numerous suggestions on how to find other players who are just about at your own level (and how to mind your chess manners when you sit down to play!).

If you're a beginner, the great joys of chess await you. If you're an intermediate player, you can find in this book a wealth of material to help you improve your game and to enjoy chess even more.

Conventions Used in This Book

Throughout this book, I use diagrams of actual chessboards to show the positions I discuss. This convention should sometimes eliminate the need for you to have a chessboard and set in order to use the book — but even so, following along with an actual board and set is better. Just note that in these diagrams, the white pieces always start at the bottom of the chessboards, and the black pieces start at the top.

Here are a few other conventions to keep in mind:

- Throughout this book, I refer to moves with chess notation, which I usually place in parentheses. You can skip over this stuff if you don't want to find out how to decipher it, but if notation interests you, you can flip to Chapter 6 whenever you're up to the challenge. (Understanding it really isn't tough, though — believe me!)

- I use **boldface** to highlight the key words in bulleted lists and the action steps in numbered lists.

- I use *italics* whenever I define a chess term. You can use the glossary as a quick reference for these terms, as well as a resource to discover other chess words.

✔ I use `monofont` to point out any websites that I recommend.

When this book was printed, some web addresses may have needed to break across two lines of text. If that happened, rest assured that I haven't put in any extra characters (such as hyphens) to indicate the break. So, when using one of these web addresses, just type in exactly what you see in this book, pretending as though the line break doesn't exist.

✔ I alternate the use of male and female pronouns by chapter throughout this book. No gender bias is intended.

What You're Not to Read

Throughout this book, I use sidebars (in shaded gray boxes) to introduce famous chess players or to add miscellaneous information you don't really need to know to play chess. I've included this information to increase your sheer enjoyment of the game. If you're crunched for time, feel free to skip the sidebars.

Foolish Assumptions

I assume that either you want to learn how to play chess, or you already know how to play chess and want to get better. I also assume that you'll be able to find someone to help you if you're a beginner and have any problems with the material in this book. (And if you don't know anyone who can, I provide plenty of websites and computer programs that can help you navigate the road through the world of chess.) After all, everyone has to start somewhere.

How This Book Is Organized

I've organized this book into six parts so you can easily find just the information you need.

Part 1: Laying the Groundwork for Champion Chess

Chapter 1 briefs you about the game of chess and familiarizes you with the board. It assumes that you do have a chessboard and set. You may proceed in any case, because this chapter contains plenty of illustrations, but your best course is to work through the chapter with a board and set of your own. In that chapter, you walk through the basic setup of the chessboard and get the scoop on some of the basic chess terminology used more extensively in later chapters.

Chapter 2 provides an in-depth look at each piece in the chess set, detailing its strengths and weaknesses and how it moves. I also clue you in on the value of the pieces, relative to one another — you need to know this information in order to make wise decisions in your game.

Chapter 3 introduces you to the basic elements of a game of chess. You find out about material, space, development, and other chess elements. After reading this chapter, you can give a rough assessment of almost any chess position.

Chapter 4 points you toward your desired destination: checkmate. Here, I show you the basics on checkmate, and I also give you the rundown on a less decisive but still forceful move — check — as well as a scenario you want to avoid if you're on the winning end — stalemate, which is essentially a tie game (in chess, that situation is known as a *draw*).

Chapter 5 covers those rules of the game that are less commonly understood by most players. These rules start at least half the arguments that break out among beginning chess players, so taking a good look at them now may save you some unpleasantness.

Chapter 6 kicks your chess knowledge up a notch, explaining the mysterious system of chess notation and showing you how to record your games for posterity — or for anyone else you want to show the game. Understanding notation also enables you to read about various games that have been previously played.

Part II: Gaining Chess Know-How

Chapter 7 deals with different types of tactical situations and combinations of those tactics. Most games are lost by mistakes made in these areas, so pay careful attention to the information in this chapter. Chapter 8 deals with another important concept: sacrifices. Sometimes, taking a hit is a wise move in order to secure a greater advantage.

Pattern recognition plays a large role in chess, because certain configurations of pieces and pawns occur relatively frequently. If you already know the ideal way to play when these configurations occur, you don't have to reinvent the wheel every game. Chapter 9 deals with pattern recognition in general, while Chapter 10 examines commonly occurring pawn formations. Chapter 11 covers mating patterns, which are recurring themes that end in checkmate.

Part III: Game Time: Putting Your Chess Foot Forward

Chapter 12 introduces the general principles of play that form the basics of chess strategy. From there, I take you through the three phases of a chess game: the opening, middlegame, and endgame. Each phase has its own nuances, and you need to understand each of them in order to play a good game. Chapter 13 is devoted to the opening, Chapter 14 deals with the middlegame, and Chapter 15 covers the endgame.

Part IV: Getting into Advanced Action

In Chapter 16, I show you the competitive side of chess, giving you the ins and outs of the various kinds of competitions you can participate in and how to go about doing so. Here, I also point out some etiquette matters that you'll want to bear in mind when you find yourself in competitive play.

Chapter 17 surfs the information superhighway for computer and online chess opportunities and offers an account of what's out there now.

Part V: The Part of Tens

Chapters 18 and 19 make up the Part of Tens, where I do a top-ten countdown on aspects of the game of chess. Specifically, in Chapter 18, I discuss the ten most famous chess games of all time; in Chapter 19, I list the ten best chess players of all time, which is always a controversial subject.

Part VI: Appendixes

Finally, I provide a glossary at the end of this book (Appendix A), in case some of these odd chess terms don't get past your short-term memory and you need to refer to them at a later time. Appendix B lists some of the best chess resources and how to connect with them.

Icons Used in This Book

The icons used in this book point you to important topics and help you pick out what you want to know. Make a mental note of the following icons to guide you on your path to chess greatness.

If you're interested in chess matters that take you beyond the introductory level, this icon points the way.

This icon wouldn't be necessary if chess didn't have so many good, general rules. Keep the rules of thumb in mind when you play. You'll be surprised how many you can retain — and how helpful they can be.

This icon points to helpful hints — anything from playing better chess to where you can find more chess stuff.

This icon warns you of impending danger that you just may be able to avoid.

Where to Go from Here

If you have no knowledge of chess whatsoever, I highly suggest that you start right at the beginning with Chapter 1. Otherwise, just remember that it's perfectly okay to skip around the book to locate the chapters and sections of most interest or use to you. Dig in!

Part I

Laying the Groundwork for Champion Chess

"I'm pretty sure it's just a sprain. He castled pretty hard at the end of that last round."

In this part . . .

1n this part, I show you how to set up a chessboard and discuss the chess pieces and the ways they move. I also cover the fundamental elements of chess: the concepts of material, development, space, pawn structure, and king safety. I then foreshadow the end of the game as I define check, stalemate, and checkmate and show you what they look like in play. I wrap up this part by covering a few special chess moves, such as castling, and introducing chess notation, which is a written record of the moves in a game.

Chapter 1

Tackling Chess Basics

. . . .

In This Chapter

▶ Discovering what chess is all about

▶ Familiarizing yourself with the chessboard

▶ Setting up your army

. . . .

*1*f you're interested in participating in an endlessly fascinating and stimu-lating mental activity — an activity that sports a rich history and may pro-vide you with countless hours of amusement — you're in luck. You can play chess.

If you're new to chess, don't despair. No chess gene decides who can and can't play; take my word for it. Everyone can learn to play a passable game of chess, and after you come on-board (no pun intended!), it's just a matter of time until you find someone you can play well against.

In this chapter, I define the game of chess, discuss the basics of how you play, and describe the materials you need.

Chesstacular! Understanding the Basics of the Game

Chess, simply stated, is a board game for two — one player uses white pieces, and the other uses black. Each player gets 16 pieces to maneuver. Players take turns moving one piece at a time, with the ultimate objective of checkmating their opponent's king.

Because chess has so many great rules and because the pieces all exercise their individuality with different moves and abilities, the game has lots of interesting nuances that you'll want to keep in mind as you play. I cover each aspect of the game in this book, so if you're a novice, you'll find sufficient infor-mation to get acquainted with chess; if you already know how to play but want to hone your prowess, you'll find plenty of information to help you do just that. This section gives you the nutshell version of all this book has to offer.

The underlying concepts

Components of a chess game can be broken down into categories that are so fundamental that they're referred to as *elements*. The element of time, known as *development,* is one example. The element of force, known as *material,* is another. If one player deploys more force more quickly than the other player, it may be impossible for the latter player to defend against a subsequent invasion. The first step in a player's progress is learning how the pieces move, so I cover the bases in Chapter 2. Gaining an appreciation of the importance of the game's elements is usually the next step, so I describe all the chess elements in Chapter 3.

The elements are all a part of what drives a game to the desired end result: *checkmate.* If the king is attacked and can't escape the attack, the aggressor has secured checkmate, and the game is over. However, checkmate doesn't always come to fruition — sometimes a game ends in *stalemate,* which is one way to draw. You can also have a situation called *check,* which is an attack on the king. One thing to note, however, is that placing your opponent in check doesn't necessarily mean you'll win — check can actually happen several times in a game, and if your opponent can effectively escape from check, you may just be wasting your time. I discuss all of these events in Chapter 4.

You also have some special moves at your disposal that your opponent (if she's a novice) may not know about — namely, en passant, promotion, and castling. To give you an edge (and a resource to help quell any arguments that may arise after you make one of these tricky moves!), I provide the inside scoop on these special moves in Chapter 5.

To make it easier to talk about what's happening on the board, someone somewhere at some point in time came up with a naming system for the exact pieces and squares, and I use those conventions throughout this book. In Chapter 6, I dive into the subject of *notation,* which expands on these naming conventions and shows you how to write the moves of a game. You really don't need to know this stuff to enjoy playing chess, but it does help to have the basic terminology under your belt, and throughout this book, you can read the extra notation information I give to you as I explain moves.

The finer points of the game

Holding an advantage in one or more of the elements of chess doesn't guarantee victory. It does, however, increase the likelihood of success. When the inevitable clash of opposing armies takes place, the resulting tactical possibilities generally favor the one with elemental advantages. These clashes usually feature common tactics and combinations such as the ones that I present in Chapter 7. Tactics decide the outcome of most of the games played at a fairly competitive level, so a good understanding of the basic tactics and combinations pays off extremely well.

One of the ways an advantage can be transformed into victory is through sacrifice. A game of chess is a constant process of giving up something to get something else. Giving up some of your force makes sense, for example, if doing so allows you to checkmate the enemy king. Chapter 8 provides examples of when sacrifices are justified.

Another key to playing chess well is the ability to recognize patterns. When you spot a pattern with which you're familiar, the right moves suddenly suggest themselves. Chapter 9 deals with building pattern recognition in chess.

Due to the starting lineup and the piece movement limitations, only the knight can move at the start of the game, so you have to move some pawns in order to get your other pieces out. The positioning of the pawns often determines the optimal positioning of the pieces. Certain pawn positions, or *formations* as players often call them, have occurred in so many games that they have their own names. Chapter 10 presents some of the more common ones and shows how the pawns guide you on where to put the pieces.

Chapter 11 illustrates a number of common ways to deliver checkmate. These types of checkmates appear so often in chess games that players refer to them as *mating patterns*.

There usually comes a time in every player's development when she's at a loss as to what to do next. Sometimes a player will see a move by a stronger player and have no idea why that move was made. At this point, the principles of play, or strategies, are necessary to make further progress. Chapter 12 provides an introduction to chess strategy.

The militaristic character of chess is undeniable, but it also holds appeal for the confirmed peacenik. Although many of the strategies of war apply equally well to chess (divide and conquer, for example), many people gain ascetic pleasure from playing or watching a well-played game. Well-known patterns can appear with an unexpected twist and delight the observer. At an advanced level, you'll discover harmonies that lie just below the surface of the moves, and a move that breaks that harmony will feel as discordant as an off-key note in music. So take heart, consider the information this book provides, and allow yourself to get comfortable with the pieces, their powers, and all the exciting aspects of this strategic, creative game. Besides, unlike real warfare, the worst you'll suffer in your chess career is a bruised ego.

Three parts that make a whole

Players divide the chess game into three phases — opening, middlegame, and endgame — to better understand the different demands of each one, but you really need to understand the game as a whole and not just in terms of its separate parts. Otherwise, playing the game can be a bit like eating Chinese food with one chopstick.

Here's a quick breakdown of what each phase entails (see Chapters 13 through 15 for an in-depth look):

- ✔ **The opening:** The main objective of the opening moves is to effectively activate your forces. The term *development* refers to this type of activation.

- ✔ **The middlegame:** This phase is where the opposing armies most frequently clash. The terms *tactics* and *combinations* are frequently used to describe these clashes.

- ✔ **The endgame:** By this phase, the forces have been greatly reduced in number, but checkmate hasn't yet been delivered.

Different ways to get your game on

If you're the type of player who wants to be tested in competition, check out Chapter 16. Chess tournaments come in a variety of flavors, and that chapter gives you the scoop. You need to know how to act as well as how to play, so I also cover chess etiquette in that chapter.

In this day and age, you don't need to be physically located next to an opponent in order to play, and Chapter 17 gives the lowdown on computer chess and chess in cyberspace. Chess on the Internet has blossomed, but you need to be aware that nothing is permanent. Although the web is ever-changing, the addresses I provide have proven to be very stable, so they should take you where you want to go.

Chessboard Chatter: Bringing Home a Board and Chess Set

So you've decided all this chess stuff is up your alley. Well, first things first — you need a chessboard and *chess set* (the collection of chess pieces). If you don't own a board and chess set, you can turn to Appendix B for mail-order information. You'll find it extremely helpful to have a board and chess set on hand when reading chess books. Some people can do without one — but some people can memorize the works of John Milton, too. (And who wants to be like that?)

In the following sections, I explain different types of boards and chess sets that are available, and I break down the layout of the board.

Throughout this book I include numerous diagrams to help you understand the game, but they don't take the place of a real set and board; these diagrams serve primarily to make certain your board is set up correctly. I urge you to get out your chessboard and set when you're reading and set up the board as the diagrams show you. That way, you get a real-life view of the moves I describe.

Finding the right board and set

Your first challenge in finding a chessboard and set is to sort through the many available types. A tremendous range in sizes, colors, and quality exists.

The name of the standard design, which is distinguished by the look of the pieces, is the Staunton. This design bears the name of the great English player Howard Staunton and was registered in 1849. Its popularity was so great that it was adopted as the one and only design allowed in official tournaments. If you play with strangers and bring anything other than a Staunton-designed set, people may assume that you're trying to psych them out by using equipment that they aren't familiar with. You probably don't want to start off on the wrong foot.

Wood sets and boards in the Staunton design are more popular at higher levels of competition, but a typical tournament set can be made of plastic pieces in classic white and black. The board is generally of a vinyl roll-up variety with white and green squares. "Why not black squares?" you may justifiably ask. "Headaches," I would answer. I've learned that staring at a high-contrast board is not advisable. Miniature traveling sets are the only exception. It doesn't matter what color they are, because the makers assume that you won't be staring at them too long (especially if you're driving!).

If price is no object, wood pieces and boards are the way to go. Wood boards provide the most soothing background possible, and the weight and feel of wood pieces are generally far more satisfying to the touch. In case you're really getting into chess and admire sets meant to be looked at rather than played with, collectible sets have a small cottage industry of their own, and these sets vary in design as well as in quality.

Getting up close and personal with your board

After you pick up your soon-to-be-beloved chessboard and set, you need to get familiar with them. The first thing to notice about the chessboard is that all the squares are the same size but alternate between two colors (a light color and a darker color). Colors are important in chess (bishops are confined to only one of them, knights go back and forth between them, and so on), which is why chess players insist that a white square needs to be in the lower right-hand corner at the start of the game. Start by whipping out the board and making sure it's facing the right direction in front of you — Figure 1-1 shows the correct orientation (if you set this book on your lap and look at the figure, you get a better idea).

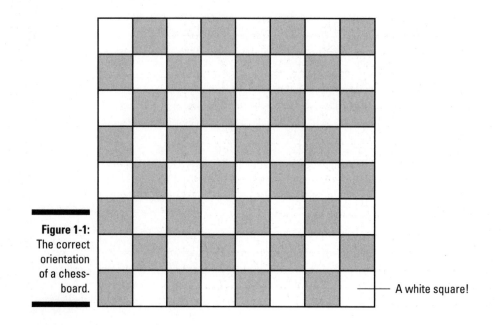

Figure 1-1:
The correct
orientation
of a chess-
board.

A white square! —

A white square should be in the lower right-hand corner as you face the board. The most common mistake among beginners is to position the board incorrectly at the start of the game. (As a matter of fact, Hollywood makes this common mistake, too. Whenever you see a chessboard positioned in a movie, check to see whether the lower right-hand square is white. Chances are it won't be!)

Consider a few fun facts while you're scoping out your chessboard:

- It's made up of 64 squares evenly divided between 32 light squares and 32 dark squares.

- It's symmetrical and square — in the geometric sense.

- The square comprises eight *ranks* and eight *files* (and a bunch of diagonals), which you'd normally call rows and columns (and diagonals!), but chess people shun such conventional language. (Using clear, easy-to-understand terms would be too easy, right?)

In the following sections, I go into more detail on the ranks, files, diagonals, and squares.

Recognizing the ranks

Ranks are rows that go from side to side across the chessboard and are referred to by numbers. Each chessboard has eight ranks, which are numbered from the *bottom* of the board (where the white pieces start) on up; see Figure 1-2.

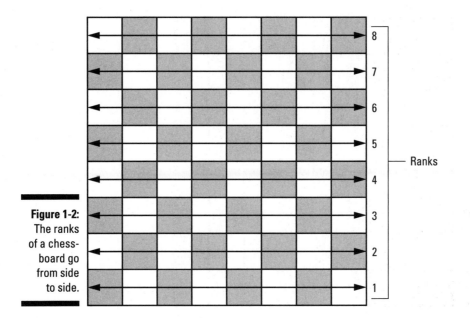

Ranks

Figuring out the files

Files are columns that go up and down the chessboard, and each board has eight of them. Because numbers indicate ranks, letters indicate files, which are labeled from left to right. Figure 1-3 shows the files.

Naming individual squares

The naming convention for ranks and files allows you to give a unique identifier to every square by using what chess people call the *file-first method.* For example, the lower right-hand square (which is white, of course) is called h1. This name is shorthand for h-file, first rank. Figure 1-4 gives the name for every square.

When figuring out the names of individual squares, it may be helpful to think of the games *Bingo* and *Battleship,* where every square has a letter and a number (and the names may be easier to figure out if you're sitting on the "white" side — or bottom — of the chessboard). Of course, in *Battleship* you get to see only your pieces and have to guess where your enemy's are. In chess, however, you know where your opponent's pieces are — you just have to guess where he's going to move them!

Digging those diagonals

As you probably expect, diagonals have names, too. Unlike ranks and files, diagonals are defined by their starting and ending squares. The starting square is conventionally given as the one with the lower rank. For example, Figure 1-5 shows the h1-a8 diagonal. Diagonals are always composed of like-colored squares. You can have light-squared diagonals and dark-squared diagonals — but never two-toned ones.

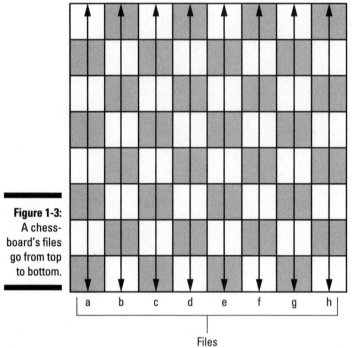

Figure 1-3:
A chess-board's files go from top to bottom.

a b c d e f g h

Files

Figure 1-4:
The squares are marked to show the letter of the file and the number of the rank.

	a	b	c	d	e	f	g	h
8	a8	b8	c8	d8	e8	f8	g8	h8
7	a7	b7	c7	d7	e7	f7	g7	h7
6	a6	b6	c6	d6	e6	f6	g6	h6
5	a5	b5	c5	d5	e5	f5	g5	h5
4	a4	b4	c4	d4	e4	f4	g4	h4
3	a3	b3	c3	d3	e3	f3	g3	h3
2	a2	b2	c2	d2	e2	f2	g2	h2
1	a1	b1	c1	d1	e1	f1	g1	h1
	a	b	c	d	e	f	g	h

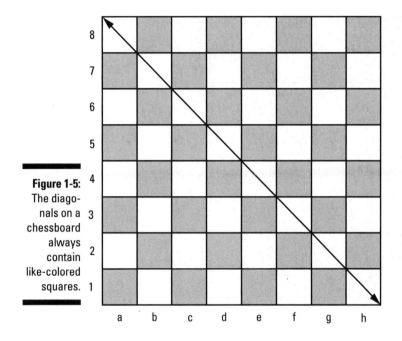

Piecemeal: Putting the Pieces on the Board

To depict the chessboard in a way that everyone around the world can understand, chess players have developed a set of symbols to represent the chessmen. Each may be represented by a one-letter abbreviation or by an icon. (See Table 1-1 for a list of all the pieces and their symbols.)

Table 1-1	Chess Pieces and Their Symbols	
Piece	*Symbol*	
King	♚	♔
Queen	♛	♕
Knight	♞	♘
Bishop	♝	♗
Rook	♜	♖
Pawn	♟	♙

I use the piece symbols here to show you how to set up the board, and I use them throughout this book to demonstrate various moves and positions. You may find it helpful to set up your own board piece by piece.

Start with the corners. The rooks go on the corner squares, as shown in Figure 1-6.

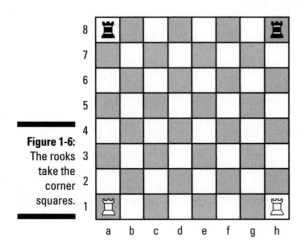

Figure 1-6: The rooks take the corner squares.

Next come the knights. Place them next to the rooks (see Figure 1-7).

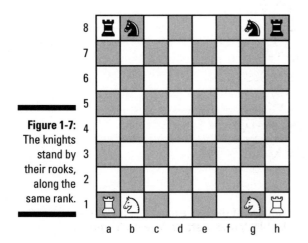

Figure 1-7: The knights stand by their rooks, along the same rank.

Then put the bishops on the board next to the knights (see Figure 1-8).

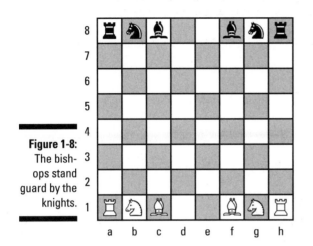

Figure 1-8:
The bishops stand guard by the knights.

After the bishops come the queens. Your board should now look like the one in Figure 1-9.

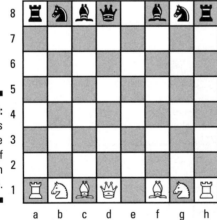

Figure 1-9:
The queens perch on the squares of their own shade.

The queens always start on a square of the same shade — the white queen starts on a light square, and the black queen starts on a dark square.

Next, place the kings next to the queens, which is only fitting (see Figure 1-10).

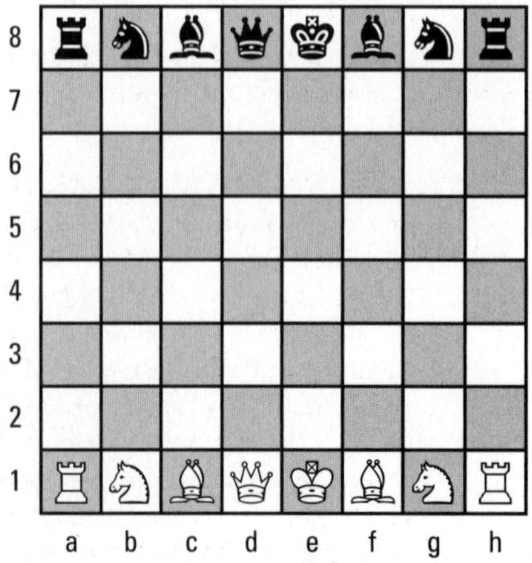

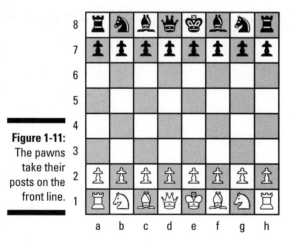

Figure 1-10:
The kings take their thrones, next to their ladies.

Finally, add the pawns straight across the rank in front of the other pieces, as shown in Figure 1-11.

Figure 1-11:
The pawns take their posts on the front line.

If you set up your chessboard by using the preceding directions and it looks like the finished one in Figure 1-11, pat yourself on the back! You're ready for a game.

A trip back in time: The origins of chess

The true origins of chess are shrouded in the mists of prehistory, which is good because it allows people to say just about anything they want about how the game started without fear of contradiction. From the evidence that does exist, the best guess is that chess, or a game very much like it, originated in Northern India sometime around A.D. 600 and eventually migrated to Europe through China and Persia (modern-day Iran). The ancient Indian game was based on Indian armies and was undoubtedly a pastime for their rulers.

No doubt, this game, called *chaturanga,* was much like present-day chess. It was played on an 8-x-8-square board and used six different kinds of pieces. The Indian Army was led by the *rajah* (king) and his chief advisor, the *mantri,* sometimes referred to as the *vizier.* The army was represented by foot soldiers, cavalry, chariots, and elephants, and the game had corresponding pieces for all these leaders and warriors.

By the time the game got to Europe, it had changed considerably and continued to change until about the end of the 15th century. The changes basically made the game more familiar to the Europeans who were then playing it. The rajah became the king, the mantri the queen, the foot soldiers the pawns, the cavalry the knights, the chariots the rooks, and the elephants the bishops. Since that time, the game has been essentially stable. Nowadays, chess is played all over the world by the same rules established in Europe in the 15th century, under the control of the Fédération Internationale des Échecs (FIDE), which is French for the International Chess Federation.

Chapter 2

Getting to Know the Pieces and Their Powers

· ·

In This Chapter

▶ Speeding along with the rook

▶ Seeing the bishop outside church

▶ Kissing the queen's hand and bowing before the king

▶ Mounting the knight

▶ Giving the pawn the time of day

· ·

*A*fter years of teaching chess to elementary school children, I think I've found the easiest way to introduce the pieces. So in this chapter I use the same method. I start with the rook because its simple up, down, and side-to-side movement is easy to grasp. Then I move on to the bishop because it, too, moves in straight lines and boldly goes where the rook can't. Kids seem to pick up these ideas right away. And what's good for kids is certainly good for older students of the game, right?

After you understand the moves of the rook and the bishop, figuring out how the queen moves is a breeze. The queen simply has the combined powers of the rook and bishop. And the king follows his queen. He moves just like her, except only one square at a time. I leave the knight and the pawn for the end because they're the trickiest to explain.

Keep in mind that chess is a science when you consider the pieces in isolation from one another, but it approaches an art when you combine the pieces in various ways. All pieces like to have company, but they're fickle; for example, sometimes a queen and a knight are happy together, and sometimes they aren't. No easy rules explain this relationship. The chess genius seems to know how to make the pieces work together seamlessly, but everyone else has to muddle along by trial and error. In Chapter 3, I consider the elements of chess from the scientific and artistic viewpoints — in isolation from one another and in combinations.

Acting Like a Chariot: The Rook

Sure, you may believe the rook is a tower or castle, but au contraire! In the history of chess, the rook actually developed from the chariot: This piece is both fast and strong, and therefore of considerable value. The rook appears a bit squatter than the other pieces, which partly accounts for the perception of it as a heavy piece (see the sidebar "Weighing in on chess heavies," later in this chapter).

This heavy aspect can be taken too far, of course. The rook is far from a plodding piece, and the player who gets his rooks into the game most effectively often turns out to be the winner. Unfortunately, this piece begins the game tucked into a corner and usually has to wait for the other pieces to settle into their preferred squares before receiving any attention.

Figure 2-1 shows where the rooks go on the chessboard.

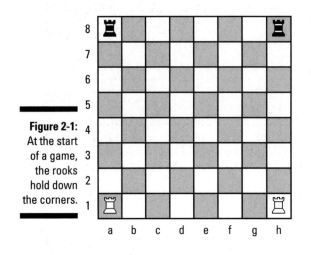

Figure 2-1:
At the start
of a game,
the rooks
hold down
the corners.

The rook has the freedom to move any number of squares, but only in straight lines up and down or side to side, as indicated by the rook on d5 in Figure 2-2a. Again, think of the chariot. After a chariot gets ahea d of steam, turning corners isn't easy. Have you ever seen *Ben-Hur?* The rook moves just like the chariot in that movie, but without the spikes.

In Figure 2-2b, you can see that the rook can't move to a square occupied by one of its own pieces, in this case another rook on f5 — nor can it jump over the piece and move to any of the other squares along that rank.

In Figure 2-3a, a white rook and a black rook are ready for battle. The white rook can't move beyond the black rook along that rank, but it can *capture* it by removing the black piece and taking its place, as in Figure 2-3b. (In chess

notation, this move is written 1. Rxf5 — see Chapter 6 for details on notation.) This concept is the same for the other chessmen (and woman) with the
exception of the king, which is immune to capture. But don't think that you
have to capture when given the opportunity. This isn't checkers!

When new players discover the power of the rook, they sometimes decide to
move the pawns that are in front of the rooks forward at the beginning of the
game (these pawns are known as the *rook pawns*). This action has the advantage of increasing the space available to the rook but is usually a poor way
to open the game. The rook must retreat when attacked by an enemy pawn,
knight, or bishop because it's too valuable to be lost in exchange for one of
them. Time is then lost shuffling the rook to and fro while the enemy pieces
come out in force. The best strategy, especially early in the game, is to move
a minimum number of pawns, get the minor pieces (knights and bishops) out,
and only then move on to the rooks.

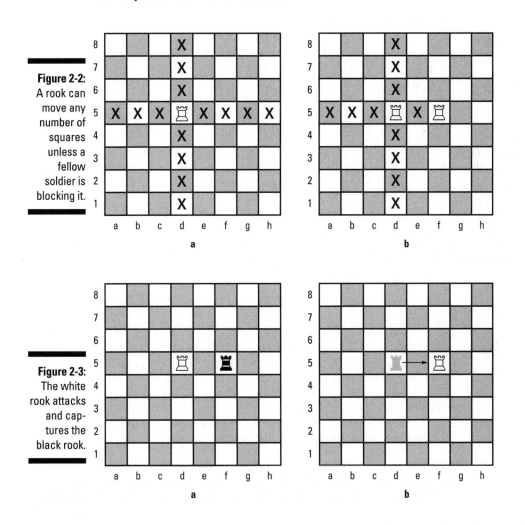

Figure 2-2:
A rook can
move any
number of
squares
unless a
fellow
soldier is
blocking it.

Figure 2-3:
The white
rook attacks
and cap-
tures the
black rook.

Weighing in on chess heavies

The rook and the queen are sometimes referred to as *heavy* or *major* pieces, because the rook and the queen, assisted by their own king, can checkmate an enemy king by themselves (see Chapter 4 for a discussion of checkmate). Minor pieces — a knight or a bishop — can't checkmate an enemy king with only their own king for assistance.

Showing Off Slender Curves: The Bishop

The bishop has a slender waist so it can slide between squares along diagonals. (Actually, I don't really know why the bishop was designed like that, but that's always how I've thought of it.) The bishop is called a *minor piece* because you can't deliver checkmate with just a bishop and its king. Go ahead, set up a board and try it (you may want to check out Chapter 4 first). If you can do it, you'll become world-famous, and I'll include you in the next edition of this book.

Figure 2-4 shows the bishops and where they start on the chessboard.

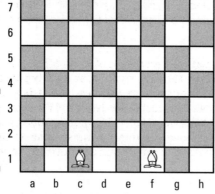

Figure 2-4: The bishops take their marks.

A bishop can move any number of squares, but only along the diagonals and until another piece gets in its way. If that piece is the opponent's, the bishop can capture it, of course, by displacing it.

Figure 2-5a indicates some possible bishop moves. Unlike the rook (which I describe in the previous section), the attacking power of the bishop depends on where the piece is located on the chessboard and ultimately its mobility or *scope,* which is simply the number of squares it can move to. The bishop attacks more squares in the center, so it's more powerful when positioned there. Unfortunately, it's also more easily attacked there. You can see in Figure 2-5a that the bishop attacks 13 squares. How many squares does it attack in Figure 2-5b? (The correct answer is 9 — don't count the square that it occupies.)

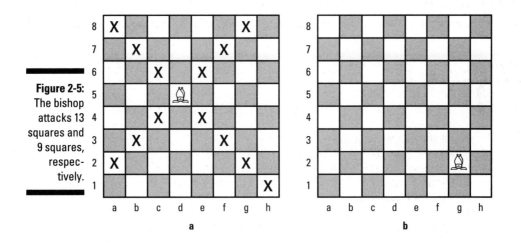

Figure 2-5: The bishop attacks 13 squares and 9 squares, respectively.

You can tell by looking at the board that some diagonals are longer than others. The diagonals that cross the board's center are longer than the ones that bisect the corners. Because the bishop doesn't like hand-to-hand combat, players often position the bishop out of the way along a long diagonal, as in Figure 2-5b.

The bishop also has a unique natural restriction of its mobility: If it starts on a light square, it remains forever on the light squares, and if it begins the game on a dark square, it must always stay on dark squares. The bishop is color-bound by birth! Fully half the board is forbidden territory! For that reason, chess people speak of having "the two bishops." In tandem, bishops can theoretically cover the entire board. However, they can never come to their comrade's aid directly, and bishops on the same team can never compensate for each other's loss.

This quality is so unusual that a special category in chess endings, called the *opposite-color bishop ending,* exists. This ending arises when each side remains with one bishop, but the bishops are on different-colored squares and are thereby sentenced to roam their own mutually exclusive halves of the board. Figure 2-6 illustrates this type of ending. These bishops are close to one another — they can get close enough to blow each other kisses — but never close enough to capture one another. (Flip to Chapter 15 for full details on chess endings.)

The bishop, like the rook, can be blocked by its own army. In fact, the least desirable placement of the bishop is behind pawns of its own color: Pawns (which I discuss later in this chapter) are the least mobile of the chessmen and can render the bishop nearly powerless, as shown in Figure 2-7a. A bishop blocked behind its own pawns is often called a "bad bishop." Enemy pawns can also restrict the bishop's mobility, as in Figure 2-7b.

However, restricting a bishop with pawns isn't always effective, because the bishop may be able to capture one of the enemy pawns. Just look at Figures 2-8a and 2-8b to see how (in chess notation, this move is written 1. Bxf3 — see Chapter 6 for details).

TIP

If you plan on using your pawns to restrict a bishop's mobility — which is a good thing to do, as long as you aren't restricting your own bishops — you'd better make certain that the pawns are adequately defended!

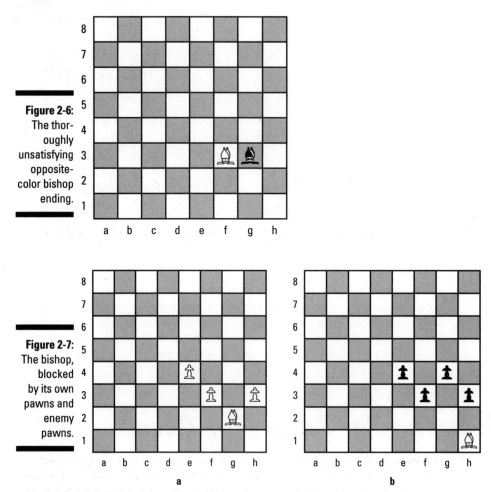

Figure 2-6: The thoroughly unsatisfying opposite-color bishop ending.

Figure 2-7: The bishop, blocked by its own pawns and enemy pawns.

a

b

What do a bishop and an elephant have in common?

The bishop evolved from the elephant, which may be difficult to imagine at first. Elephants don't have slender waists, at least not the elephants I've seen. However, if you think about the ancient Indian soldier sitting *atop* an elephant and tossing down spears at the enemy, or if you visualize the medieval archer in a castle tower firing arrows down on a hapless foe, you can understand how this development came about. The bishop doesn't like hand-to-hand fighting and is at its best when attacking from long range. If you think about it, would you rather be shooting arrows safely out of harm's way or down in the trenches getting trampled? Archers weren't stupid.

Why, then, is the piece called a bishop and not an archer? Oddly enough, it's simply because the look of the carved piece resembled a bishop's miter (the pointed hat that bishops wear) to medieval Europeans. What probably started as an off-hand remark soon became a custom.

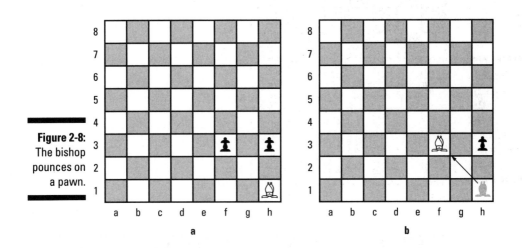

Figure 2-8: The bishop pounces on a pawn.

a

b

WARNING!

Bishop moves are relatively easy to master, but their long-range attacking ability is often surprising. Many are the times when I've been shocked to see my opponent's bishops spring from one corner of the board to the other. Just because your opponent's bishops aren't close to your pieces doesn't mean they aren't attacking you!

Flaunting Her Power: The Queen

The most powerful piece is the queen. A piece's power is directly related to its mobility, and the queen is the most mobile. Although the queen is the most powerful piece, she must be very careful when engaging enemy forces because she's so valuable. If rooks or minor pieces attack her, she's often forced to retreat or be lost. Treat the lady with kid gloves!

Figure 2-9 indicates where the queens are placed at the start of the game.

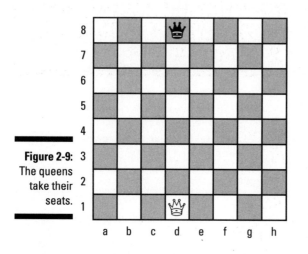

Figure 2-9:
The queens take their seats.

REMEMBER

The queen's moves are simply the combination of the rook's up-and-down, side-to-side moves and the bishop's diagonal moves — basically, she can move any number of squares in any direction. Her only restriction is that she can't jump over pieces. The queen captures an opponent by taking the opponent's place on the board.

To get an idea of the queen's strength, just put one in the middle of an empty chessboard — which, by the way, is a situation that will never happen if you're playing chess by the rules! When placed in the center of the board, the queen can cover 27 squares and can move in eight different directions, which you can see in Figure 2-10.

The queen covers fewer squares when placed on the side of the board, so her powers are slightly reduced in that case. However, it's far too dangerous to post the valuable queen in the center of the board too early in the game, where members of the opposing army can harass her. Far more commonly, you see chess masters post the queen in a more conservative position early and wait to centralize her later, when pieces have been exchanged and the danger to her reduced.

TIP

The queen is not only the most dangerous chess piece, but also the most powerful! Moving her into positions where she can be easily attacked is generally frowned upon. Let your other pieces and pawns fight the early fight, and bring the queen into the game after some of the dust settles. If your opponent moves the queen to your side of the board early on, take heart! The move is probably a mistake. Look for ways to move your pieces so they attack the exposed queen and force her to retreat.

The birth of the queen

The queen evolved from the Indian vizier who was the king's chief minister or advisor. Originally a weak piece, the queen was given its great powers toward the end of the 15th century. Whether this bestowal was an act of chivalry or just another attempt to speed up the game remains unclear. It seems certain, however, that medieval Europe was accustomed to powerful queens — and this reality can also explain the gender change.

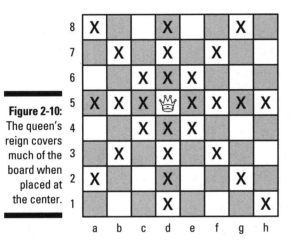

Figure 2-10: The queen's reign covers much of the board when placed at the center.

Moving One Square at a Time: The King

The king isn't the most powerful chess piece (the queen is — see the preceding section for details), but he's the most important (and in conventional chess sets, he's the tallest). When someone attacks your king, you must defend him. If your king is attacked and you can't defend him, then you have checkmate . . . and the game is over (see Chapter 4 for information on checkmate). But you never actually capture the king; you simply force him to yield. Thousands may die on the battlefield, but royalty respects royalty. (Yet don't forget that the king can capture, just like the other pieces, by taking over an opponent's square!)

Figure 2-11 shows where the king resides on the chessboard at the start of the game.

The king can move one square in any direction, except for the one-time possibility of castling (see Chapter 5 for details on this special move). The kings may never get too close to one another but must remain at arm's length (at least one square away) because one king may never put the other in check. You can see the king's possible moves for yourself in Figure 2-12.

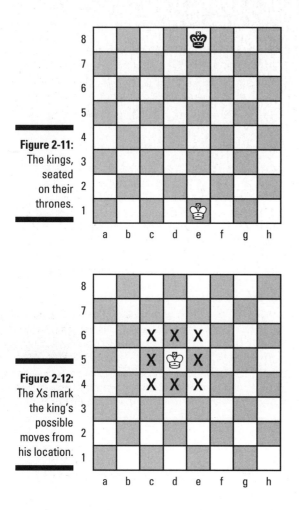

Figure 2-11:
The kings, seated on their thrones.

Figure 2-12:
The Xs mark the king's possible moves from his location.

You may expect a king to lead his troops into battle, but that analogy doesn't quite work because the king usually hides away in a corner behind pawns until it's safe to come out. Generally, when the king becomes active, the *endgame* (when most pieces have been captured) has begun. During the endgame, the king can become very powerful, and you should consider bringing him to the center. But a king in the middle of the board during the middlegame is a recipe for disaster (check out Chapters 14 and 15 for details on middlegame and endgame strategy).

Galloping in an L-Formation: The Knight

The knight is a tricky piece, and getting comfortable with its movements usually takes a little practice. As its shape suggests, the knight derives from the cavalry of the armies of old. Because it can't deliver checkmate against an opponent with only its own king to help, the knight is a minor piece, as is the bishop — but the knight's powers are very different. Unlike the long-range bishop (which I describe earlier in this chapter), the knight loves combat in close quarters and is usually the first piece moved off the back rank and the first to come into contact with the opposing army. The knight is indeed hopping mad and ready to fight!

Figure 2-13 shows the knights' starting place.

I like to think of the knight as a medieval knight on horseback with a lance. You can't throw a lance very far, but if the bad guys get too close, they're likely to get stabbed. Oddly, if an enemy can get past the lance and closer still to the knight, the knight is defenseless. (The knight would need to dismount, drop its lance, and draw a sword to fight at very close range — but this is too time-consuming, besides being against the rules of chess!) Strangely enough, although the knight is a strong attacking piece, it can't control the squares right next to it.

The easiest way to understand the knight move is to think of it as an L-shape in any direction: two squares up and one over, or one square down and two over, or any such combination of two squares plus one. The knight captures just as the other chess pieces do, by replacing the piece or pawn occupying the square it lands on — *not* the players it jumps over. Figure 2-14a illustrates where the knight can move from the center of the board. The knight controls eight squares when positioned in the center of the board as opposed to two when it's in one of the corners, as Figure 2-14b illustrates.

The knight must always move to a different-colored square than the one it occupies. This alternation between colors is true of no other piece. If the knight is on a light square, it must move to a dark square, and vice versa.

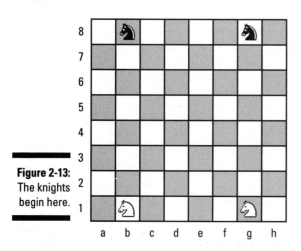

Figure 2-13: The knights begin here.

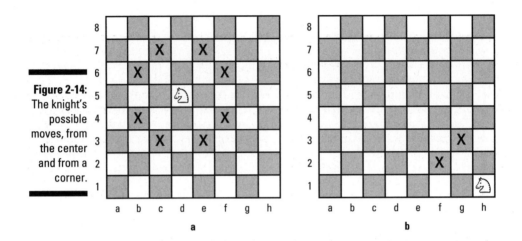

Figure 2-14:
The knight's possible moves, from the center and from a corner.

The knight is much more effective when centralized — or positioned so that it occupies or attacks one of the four central squares. However, unlike the other pieces for which this general rule also holds true, the knight loves to be in the center of the action and is forced to retreat only when attacked by the lowly pawn (which I describe in the following section). Otherwise, the knight just holds its ground and dares you to capture it. The knight considers charging off into battle an honor and hates to watch while others are left to carry the day.

The knight's truly unique power is its ability to leap over chessmen, either its own or those of the enemy. In fact, this piece is the only one that can move off the back rank at the start of the game without a preliminary pawn move, as illustrated in Figure 2-15.

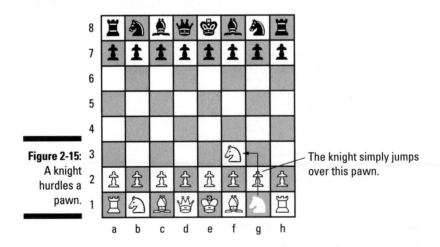

Figure 2-15:
A knight hurdles a pawn.

The knight simply jumps over this pawn.

The knight's tour

The knight's tour is an interesting exercise where you position the knight anywhere on the chessboard and then move it to every other square on the board, without ever landing on the same square twice. Grandmaster George Koltanowski was famous for the knight's tour and could do it without seeing the board (calling out the name of the square where the knight was to move). In fact, he once did it in front of more than 300 enthralled spectators on the occasion of his 90th birthday!

Scooting Around as the Army's Runt: The Pawn

Although chess people sometimes refer to all the chessmen collectively as pieces, they don't really consider a pawn to be a piece. If you lose a knight, you can either say, "I lost a knight" or "I lost a piece," but if you lose a pawn, you don't say, "I lost a piece." You say, "I lost a pawn" instead. (Why? Because that's just the way chess people talk.) Pawns are only pawns, but chess has a lot of them! Figure 2-16 shows how the pawns are set up at the start of the game.

The pawns are the foot soldiers of chess, and you know how foot soldiers are treated. Their powers are very restricted. The pawn can move only one square forward, except on its very first move, when it has the choice of moving one or two squares forward. A pawn can't move backward or sideways — *only forward*. Figure 2-17 shows the options for the white pawns at the starting line.

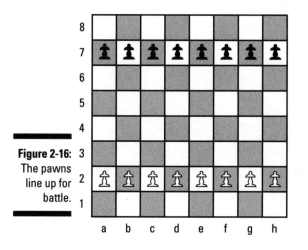

Figure 2-16: The pawns line up for battle.

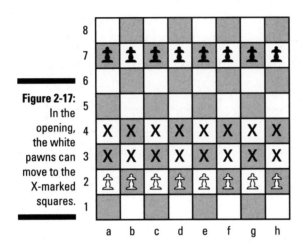

Figure 2-17: In the opening, the white pawns can move to the X-marked squares.

The pawn, unlike a piece, captures differently than it moves. It captures diagonally, one square forward to either side. But it still takes the opponent's place on a square when it captures, just as the other chessmen do. Figure 2-18 illustrates the pawn's capturing ability.

In Figure 2-19a, an enemy pawn occupies one of the squares that the white pawn can attack. Figure 2-19b shows how the white pawn captures the black pawn (although the black pawn could have captured the white pawn if it were black's turn!).

If no member of the opposing army occupies a square that the pawn attacks, then the pawn can move forward. If a piece or another pawn is in front of it, but nothing is on the squares the pawn can capture, the pawn is stymied and can't move; chess players say the pawn is *locked*. In Figure 2-20, the pawns on d5 and d6 are locked . . . by each other.

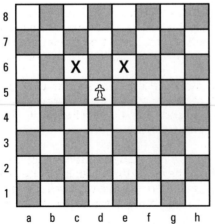

Figure 2-18: The white pawn can capture an opponent on either of the X-marked squares.

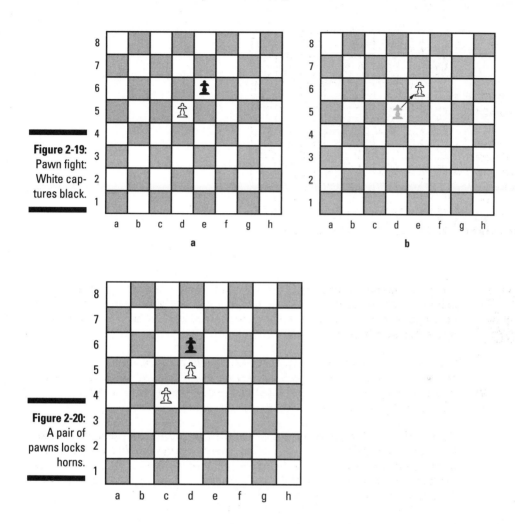

Figure 2-19: Pawn fight: White captures black.

a

b

Figure 2-20: A pair of pawns locks horns.

When two pawns are locked together as in Figure 2-20, you should try to bring another pawn alongside to help out. This strategy is so common that it's referred to as a *lever*. You can see where that term comes from, because the second pawn attempts to pry the first one free. Figure 2-21 illustrates the use of the lever.

I find it helpful to think of the foot soldier holding a spear and a giant shield. The shield is in front of the foot soldier so that the soldier can thrust only to the right or left side of the shield and can't thrust in front of it. The soldier needs a comrade in arms to come to his aid.

With the additional pawn's aid, now two of the pawns can capture each other. If the black pawn captures the white pawn, the remaining white pawn is free to move. Often the lever can be used to pry open an otherwise locked position, a technique that's seen over and over again in the games of the masters.

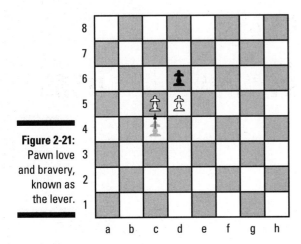

Figure 2-21:
Pawn love
and bravery,
known as
the lever.

Because pawns can be stopped in their tracks so easily, chess players have discovered that pawns are most powerful when they stay by each other's side. This way, two pawns — or *pawn duos* — can guard the square in front of the other. By helping each other out, both pawns become more mobile, and their influence on the game grows.

You need to know a few more things about pawns, but I don't discuss them in this chapter. I cover pawn promotion and something called *en passant* (or "in passing") in Chapter 5, which deals with special moves. The pawns' placement is collectively referred to as the *pawn structure,* and I examine this concept in detail in Chapter 3. I also devote a whole chapter to pawn structures that are associated with particular openings — see Chapter 10 for information on *pawn formations.*

Pawns: The soul of chess

Although the pawn is the lowliest of the chess pieces, some people have called it the "soul of chess." This is what the great master François-André Danican Philidor (1726–95) meant when he said, "The pawns are the very life of the game." This honor is due to a number of factors:

✔ A chess set has more pawns than anything else.

✔ The pawns can dictate whether the other pieces have maneuvering room.

✔ No piece wants to be exchanged for a poor pawn, so other pieces have to back down or move around them.

✔ Pawns can't move backward, so each move is a commitment and should be made only after due consideration.

Chapter 3

Exploring the Elements of Chess

The elements of chess — space, material, development, king safety, and pawn structure — are the basic building blocks of the game. By grasping the individual elements, you dramatically increase your knowledge of chess. Of course, understanding the elements in isolation from one another is far easier than understanding them in combination.

Unfortunately, the elements are always interacting with each other, as if they were volatile gases. Sometimes one element is far more important than all the others combined; other times, a dynamic balance exists among them all. When you come to understand each element's relationship to the others — in any given position — you'll have approached chess mastery.

In this chapter, I introduce you to these interacting elements, first explaining them individually and then showing you how they all interact.

Hogging the Board: Space

Space may be the final frontier to some people, but it's an essential element in the chess world. Chess really is a game of spatial conquest. All things being equal, the player who controls the most space controls the game: Maneuvering your pieces is easier when you have space than when you don't. When you don't have space, you can't always get your pieces to the right place at the right time. Imagine trying to get from one side of the battlefield to the other when your own soldiers keep getting in your way.

In the following sections, I describe the strategies you need to control plenty of space on the chess board.

The battle for space is fiercest in the center of the board. Controlling squares e4, e5, d4, and d5, as well as the squares adjacent to them, is like seizing the high ground in a skirmish. (See the later section "Maneuvers with minor pieces" for more information about the space at the center of the board.)

Avoiding that cramped feeling

If you're losing the space war, chess people say that your game is *cramped*. For example, if your opponent's maneuvers leave all your remaining pieces stuck in a corner, you're definitely cramped. A move that secures a spatial advantage for you by restricting your opponent's space is a *cramping move*. On the other hand, a *freeing move* is a move that gains back space. I expand on these ideas in Chapter 10.

Gaining control

Space is little more than the number of squares you control. *Control* refers to the number of squares attacked — not necessarily occupied — by your pieces and pawns. (*Attacked* squares are those squares that your pieces can go to on your next move or that pawns can capture on.) If your opponent attacks the same squares, then these squares are *contested* and aren't clearly controlled — and no one gets to claim them as space.

If a square is contested, you can use a kind of chess arithmetic to determine which side is more likely to end up controlling it. You can count the number of your pieces attacking the square and then count the number of your opponent's pieces contesting it. The side with the highest number is the side most likely to seize control.

Employing space strategies from the get-go

Each side starts the game with the same amount of space. At this point neither side controls any squares on the opponent's half of the board (of course!). In the following sections, I describe typical opening moves by black and white as well as maneuvers by minor pieces that you can use to secure space.

Typical opening moves by white and black

Because white has the benefit of the first move, white almost always secures a temporary spatial advantage by putting a pawn or piece on a square that allows it to attack and, at least temporarily, control squares on the other half of the board. Figure 3-1 illustrates the most common opening move (1. e4; see Chapter 6 if you need help deciphering the notation in this chapter).

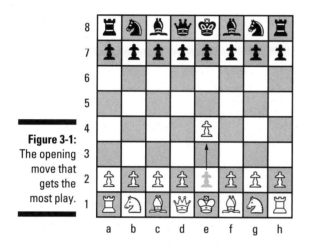

Figure 3-1:
The opening move that gets the most play.

If you already know how pawns move, you can readily see that the pawn on e4 now attacks two squares on the opponent's side of the board. These squares, d5 and f5, are shown in Figure 3-2. (For a refresher on how pawns attack versus how they move, see Chapter 2.)

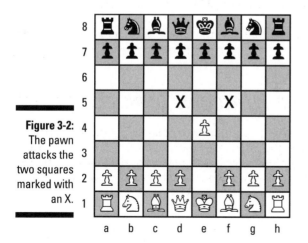

Figure 3-2:
The pawn attacks the two squares marked with an X.

Typically, but not always, black opens with a move that evens up the space game. This action-reaction is sometimes referred to as the *dynamic equilibrium* of chess, which is just a fancy way of saying that one side can usually reestablish the initial equality on her turn. For example, black can reply on the next move with the same results by moving the king's pawn (in other words, the pawn directly in front of the king) to e5 (see Figure 3-3).

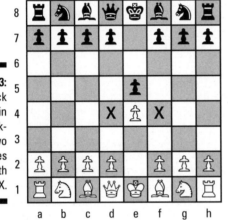

Figure 3-3: Black replies in kind, attacking the two squares marked with an X.

Notice how white holds a spatial advantage after the first move, but black immediately reestablishes spatial equality. Because white moves first, the trick is to play in such a way that black can't simply copy white's moves. In this way, white tries to force a concession from black and secure a lasting advantage. If black could always copy white's moves, the game would be a draw.

Maneuvers with minor pieces

Space is more important in the opening and middlegame phases of chess than it is in the endgame. This idea is true because, by definition, the endgame has the fewest pieces on the board. Getting cramped by a handful of pieces in the endgame rarely happens — you have to be sort of clumsy to trip over your own pieces.

The key to controlling space in the opening is to control the *center.* In Figure 3-4, the key central squares are indicated.

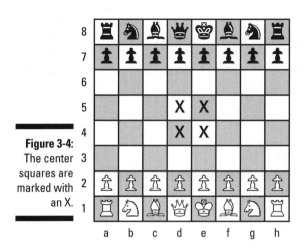

Figure 3-4: The center squares are marked with an X.

The most common opening strategy in chess is to try to maneuver your minor pieces (the bishops and the knights) and central pawns so that they control the four center squares and strike out into enemy territory. The minor pieces increase in power when mobilized toward the center. If you can post your pieces there and prevent your opponent from doing the same, you secure greater control over the center and a spatial advantage, and your pieces become stronger than your opponent's.

In Figure 3-5, white has moved its pawns and knights to control the center. Black has been busy moving the pawns on the a- and h-files and is already behind in the battle for space.

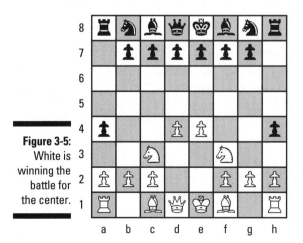

Figure 3-5: White is winning the battle for the center.

Chess isn't a static game — it's important not only to establish a spatial superiority but also to maintain it! Having one or two pieces cross over into enemy territory does little good if they're cut off from the rest of your troops. You must keep the supply lines open and invade only when you can adequately support the advanced pieces.

Central control makes use of the old adage "divide and conquer." If you split your opponent's army into two camps, you can bring a decisive amount of force into one arena before reinforcements arrive.

Considering the laws of space

Following is a list of the laws of space, but don't try to memorize it. No chess master ever does. Just become familiar with these concepts in a general way, and they'll become second nature soon enough.

- ✔ Use your center pawns to gain space in the early phase of the game.
- ✔ Invade only if you can support your pieces. In other words, keep a piece's lifelines open, or don't go there in the first place.
- ✔ Control the center before attacking on the *wings* (sides of the board).
- ✔ Don't lock in your bishops behind your own pawns.
- ✔ If your opponent is cramped, try to prevent freeing moves.
- ✔ Exchange pieces to help relieve a cramped position. (See the later section "Adopting material strategies" for more about exchanging pieces.)
- ✔ If your opponent is attacking on a wing, strike back in the center!
- ✔ After you gain control of a square in enemy territory, try to occupy the square with a knight.
- ✔ During the endgame, consider bringing the king to the center of the board.

Getting the Most Bang for Your Buck: Material

Naturally, some chess pieces are more powerful than others. The *material* element is concerned with this relative strength of the pieces.

Material superiority can be decisive when everything else is equal. If you can win one pawn, you can usually win another or force further concessions from your opponent. A material advantage of a single pawn is often decisive in games between masters. A material advantage equivalent to a rook is usually enough to win, even for inexperienced players.

In the following sections, I talk about the values of chess pieces and go over a few basic material strategies.

Valuing your pawns and pieces

Chess players attempt to quantify the power of the pieces by assigning them a numerical value. The pawn is the basic unit of chess and is assigned a numerical value of one. The other pieces are evaluated relative to the pawn's value. Therefore, if a pawn is worth one point, a knight is worth more: three points. In other words, you lose two points in the element of material if you trade a knight for a pawn. You'd need to capture at least three enemy pawns (or one knight) to compensate for the loss of your knight. (Of course, every rule has its exceptions. See the nearby sidebar "Bishops and knights aren't created equal" to find out why a bishop isn't an even trade for a knight, even though bishops and knights have the same relative value.)

Table 3-1 shows the relative values of the pieces. *Note:* Assigning a value to the king is futile, because its loss means the loss of the game!

Table 3-1	The Relative Values of Chess Pieces (In Terms of the Pawn)
Piece	*Value*
Pawn	1
Knight	3
Bishop	3
Rook	5
Queen	9

Pieces themselves gain or lose power depending on their positioning. Having an advanced pawn deep in enemy territory may be far more important than having a measly knight tucked away in a corner. A bishop locked behind its own pawns may not be worth a fraction of a free roaming knight. These values are relative and can change many times over the course of the game. Nevertheless, remembering the piece's relative value when you consider trading it for another is a useful guide. If you give up your rook or queen for a pawn, you'd better have a darned good reason!

Bishops and knights aren't created equal

Although the bishop and knight are considered to be of equal relative value, chess masters have learned over time to value the bishops slightly more. Some people assign the bishop a value of 3¼ points. Having the two bishops control both light and dark squares is especially important. In tandem, they're usually considerably more powerful than two knights or a knight and a bishop.

Adopting material strategies

A good rule is to exchange pieces when you have an advantage in material. This strategy is referred to as *simplification*. For example, if you have an extra pawn, but both you and your opponent have a bishop, winning is usually easier if you trade your bishop for your opponent's and play the rest of the game with just kings and pawns.

Material superiority takes on added importance the closer you come to an endgame. A single pawn advantage may mean little in the opening, but it may be decisive in the endgame. The strategy of simplification illustrates how you can force additional concessions from your opponents. If you keep offering to exchange pieces and your opponents keep refusing, they'll be forced to retreat. The result? You wind up with a spatial advantage, too! (I talk about space in detail earlier in this chapter.)

Because the side with an edge in material is the one that desires exchanges, logically, you should avoid the swaps if you're behind.

The intentional loss of material in return for an advantage in another element is referred to as a *sacrifice*. Sacrifices are near and dear to the heart of chess players who know that if they don't obtain an immediate advantage, time will work against them. The closer you get to an endgame, the more important the extra material becomes, so the risky maneuver of sacrificing is considered courageous by some and foolhardy by others. You can often tell a lot about chess players by watching how they risk or conserve their material! Chapter 8 deals with the most common types of sacrifice in chess.

The following points regarding material are meant to serve as guidelines rather than as rigid rules. Every time chess players try to devise a rigid rule, some smart aleck comes along and breaks it successfully! Nevertheless, it's useful to at least think about the concepts presented here:

✔ When you're ahead in material, force exchanges and steer toward the endgame. Simplify!

✔ Open files and diagonals when possible so that you may use them to engage the enemy and force further concessions. (See Chapter 1 for an introduction to files and diagonals.)

✔ If your opponent captures a piece, you should almost always try to restore material balance by capturing one of your opponent's pieces.

✔ If possible, win material without sacrificing some other element.

✔ Material is usually more important than the other elements, so take it if you can — unless you have a really good reason not to.

✔ If you're behind in material, avoid exchanging additional pieces, but don't become passive. You must attack!

Positioning Pieces in Good Time: Development

Development is the element of time. In chess, players take turns moving. You can't pass or give up a turn, so you must make a move at every turn. Not all moves are equal, however, and only those moves that contribute to the increased mobility of your pieces are said to be *developing moves*. In practice, nearly every time a piece moves from its original square, that move is a developing one.

In the following sections, I talk about different development strategies, such as gaining a tempo and making a gambit.

You want to use the element of time to place your pieces on effective squares as efficiently as possible. Moving a piece a second or third time before moving the others is usually a waste of time. Move it to a good square and then move another piece to another good square. If you keep doing that, you'll develop appropriately.

Gaining a tempo

If your opponent is playing developing moves and you're just marking time, you'll soon lose the game. Every move is a precious resource, not to be wasted! Chess players call a move a *tempo*. For example, one often hears, "I just gained (or lost) a tempo." This lingo means that you have (or have allowed your opponent to get) the chance to move, in effect, twice in a row! Figures 3-6 and 3-7 show white losing time by moving one piece too often:

✔ Figure 3-6a reflects a standard opening position known as Petroff's Defense after the white and black pawns move to e4 and e5 respectively, and the white and black knights move to f3 and f6 respectively (1. e4 e5 2. Nf3 Nf6). Figure 3-6b shows white making a mistake by moving her knight a second time, to g5.

✔ Black exploits white's mistake by moving the h-pawn to h6 (3. ... h6), as Figure 3-7a shows. To avoid being captured by the h6 pawn, the white knight moves back to f3, as shown in Figure 3-7b.

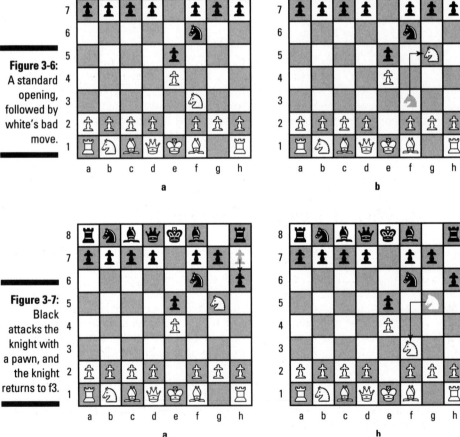

Figure 3-6:
A standard opening, followed by white's bad move.

a

b

Figure 3-7:
Black attacks the knight with a pawn, and the knight returns to f3.

a

h

Now it's black's turn to play again. By comparing Figure 3-6a with Figure 3-7b, you can see that black not only got to move the pawn from h7 to h6 but also gets another turn — in chess speak, black has gained a tempo. White has just wasted time and has lost a tempo.

Sometimes the concept of gaining or losing a tempo is very subtle. For example, you can develop a piece to a reasonable square but, as the course of events unfolds, discover that your piece really belongs on another square. You may be forced to reposition the piece to where it really belongs. Such a move can be a loss of tempo.

White begins the game and has, by definition, a slight edge in time. White can either squander this advantage easily or make use of it. The advantage that comes with an edge in the element of time — or development — is often called the *initiative*. Thus, by virtue of the first move, white is given a slight initiative at the beginning of the game. This advantage is often compared to having the serve in tennis, and in the hands of the grandmasters, the advantage of having white is quite significant.

The most common error that beginners make is to lose a tempo by giving check (for more on check, see Chapter 4). Some inexperienced players give check at every opportunity, but such a course of action isn't always wise. Sometimes the checking piece is later forced to retreat, and a tempo is lost. If you plan on checking the king, make certain that you have a concrete reason for doing so. Chess players have a saying: "Monkey sees a check, monkey gives a check." Don't be a monkey! Check isn't important by itself — checkmate is!

Making a gambit (maybe)

Very often you can sacrifice a small amount of material for an advantage in development. Many openings sacrifice a pawn for this reason, and those openings (and the sacrifices themselves) are called *gambits*.

A gambit is usually more effective for white than for black because white already has the initiative and can add to it at the small cost of a pawn. Gambits tried by black usually offer fewer chances for the initiative and often wind up as a simple loss of material. (For more on the gambit sacrifice, see Chapter 8.)

The general idea is that it takes time to capture the pawn. The move one player spends on the pawn capture will be used by the gambit player on development. Will the lead in development be worth the material sacrifice? It depends on whom you're playing!

Risky development: The Center Counter

One opening that you occasionally see in grandmaster play is the Center Counter. The chief draw-back to this opening is that the black queen is developed too early and comes under attack. When the queen is forced to retreat, white gains a tempo. Here are the usual opening moves of the Center Counter.

White moves out the king pawn two squares, and black makes a plausible reply to white's first move by advancing the pawn in front of its queen two squares (see the following two figures). This move has the advantage of opening lines for the bishop and the queen and contesting white's control of the center. The drawback of this move will become clear in just a moment.

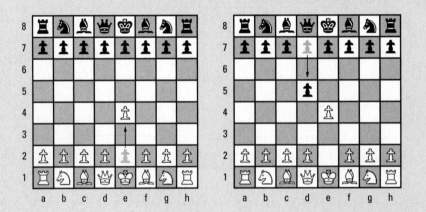

White captures the black pawn and is temporarily ahead in material. Black now recaptures the white pawn to reestablish the material balance (see the following two figures).

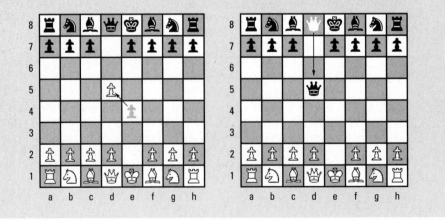

White can now develop its knight and simultaneously attack the black queen (see the following figure).

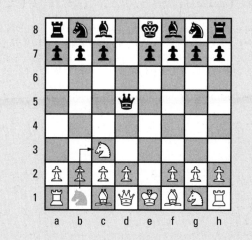

The white knight develops with tempo, taking up its natural position and also attacking the black queen. Because the knight is worth three pawns and the queen worth nine, black can't afford to ignore this threat and must move the queen again. White has won a tempo!

Protecting the Head Honcho: King Safety

Of all the elements, king safety can be the most dramatic. If the king is in jeopardy, nothing else matters. It doesn't matter how many pieces you have in your pocket if your king is checkmated, because that's the end of the game. I explain checkmate in Chapter 4 — but even if you don't know what checkmate is now, you probably realize that you need to protect your king. History has taught that by making a few early defensive moves to secure the king's position, you can go about your prime objective: attacking the opponent unhindered. You can't put a price on peace of mind.

Many chess games begin with one or two pawn moves and the development of two or three of the minor pieces. The next step is usually to bring the king to safety by *castling,* a move that allows you to place your king closer to one of the corners (see Chapter 5 for this special move), which is usually farther from the action and behind other pawns and pieces.

Understanding the importance of king safety by looking at the quickest checkmate

If you're wondering how important the element of king safety is in chess, studying the quickest possible checkmate may help. With the first move, white advances the pawn in front of her kingside knight two squares. Black takes the opportunity to strike back in the center and to open lines for her bishop and queen by moving the king's pawn (see the following two figures). Keep in mind that the best strategy for countering an advance on the wing is to advance in the center.

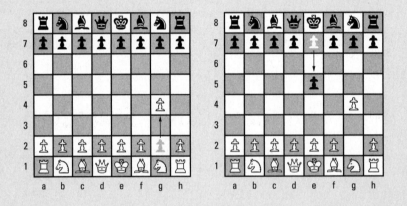

Now white really makes a huge mistake by advancing her king's bishop pawn to attack black's pawn, which opens a line against white's king. Does black have a piece that can make use of it? Indeed, black does, and white's disregard for king safety is quickly punished. Checkmate in two moves! The black queen attacks the white king along the diagonal, and white has no defense. (See the following two figures.) The king can't move out of check, no defender can move in the way, and no piece or pawn can capture the black queen. This is an extreme example of the price you pay for ignoring the safety of your king, but believe me, you'll encounter others!

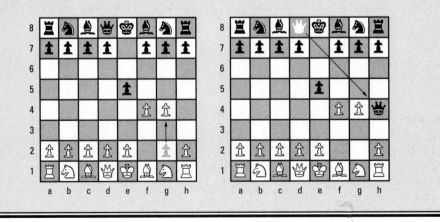

This early castling and king safety strategy is evident in countless openings that are otherwise completely different. The main idea is to engage the enemy only after the king is secure. Protecting the king with all your pieces is inefficient, so good chess players usually leave the guard duty to one or two of them along with the pawns. A knight is an excellent defender of the king and puts up fierce resistance in the face of an attack. With the help of a few pawns, a knight can usually hold down the fort.

Be careful about opening up lines of attack for your opponent against your king or moving the pawns away from your castled king, who's now in a corner of the board. Check isn't checkmate, but it does force your hand because you can't ignore it. In addition, although you can find master games where the king is left in the center, this strategy is the exception. Until you get a great deal of experience in chess, you're better off following the tried-and-true method of protecting your king before launching an attack.

Working Together: Pawn Structure

A pawn is considered the soul of chess because, very often, the mobility of the pieces depends upon the positioning of the pawns (you can read about some specific pawn formations in Chapter 10). Also, as the endgame approaches, the pawns tend to become more valuable. The famous Australian chess player Cecil Purdy (1906–79) once wrote, "Pawn endings are to chess what putting is to golf." I couldn't have said it better myself.

A general rule is that mobility is the key to the power of any chess piece. This rule is true even of the lowly pawn. The pawn's mobility is clearly tied to its ability to advance, because it can't retreat. The best pawn *structure,* or the relationship of the pawns to one another, appears at the start of the game (see Figure 3-8). All the pawns are mobile, and their structure is unbroken. Unfortunately, to get the pieces out, the pawn structure must be altered.

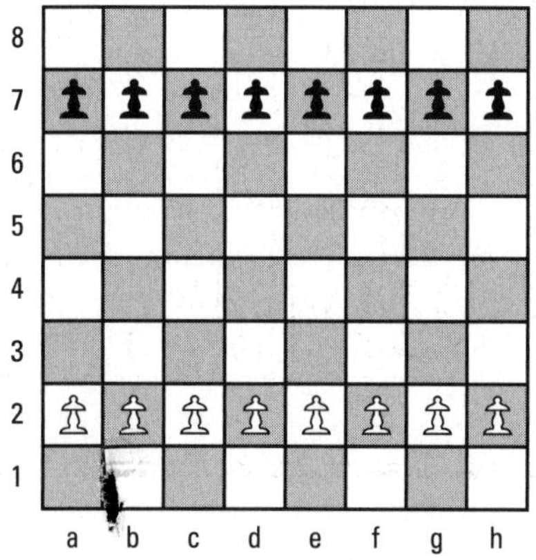

Figure 3-8:
The ideal pawn structure (the beginning of the game).

In the following sections, I describe a variety of different pawn structures and provide tips for using them.

Two at a time: Pawn duos

Pawns can't attack the square directly ahead of them, so their mobility often depends on help from another pawn. This limitation is why pawns are stronger together, or in pawn duos, than they are alone. Figure 3-9 illustrates a pawn duo. In a pawn duo, the pawns can guard the squares in front of each other and support one another should either of them advance. These pawns are mobile.

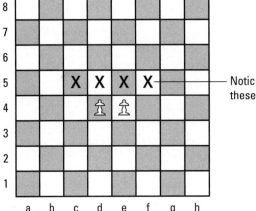

Figure 3-9: Pawns find strength in numbers, such as in this pawn duo.

Notice how many squares these pawns attack!

In Figure 3-10, the white pawns are still mobile, but their potential to advance is restricted by the black pawns. You usually want to control a square prior to occupying it, but doing so is difficult in this case because the squares in front of the pawns are contested — the white pawns and the black pawns attack the same squares, which are marked by Xs.

Figure 3-11 shows a position where all the pawns are locked: Neither side can advance, and the pawns require assistance before progress can be made. Locked pawns lead to what chess players call *closed positions,* which are characterized by slow maneuvering rather than by sharp hand-to-hand fighting. You can now see how the pawn structure dictates the further course of action, right?

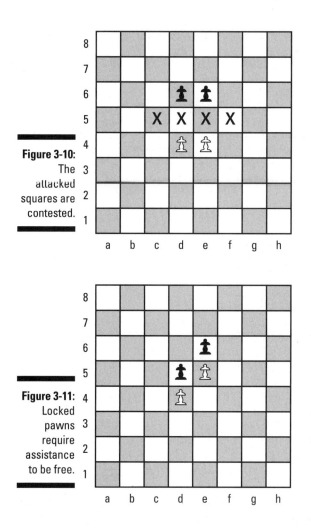

Figure 3-10:
The attacked squares are contested.

Figure 3-11:
Locked pawns require assistance to be free.

Promote the little guys: Passed pawns

Pawns play a critical role throughout the game of chess. During the endgame, they take on added significance because of the possibility of promotion (see Chapter 5 for the lowdown on pawn promotion). When pawns reach the eighth rank, you may promote them to any piece other than the king.

If pawns are locked or otherwise immobile, the chances of promoting them are remote. However, if the pawn has a free path ahead of it — unobstructed by other pawns — the chances of promoting it are considerably greater. Such a pawn is called a *passed pawn*.

In Figure 3-12, the white pawn on the far left is a passed pawn. No black pawn is between it and the eighth rank — and no black pawn can capture it.

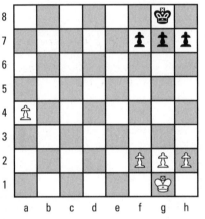

Figure 3-12: Nothing can stop the a4 pawn from being promoted.

Passed pawns must be pushed! In other words, you must advance them toward the eighth rank. A passed pawn becomes a tangible advantage whenever it's free to advance and is adequately supported so that it can't simply be captured. A passed pawn may force the opposing forces to assume a defensive posture in order to halt the pawn's advance, or it may deflect enemy pieces away from the real action.

The best kind of passed pawn is the protected one (see Figure 3-13). Such a pawn has not only an unobstructed path to the eighth rank but also the support of one of its peers. In this case, the black king can't capture the white pawns. If it ever moved to capture the d-pawn, the e-pawn would move to the eighth rank and promote.

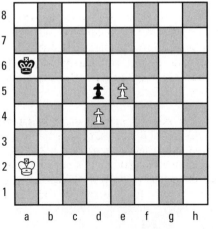

Figure 3-13: The protected passed pawn on e5 has a clear path ahead.

The protected passed pawn can be opposed only by pieces, which often keeps those pieces from doing more productive work. If one of your pawns is tying down an enemy piece, it's reducing that piece's mobility and therefore its power.

Mobility is key: Isolated pawns

Pawns are considered *isolated* when they don't have any pawns from their own team by their side. In Figure 3-14, the white pawn on d4 is isolated.

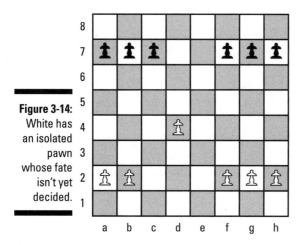

Figure 3-14: White has an isolated pawn whose fate isn't yet decided.

Isolated pawns may or may not be passed pawns (which I discuss in the preceding section). If they're passed or mobile, they may become strong. If they aren't passed or are immobile, they may become weak. Because isolated pawns don't have any supporting pawns and can't control the square directly in front of them, they may easily become blocked (blockaded).

Aaron Nimzowitsch, who wrote extensively on the subject of pawns, demonstrated that a mobile, isolated pawn may provide a sound basis for attack and that on the other hand, an immobile (blockaded), isolated pawn may become subject to attack. The pieces must then defend the threatened pawn, and pieces don't like to be on guard duty for pawns — that duty offends their lofty sense of self.

To immobilize your opponent's isolated pawn, you can blockade it. The knight is an ideal blockader. A knight camped in front of an isolated pawn can't be driven off by pawns, and the knight stands its ground in the face of attack by any other piece. The queen, in comparison, is a poor blockader because she must retreat in the face of attack by knights, bishops, or rooks and can't maintain the blockade. After a blockade is broken, the isolated pawn becomes mobile and gains strength.

Left behind on open files: Backward pawns

The kissing cousin to the isolated pawn that I describe in the preceding section is the backward pawn. A *backward pawn* still has one or more pawns on adjacent files, but those pawns are more advanced. It may be difficult or even impossible for the backward pawn to catch up with its sidekick(s), and, in that case, such a pawn is, in effect, isolated. The backward pawn (like the white pawn on d2 in Figure 3-15) may come under pressure from the enemy's big guns because the file is open, allowing the opponent's queen and rooks to attack the backward pawn.

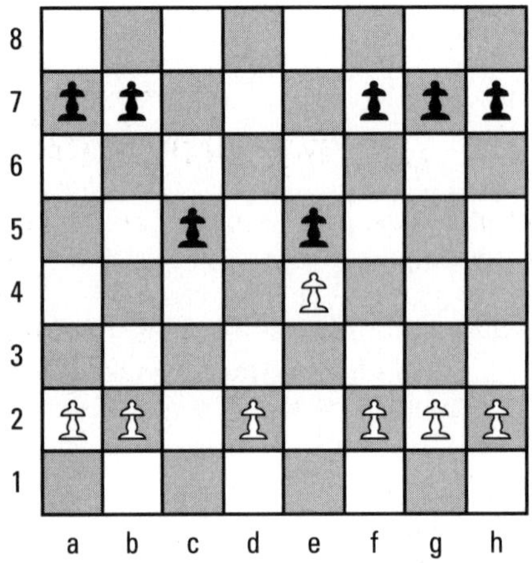

Figure 3-15:
The backward pawn on d2 is at risk.

You should avoid having a backward pawn in most cases because you may end up using your pieces to guard the relatively insignificant pawn. The pieces then become listless and bored — and of no use to anybody.

On the verge of backward: Hanging pawns

Hanging pawns are the second cousins once removed of the backward pawn that I describe in the preceding section. The *hanging pawns* are in a pawn duo, which is strong in and of itself, but they don't have any other supporting pawns around them. This lack of support means that if one of those two pawns advances, the remaining pawn will become a backward pawn. If you advance one, try to advance the other to reestablish the pawn duo. In Figure 3-16, the advanced white pawns on c4 and d4 are hanging pawns.

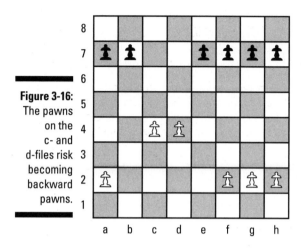

Figure 3-16:
The pawns on the c- and d-files risk becoming backward pawns.

In front of a pawn sibling: Doubled pawns

Doubled pawns are produced when one pawn captures an opponent's piece or pawn and moves in front of another pawn of the same color. Figure 3-17 gives an example of doubled pawns. The black pawns in the upper-left corner of the board are now crowded together. When the pawn on d7 moved to capture a piece on c6, it created doubled pawns. Although four pawns occupy this corner, they really have the mobility of three.

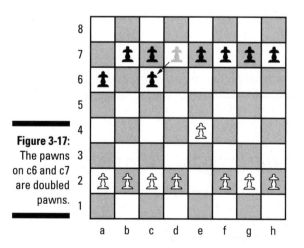

Figure 3-17:
The pawns on c6 and c7 are doubled pawns.

When such a situation happens, the pawns lose the ability to protect one another and reduce the chances of using each other as a *lever* (the act of dislodging an enemy pawn from blockading your own; see Chapter 2). Most importantly, the pawns' mobility — especially that of the trailing pawn — is significantly reduced. If three pawns of the same color are on the same file, they're called *tripled pawns,* and protecting all of them is very difficult.

If you have the misfortune of finding yourself saddled with pawns that are doubled (or tripled) and also isolated, you'll have a very hard time straightening them out. The only remedy is to use one of the pawns in a capture. Because a pawn captures diagonally, it would move to an adjacent file. Prevention is the best cure, so try not to allow your opponents to capture your pieces when you can only recapture by doubling your pawns.

Lines in the sand: Pawn chains

Pawn chains are pawns that are lined up along a diagonal, with each pawn supporting a more advanced one until they reach the head of the chain. These pawn chains represent a line drawn in the sand and make it difficult for the enemy to cross over. Figure 3-18 shows two pawn chains, one for white and one for black.

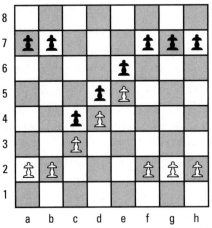

Figure 3-18: Both white and black have established a pawn chain.

Because other pieces have a difficult time crossing the pawn chain and coming into contact with each other, this arrangement can make for a long game with few exchanges — so whether you decide to create a chain depends on whether you like such games. A pawn chain also divides the board into two camps: one where the white pieces have more freedom to move about, and another where the black pieces can roam more freely. If you can crash through a pawn chain, however, you almost certainly can obtain the advantage.

The weakest link of the pawn chain is at the *base,* which is the rearmost pawn — the one that starts the chain. From white's point of view, this pawn is the one that's closest to or on the second rank. If you destroy the base, you weaken the pawn chain. After you remove one base, another base is established, but each becomes easier to attack and destroy. If you can't attack the base of the chain, attack at the head. This strategy isn't as effective, but it may create weaknesses in the chain that you can exploit later.

All together now: Pawn tips for the road

You don't need to memorize the following pawn tips. Give them a good once-over and move on. But if you remember any of them, you'll be ahead of the game!

- ✔ Try to keep your pawn structure intact.
- ✔ Because some pawns must be advanced, try to keep them mobile or in pawn duos because immobile pawns are easy to attack.
- ✔ If some pawns become locked, use other pawns to pry them free.
- ✔ If you have an isolated pawn, keep it mobile to keep it strong; if your opponent has one, blockade it!
- ✔ Create a passed pawn and, when possible, a protected passed pawn.
- ✔ Push your passed pawns toward the eighth rank and promote them if you can.
- ✔ Attack backward pawns with the heavy pieces (the queen and rooks) to force your opponent to defend them.
- ✔ Try to provoke a hanging pawn into an advance and then blockade the hanging pawn to immobilize it.
- ✔ Avoid doubling your pawns, but if you can't, try to exchange one of the doubled pawns to repair your pawn structure.
- ✔ Attack pawn chains at the base, where they're weakest.

Chapter 4

Going after the King: Check, Stalemate, and Checkmate

*T*he object of the game of chess is to checkmate your opponent's king. Simply attacking the king isn't enough — you have to attack him in such a way that he can't escape. If you achieve that result, my friend, you win the game — time for a victory lap (in private, of course — no need to be rude)!

You always want to deliver checkmate if at all possible. Unfortunately, your opponent is trying to checkmate you at the same time! Sometimes you have such an overwhelming advantage that your opponent's resistance is futile. But because not all games are the cut-and-dry win/lose sort, you need to be aware of a couple other situations that pertain to the end result. In this chapter, I distinguish the differences between check, checkmate, and stalemate.

Check 'Em Out: Attacking the Enemy King

To *give check* simply means that you're attacking the enemy king. In Figure 4-1, white has a king and queen to black's lone king. The black king is currently in check because the white queen has moved to the g-file (1. Qg6+) and is now attacking it. (See Chapter 6 for the scoop on deciphering chess notation, which I include throughout this chapter.)

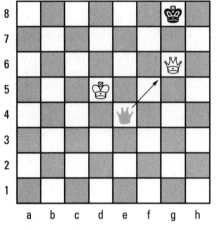

Figure 4-1:
The white
queen
moves to a
position to
attack the
black king.
Check!

Because check is an attack on the king, the victim can't ignore it. If your opponent puts your king in check, you have three ways to respond:

✔ Capture the attacking piece.

✔ Move a piece between the checking piece and the king to block the attack.

✔ Move your king out of check.

In the example shown in Figure 4-1, the black king's only option is to move out of check because black doesn't have any other pieces on the board. Here, the king can move to either f8 or h8.

One of the important things to remember when playing chess is to postpone immediate gratification. Sometimes, giving check (especially early on) can backfire. If your opponent escapes the check by blocking your attack, for example, you may be forced to retreat. Make certain that when you give check, it somehow helps your cause; to give check and then be forced to retreat is simply a waste of time. Experienced players give check only if it improves their position. For example, if the king has to move early in the game to escape a check, he loses the ability to castle (see Chapter 5 for more on castling). If you play a check that ruins your position, you may say, quite correctly, that your check bounced!

You may actually say "check" when you attack your opponent's king, but doing so isn't mandatory, and experienced players usually don't. If you do say "check," say it in a low voice so as not to disturb other players. Pumping your fist in the air and yelling, "Check . . . Yessssss!" is considered bad taste. (Under no circumstances is it correct to do a dance. Chess players try to keep their emotions under control at all times.)

Not all checks are created equal

The nastiest check short of checkmate is the *discovered check*. This type of check occurs when you move a piece out from between another of your pieces and the enemy king, and your second piece then gives check. That is, its check is suddenly "discovered" because the intervening piece is now gone, and the second piece now has a line of sight — and movement — to the opposing king. The piece you move to reveal the check can thus move anywhere and capture anything in its power with immunity, because the other side must respond to the check. If the piece you move also gives check, the combination is called *double check*. The enemy king is forced to move, because running like mad is the only way to ward off both attacks.

When you can keep checking the enemy king on every turn but can't checkmate it, you have *perpetual check*. Perpetual check results in a *draw,* because checkmate is impossible. The king can escape any individual check, and the king has no prospects of avoiding future, continuous checks, so neither side can win. This type of check can be a handy strategy if you're losing. (Getting a draw isn't such a bad thing if it takes the place of a loss!)

If your opponent is sure to lose but postpones defeat by giving a pointless check, the move is known as a *spite check*. Spite checks are considered an example of bad chess manners. Don't check out of spite!

Stuck in a Rut: Stalemate

Stalemate occurs when one side has no legal moves left to make and that person's king isn't in check. In chess you can't pass up your turn — you always have to move. However, if your opponent puts you in a situation where you can't make a move, the game is declared *drawn* due to stalemate. (If one side has no legal moves and *is* in check, you're in an entirely different situation — checkmate! See the next section.)

Keep in mind that moving your own king into check is illegal, which means any square attacked by an opponent's piece or pawn is off limits.

King and queen versus king is the easiest two-piece combination for accomplishing checkmate, but you must be sure to guard against delivering a stalemate. Because the queen can control so many squares, stalemating the opposing king by accident is quite easy! If, for example, it's black's move in Figure 4-2, the game is a stalemate. The black king isn't in check and has nowhere to go, because every square it could theoretically move to (e7, e8, f7, g7, or g8) is under attack by the white king or queen.

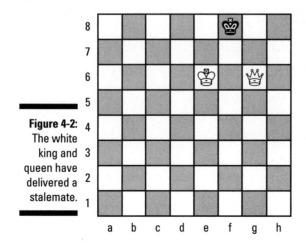

Figure 4-2:
The white
king and
queen have
delivered a
stalemate.

No Escape for Ye King: Checkmate

Checkmate occurs when one king is in check and can't escape and therefore signals the end of the game. Checkmate can occur at any time, with any number of pieces on the board, but it's good to become proficient at delivering checkmate with as few pieces as possible.

Check out Figure 4-3 to see an example of checkmate. The black king is initially placed in check when the white queen moves to f7 to attack him (1. Qf7). But the black king has no legal moves:

- ✔ He can't capture the queen because the white king is guarding her.

- ✔ He has no other black piece to block the check.

- ✔ He can't move out of check to a square that isn't also under attack.

Therefore, black is checkmated, and white cries victory. Remember the old adage, "It is better to give checkmate than to receive it!"

The checkmating process is accomplished by *cutting off squares* (systematically reducing the number of squares to which the king has access). When you cut off squares, you use your own king and whatever piece or pieces you have left to force your opponent's king to an edge of the board, where it's easiest to deliver checkmate. Kings can't check one another, so if the only pieces left are the two kings, the game ends in a draw.

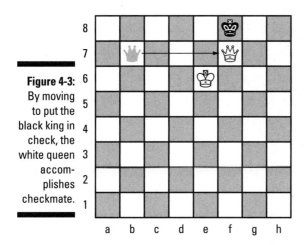

Figure 4-3:
By moving to put the black king in check, the white queen accomplishes checkmate.

Just as the king can't deliver checkmate on his own, no single piece can deliver checkmate without the help of the king. Other than the powerful queen, a lone piece can't even force the enemy king to the edge of the board where the king is most easily checkmated. You must advance your own king into a position where it can help drive back the enemy.

In the following sections, I describe a couple of techniques for delivering checkmate: using the king with the queen and using the king with the rook.

Cutting off squares with the king and the queen

Because the queen is the most powerful piece, a checkmate with king and queen against king is fairly easy to administer. The key to delivering checkmate with the queen is to drive the enemy king to any edge of the board and watch out for moves that may lead to stalemate (which I describe earlier in this chapter).

Figure 4-4 sets the stage for an impending checkmate — check out the starting positions of the black king and the white king and queen. The black king is on d5, the white king is on g8, and the white queen is on g6.

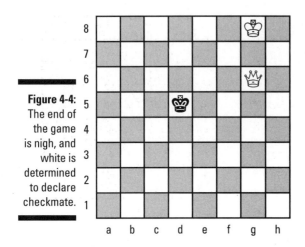

Figure 4-4:
The end of the game is nigh, and white is determined to declare checkmate.

White cuts off squares by moving the queen to the left one square to f6 (1. Qf6), as shown in Figure 4-5a. (The squares that are now cut off from the black king are marked with Xs.) The black king has only three squares from which to choose — c4, c5, and e4 — so he retreats to e4 (1. ... Ke4); see Figure 4-5b.

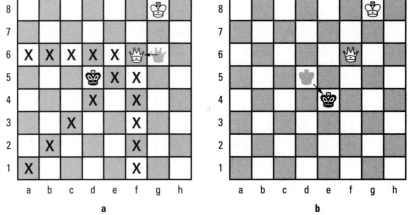

Figure 4-5:
The white queen cramps the black king's space, and the black king moves.

To support his queen, the white king advances to f7 (2. Kf7); see Figure 4-6a. Even the mighty queen can't deliver checkmate without the help of the king — she'd spend all day in a never-ending game of cat and mouse. The black king will try to stay in the center of the board for as long as possible, because he knows that the edges of the board are danger zones. The king moves back to d5 (2. ... Kd5), as Figure 4-6b shows.

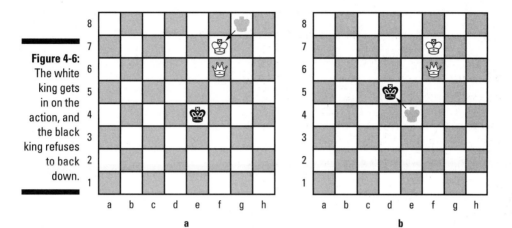

Figure 4-6: The white king gets in on the action, and the black king refuses to back down.

a   b

Keep in mind that the best defense against checkmate is to stay as far away from the edges of the board as possible.

By moving even closer to the black king (3. Qe6+), the white queen can cut off even more squares, as shown in Figure 4-7. (The Xs in Figure 4-7 show the squares that are cut off.) The queen is checking the black king in this figure (I discuss checking earlier in this chapter), but the real objective is to cut off more squares.

By comparing the setup shown in Figure 4-7 to the one in Figure 4-4, you can see how white is shrinking the number of squares available to black's king.

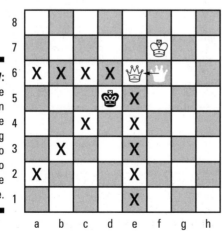

Figure 4-7: When the white queen attacks, the black king has only two squares to which he can move.

✔ In Figure 4-4, the sides of the greater square within which black resides are a1 to a6, a6 to g6, g6 to g1, and g1 back to a1.

✔ In Figure 4-7 the square is smaller, and the sides are a1 to a6, a6 to e6, e6 to e1, and e1 to a1.

Chess players sometimes call this sequence *shrinking the square.* If you cut off too many squares, however, you run the risk of giving stalemate — so be careful and make sure that if the king isn't in check, he has at least one square to which he can move.

As black has no other choice in Figure 4-7 but to move away from the queen to one of the open squares, white can continue to cut off squares by chasing after the black king until he's forced to the edge of the board. By then bringing the king to his queen's side for support, white secures an inevitable checkmate, as shown in Figure 4-8a.

Notice that the safest way to avoid stalemate is to force the opposing king to the edge of the board, use your queen to keep it trapped there, and then advance your king. Keep the queen at a safe distance from the opposing king, let your king stroll up to lend support, and then deliver checkmate with the queen as shown in Figure 4-8b.

Figure 4-8:
The black king finds himself backed into a corner and succumbs to checkmate.

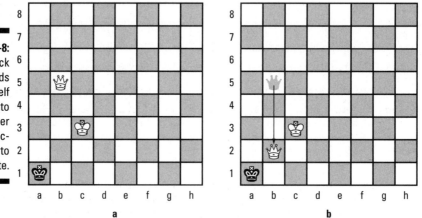

a

b

Checkmating with the king and the rook

Achieving checkmate with the king and rook follows the same general principle as that of using the king and queen (described in the preceding section); however, this method takes longer to achieve because the rook isn't as powerful as the queen. Although the steps are long and tedious, they're essential to know if you want to be able to checkmate your opponent; the figures throughout this section demonstrate how to force the opposing king to the side of the board by using your rook and king.

The king and rook must be used in tandem in order to force the enemy king away from the center and toward an edge of the board. You use the edge of a board the way a cornerback uses the out-of-bounds line in football to help defend against a wide receiver.

Step 1: Advance the king to help cut off squares

With the rook cutting off squares, the first step of this type of checkmate is to advance the king to help cut off more squares. With the white king at his back, the white rook in Figure 4-9a is cutting off squares from the black king. (In this position, the white king is supporting the rook so that black can't capture it.) The black king is forced to retreat, in this case to c5 (1. ... Kc5); see Figure 4-9b.

Figure 4-9:
The white rook limits black's choices, so black responds accordingly.

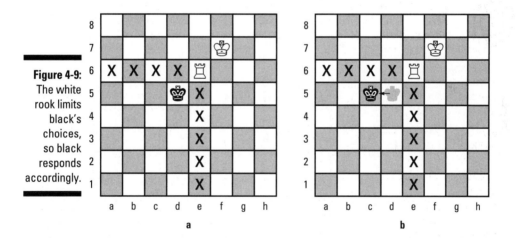

The white king advances to f6 (2. Kf6) in preparation to help cut off more squares, as shown in Figure 4-10a. The black king moves back to his original post in the center of the board (2. ... Kd5), trying to stay as far away from the edge as possible (see Figure 4-10b).

The white king advances again, this time to f5 (3. Kf5); see Figure 4-11a, and the black king is once again forced to retreat, again to c5 (3. ... Kc5); see Figure 4-11b. (Black could have moved to d4, of course, but the principle of cutting off squares remains the same.)

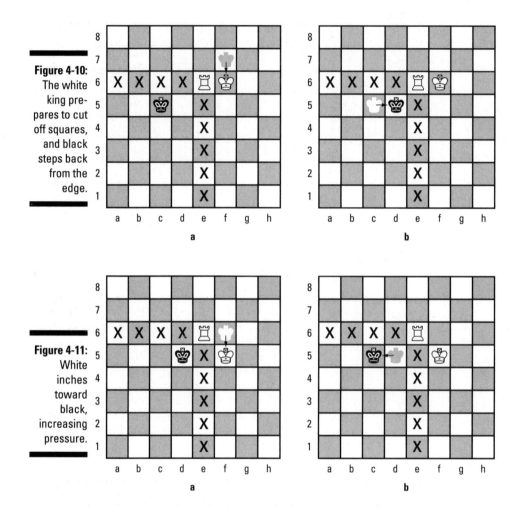

Figure 4-10:
The white king prepares to cut off squares, and black steps back from the edge.

Figure 4-11:
White inches toward black, increasing pressure.

In Figure 4-12a, notice how the white king has moved to e4 (4. Ke4) and is now cutting off squares d3, d4, and d5. An important part of this strategy is to advance the king off to the enemy king's side, not in front of it. The reason for this course of action becomes clear in the next step, which I detail in the following section. The black king responds by moving to c4 (4. ... Kc4), trying to stay as far away from the edge of the board as the white pieces allow (see Figure 4-12b). Now, however, the white king has advanced far enough to move onto phase two of the operation.

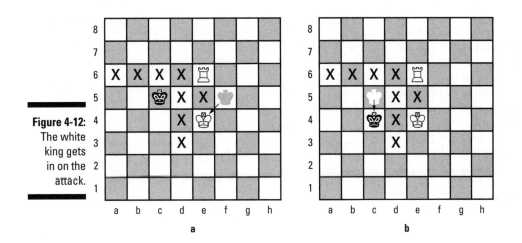

Figure 4-12: The white king gets in on the attack.

Step 2: Force the enemy king toward the edge

In phase two of the checkmating operation, the white rook and king combine forces to drive the black king closer to the edge of the board. The rook checks the black king by moving to the c-file (5. Rc6+), as Figure 4-13a shows, forcing black to move closer to the edge. The black king moves to b5 (5. ... Kb5), which is closer to the edge, but in turn he attacks the undefended rook — see Figure 4-13b.

The white king advances to d5 (6. Kd5) in order to defend the attacked rook and continue to help cut off squares, as shown in Figure 4-14a. As a result, the black king is forced yet again to give ground. To maintain a little space from the edge, black moves straight down to b4 (6. ... Kb4); see Figure 4-14b.

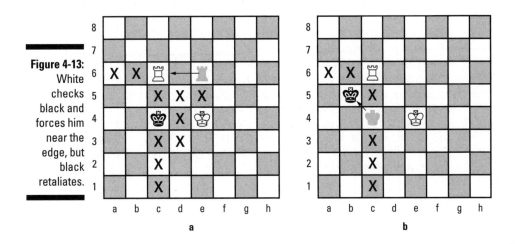

Figure 4-13: White checks black and forces him near the edge, but black retaliates.

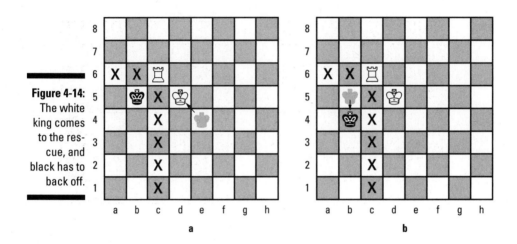

Figure 4-14: The white king comes to the rescue, and black has to back off.

Step 3: Cut off more squares

Now that white has accomplished the preliminary objective of forcing the black king to retreat toward the edge of the board, white must return to the idea of cutting off squares in order to drive the enemy king farther back. In Figure 4-15a, white advances the rook to c5 (7. Rc5) in order to cut off more squares. In Figure 4-15b, the black king retreats to b3 (7. ... Kb3), continuing to stay away from the edge of the board.

Next, white uses the rook once more to cut off additional squares by moving it to c4 (8. Rc4), as shown in Figure 4-16a. The black king again retreats down the b-file (8. ... Kb2); see Figure 4-16b. See a pattern yet? Notice how the white rook is cutting off the black king's access to all the squares except for the three in the lower-left corner.

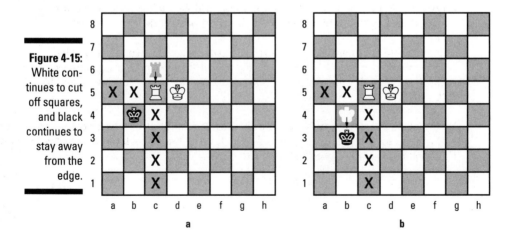

Figure 4-15: White continues to cut off squares, and black continues to stay away from the edge.

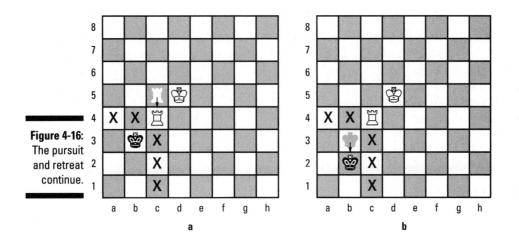

Figure 4-16: The pursuit and retreat continue.

Step 4: Advance the king and cut off even more squares

Now that additional squares are cut off, white returns to the theme of advancing the king, alternating between the two themes of advancing and cutting off squares. This step is simple: You cut off squares when you can and advance the king when you can't.

In Figure 4-17a, the white king advances to d4 (9. Kd4) so he can stand beside the rook. This approach demonstrates why it takes so long to actually achieve the checkmate. The process itself is fairly simple; the aggressor makes the same kind of moves over and over again, but because the king is needed to force a checkmate (and the king moves only one square at a time) and because the rook is less powerful than the queen, it takes quite a number of moves in order to execute the plan. In Figure 4-17b, black moves the king to b3 (9. ... Kb3) to attack the rook. However, because the white king is protecting the rook, the attack is meaningless. Still, black has nothing better to do — white is guiding him through a slow and painful death.

In Figure 4-18a, the white king continues to advance toward the lower-left corner by moving to d3 (10. Kd3). In Figure 4-18b, the black king is forced to retreat as usual. He moves to the only other square away from the edge, b2 (10. ... Kb2).

In Figure 4-19a, white returns to the theme of using the rook to cut off squares by moving to c3 (11. Rc3), finally forcing the black king to the edge of the board (11. ... Kb1); see Figure 4-19b.

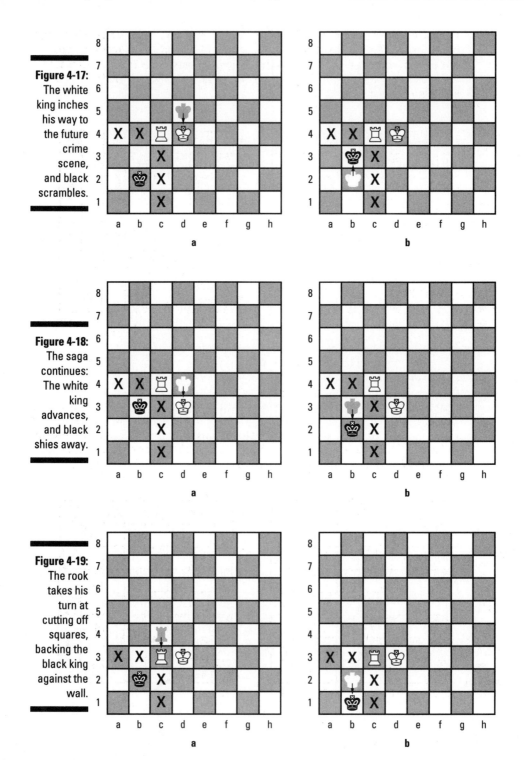

Figure 4-17: The white king inches his way to the future crime scene, and black scrambles.

Figure 4-18: The saga continues: The white king advances, and black shies away.

Figure 4-19: The rook takes his turn at cutting off squares, backing the black king against the wall.

By advancing the rook to c2 (12. Rc2), white traps the black king on the edge of the board (see Figure 4-20a). The process of cutting off squares is complete, and white can now take the final steps toward delivering checkmate. All black can do is shuffle back and forth in the lower-left corner (12. ... Ka1); see Figure 4-20b.

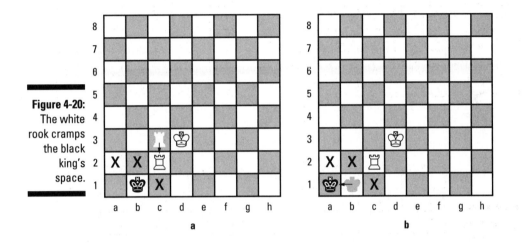

Figure 4-20: The white rook cramps the black king's space.

Step 5: Deliver checkmate!

To deliver checkmate, white simply needs to move the king into the proper position to relieve the rook of the task of cutting off squares along the second rank. To head for that goal, the white king marches to c3 (13. Kc3), as shown in Figure 4-21a. Black still has no choice but to shuffle back and forth, so he scoots to b1 (13. ... Kb1); see Figure 4-21b.

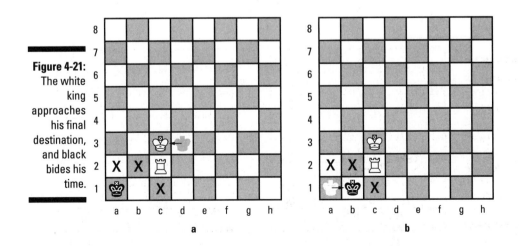

Figure 4-21: The white king approaches his final destination, and black bides his time.

White continues the march of the king in Figure 4-22a by moving to b3 (14. Kb3), but the black king can only move back into the corner (14. ... Ka1) and await his fate (see Figure 4-22b).

The time has come to deliver checkmate — finally! The rook moves to c1 (15. Rc1#), and black can't move anywhere without being captured (see Figure 4-23).

Keep in mind that the preceding series of moves is much easier to play than to explain. But you must practice this elementary rook-and-king checkmate until you understand it entirely.

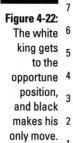

Figure 4-22: The white king gets to the opportune position, and black makes his only move.

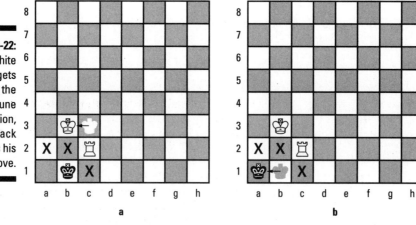

a

b

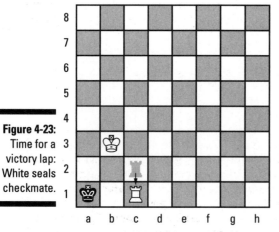

Figure 4-23: Time for a victory lap: White seals checkmate.

Chapter 5

Making a Few Special Moves

If you play enough chess, you eventually run into someone who plays by a different set of rules than the official ones. Such players may have learned chess from someone who knew most of the rules and fudged on a few others. Unfortunately, unless you lug a rule book around with you, convincing these people that you do know the correct rules may be difficult.

In this chapter, I deal with the moves that are most often confused in one way or another: en passant, promotion, and castling. Knowing these special moves may not help you avoid the occasional disagreement, but you can at least argue with an air of authority — and for some chess buffs, that's almost as good as winning. And knowing all the options available to you in the game always pays off . . . sooner or later. (*Note:* I use chess notation throughout this chapter; see Chapter 6 for the full scoop on deciphering this notation.)

Capturing a Pawn at Your Side: En Passant

French for "in passing," *en passant* is a special method of capturing available only to a pawn on its fifth rank. In the following example, the black pawn is on black's fifth rank. Such a pawn can capture another pawn if the latter attempts to pass by the first one on an adjacent square. The capturing pawn moves diagonally one square forward and captures the pawn as if it had moved only one square forward rather than two. (As I explain in Chapter 2, a pawn can move one or two squares forward on its first move; after that, it can move only one square forward.) Multiple en passant captures can occur in a game, but you have to make each capture immediately. Only at the end of a pawn's first move, and only if it moves forward two squares, can you capture it en passant — it's now or never.

The following example illustrates an en passant capture. In Figure 5-1, the white pawn on d2 is on its starting square and is ready to move. (*Note:* To make the en passant capture crystal clear, I left the other pawns and pieces off the board — in real play, of course, those pieces would be there.)

White moves the pawn forward two squares (1. d4); see Figure 5-2a. For one move — and one move only — black can legally capture white's pawn (1. ... exd), just as though the pawn had moved forward only one square; in making the en passant capture, black's pawn takes the position that the white pawn would have occupied by moving a single square (see Figure 5-2b).

Of course, if your opponent doesn't know about the en passant capture, this ploy comes as quite a shock. Even worse, if you explain that you simply captured en passant, you may be accused of playing by French rules. Calmly explain that chess is an international game and that the en passant rule was adopted in the 15th century. You may also add that the rule was universally accepted by the late 19th century. If you're playing a casual game just for fun, however, the sporting thing to do is to allow your opponent to take back her move. But if the match is a tournament game, you must insist on your rights. The fact that you know this rule and your opponent doesn't isn't your fault!

En passant comes with a few details you want to note. They include the following:

✔ The captured pawn must move two squares for en passant to be valid.

✔ If you don't capture right away, you lose the right to do so.

✔ You aren't required to capture en passant; in fact, sometimes this capture isn't the best move on the board. For example, if a different move would place your opponent in checkmate, then you definitely want to forgo the en passant capture. (Flip to Chapter 4 for the basics on checkmate.) But capturing en passant may be a good idea if it interferes with your opponent's plan.

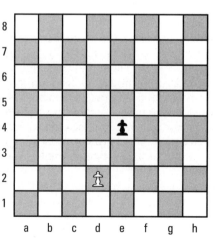

Figure 5-1: The pawns are nearly ripe for an en passant capture.

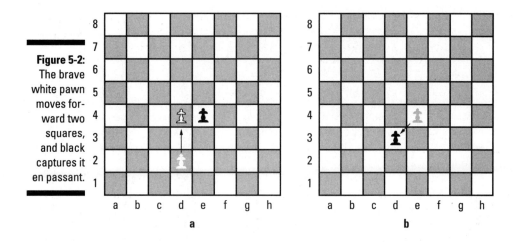

Figure 5-2: The brave white pawn moves forward two squares, and black captures it en passant.

Boosting Your Pawns' Powers: Promotion

After a pawn reaches the end of the board, you can *promote* that pawn to any piece of your choosing, except the king (each color can have only one king). In essence, after its promotion, the pawn is exchanged for that other piece (you take the pawn off the board and put the other piece back on in its staid) — not bad for a lowly pawn.

Almost always, players make the pawn into a queen, because the queen is the most powerful piece on the board (head to Chapter 2 for more on the pieces and their powers). Theoretically, you can have nine queens at one time — the eight promoted pawns and the original queen. Quite a harem for the king! (This scenario, however, is quite unlikely.) Only in odd, problem positions do players promote a pawn to anything other than a queen (for example, when a queen would produce stalemate, as I describe in Chapter 4). This condition is known as an *underpromotion*.

In the following example, white is a pawn ahead of black but can't checkmate the black king with only the pawn and king. (Wonder why? Chapter 4 has all you need to know about checkmating.) White moves the pawn to the eighth rank in order to promote it (see Figure 5-3a). In this case, promoting the pawn to a queen makes sense, especially because the newly promoted queen immediately delivers checkmate (see Figure 5-3b). Promoting the pawn to a rook will also deliver checkmate in this particular example, however, so either choice is equally powerful here. Underpromoting to a knight or bishop would be folly, because these pieces can't checkmate the king by themselves.

The three-king circus

The famous chess teacher George Koltanowski was fond of telling the following story: He was teaching the rules of the game to a brand-new student, and the student was eager to play a game right away. George easily set up a *mating net* (a situation where checkmate is eventually unavoidable) in which the student's king couldn't escape checkmate. While George was setting up the checkmate, the student was busy pushing a pawn toward the queening square. George saw that the pawn could queen, but he didn't mind because he was going to deliver checkmate on the very next move.

George was stunned when the student pushed the pawn to the queening square and promoted it to — a king! Seems that George had told the student that the pawn could be promoted to any other piece and forgot to mention the restriction involving kings. The student made him stick to his own rule! This case may be the only one involving more than two kings on a chessboard. With a sly wink, George always ended the story by saying he played a move that checkmated both kings simultaneously!

Figure 5-3:
White promotes its pawn to a queen and immediately delivers checkmate.

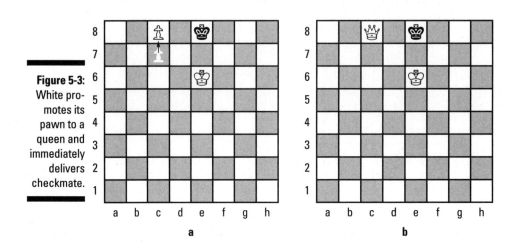

Players often call the square on which a player can promote a pawn the *queening square,* in this case the c8 square, because in all likelihood, the pawn becomes a queen after reaching that square. Controlling the queening square with one or more pieces is important so that, should your opponent's pawn reach that square, you can capture the new queen right away.

Guarding Your King and Putting a Rook in Motion: Castling

Castling is a move that safeguards the king and activates a rook at the same time. It's also the only time in chess when you can move two pieces at once. You may castle on the *kingside* (right, from white's point of view) or on the *queenside* (left), but the rule is the same: The king moves two squares to the right or left, and the rook slides around the king and occupies the square adjacent to the king, ending up on the king's opposite side.

Check out the starting position of the king and rooks in Figure 5-4 (note that I didn't include the other pieces on the board in order to make the castling move easier to see).

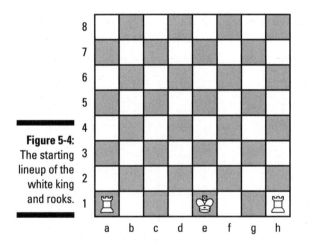

Figure 5-4:
The starting lineup of the white king and rooks.

White can castle kingside (see Figure 5-5a) or queenside (see Figure 5-5b). In both cases, the king moves two squares to the side and the rook slides around to the other side of the king.

The correct method of castling involves touching the king first. Technically, if you touch the rook first, you must move that piece and *only* it. Avoid fights and always castle by moving the king first! (For more on chess etiquette, flip to Chapter 16.)

Now that you know what castling looks like, you need to be aware that this move isn't always legal. Many a complaint has been made regarding this technicality! You *can't* castle in any of the following situations:

✔ If another piece is between the king and rook.

✔ If the king has already moved.

✔ If the rook has already moved (however, you may be able to castle by using the other rook).

✔ When in check.

✔ If the king must pass through a square controlled by the opponent. You can't castle through check.

You *can* castle even if either of the following is true:

✔ The rook is under attack.

✔ The rook (but *not* the king) must pass though a square controlled by the opponent.

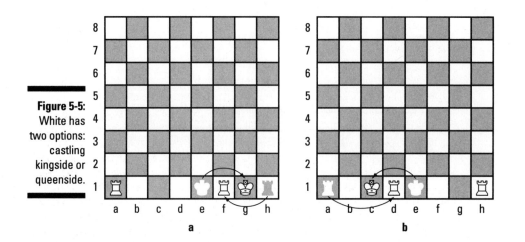

Figure 5-5:
White has two options: castling kingside or queenside.

Even champions can forget when to castle

Even the best players get confused sometimes. Viktor Korchnoi (1931–) was a leading contender for the world championship title for nearly two decades beginning in the 1970s. But during one tournament game, he moved his king, later on moved the king back to its original square, and still later castled! Neither he nor his opponent noticed the illegal move!

Chapter 6

Got Notation? Reading and Writing about Chess

- -

In This Chapter

▶ Labeling each piece

▶ Recording moves

▶ Singling out a piece when two are in question

▶ Putting in your two cents about a game

▶ Finding chess in your daily paper

- -

Chess notation has an important role in the world of chess because it preserves the game's history. It allows people to record games for posterity and gives them the chance to review the history of the game's development to date. Notation also allows people to overcome language barriers and communicate with one another in a universally understood manner. As such, official competitions require that someone record every single move with chess notation — but, fortunately, you don't have to mess with it when you're playing for fun! Even so, the notation is good to know because it allows players to communicate concisely and enables you to become a more knowledgeable member of the chess community.

Many kinds of chess notation exist, from *forsythe* (a notation that computers understand) to different notations for various languages. One kind of notation, however, is universally understood, and it's the one I describe in this chapter: *algebraic,* which uses a single letter and number to name each square and a letter for each chess piece. This notation system has replaced the older English *descriptive* notation — which used an abbreviated form of a verbal description of the moves — because chess is for all people, not just English-speaking people.

Note: Although algebraic notation looks goofy and is hard to make sense of at first, believe me, getting used to it takes just a little bit of practice. This notation tries to keep things as simple as possible, but some situations that arise may still be confusing. Some people use the fewest characters possible while still avoiding ambiguity, and others spell out moves in more detail. In this book, I lean more to the spell-it-out side.

Keeping Track of the Pieces

Each chess piece needs to be referred to by some notation; so does each square of a chessboard. (Flip to Chapter 1 for the scoop on naming individual chessboard squares.) The king is indicated by K, the knight by N (because K is already taken!), and so on. The pawn, poor thing, doesn't have any identification. If the notation, which I get into in the next section, doesn't indicate a piece, you can assume that the move in question involves a pawn. Table 6-1 shows the notation for the pieces.

Table 6-1	Chess Piece Notation
Piece	*Notation*
King	K
Queen	Q
Knight	N
Bishop	B
Rook	R

The letters must be capitalized to indicate pieces; otherwise, they indicate squares.

Writing the Moves of a Game

You can write any conceivable chess move by using algebraic notation. Every piece is identified, and so is every square. A complete description of the game is called the *score* of the game, and the paper you write the score on is called the *score sheet*.

In the following sections, I explain how to describe openings, captures, exchanges, castling, and promotions in notation.

Describing a typical opening

Take a look at how algebraic notation works in practice by examining one of the most common openings, the Ruy Lopez, or Spanish Game (see Chapter 13 for details on this opening). Each move is numbered and includes one move by white and one move by black (except in the third step, which I explain a little later in this section). The opening moves of the Ruy Lopez are written as follows:

1. e4   e5

2. Nf3   Nc6

3. Bb5

White moves first, followed by black, so it follows that white's first move was to e4, and black's was to e5.

Keep in mind that the absence of a piece designation (a capital letter) indicates a pawn move. Only one pawn can move to e4 for white and only one to e5 for black, because pawns must move straight forward. (Chapter 2 tells you all about a pawn's available moves.) Figure 6-1 shows where white and then black moved their pawns.

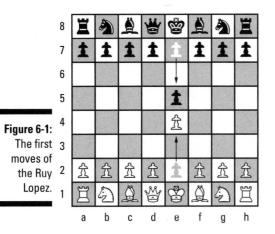

Figure 6-1:
The first moves of the Ruy Lopez.

For the second set of moves, the white knight moves to f3, and the black knight moves to c6, as shown in Figure 6-2.

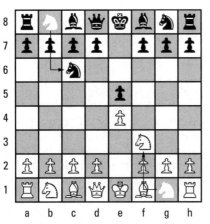

Figure 6-2:
The white knight gallops to f3, and the black knight trots to c6.

Now, white moves the bishop out to attack the knight. Note that a capital *B* means bishop, and a lowercase *b* refers to the b-file. Figure 6-3 shows the white bishop moving out to the b5 square.

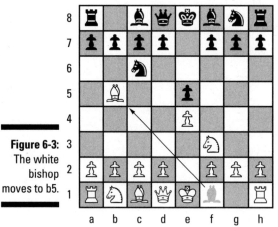

Figure 6-3:
The white
bishop
moves to b5.

Notice that I didn't give the corresponding black move in the notation for the third step of the Ruy Lopez opening. You'll often see this omission in chess books when a move by white lends itself to a comment. Because I give the white move alone, I can also give the black move alone (but still next to a "3" because it's part of the third set of moves). However, if I give the black move alone, I need to precede it with an ellipsis (...), which is the conventional way of indicating a stand-alone move by black.

Indicating captures

To indicate a capture with chess notation, you use an *x* along with the name of the square where the capture is made; you also note either the file of the attacking pawn or the symbol for the piece itself (such as B for a bishop). To set up a situation that's ripe for capture, imagine a game that begins with white moving a pawn to e4, followed by a black pawn move to e5. White then moves another pawn to d4. The notation looks like this:

1. e4   e5

2. d4

Figure 6-4 shows these first few moves.

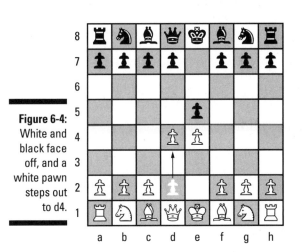

Figure 6-4:
White and black face off, and a white pawn steps out to d4.

Now black has the option of capturing the white pawn on d4 with its pawn. This capture is written as follows, and Figure 6-5 illustrates it. (Keep in mind that a black move written without the preceding white move is indicated by the use of the ellipsis, as I've done here.)

2. ... exd (or 2. ... exd4, which is more precise)

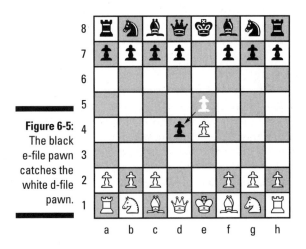

Figure 6-5:
The black e-file pawn catches the white d-file pawn.

Either notation is correct, because the black pawn can only capture on that one square on the d-file. You may also have noticed that only the file (e), not the file-rank (e5), of the attacking pawn is given. You can leave off the rank because black has just one pawn on this e-file, so the rank is understood.

Sometimes, in place of the notation 2. ... exd, you'll see simply 2. ... ed (minus the *x*). People who write notation this way don't think that indicating captures is necessary, but most people feel that using the *x* to indicate a capture makes following the game easier. In any case, you may see either convention used in other chess books.

Noting an exchange and a castle

Going back to the Ruy Lopez that I discuss in the earlier section "Describing a typical opening," one common variation is called the *exchange variation*. This situation occurs when white captures the black knight with the bishop (or exchanges the bishop for the knight; see Chapter 3 for info on exchanges). Set the pieces back to their starting positions and see whether you can follow some of this notation on your own chessboard:

1. e4   e5

2. Nf3   Nc6

3. Bb5   a6

4. Bxc6

If you're able to follow the preceding moves, you can tell that black, on his third move, moves a pawn to a6, and that white, on his fourth move, captures the black knight that occupied c6. Figure 6-6 shows the result of this capture.

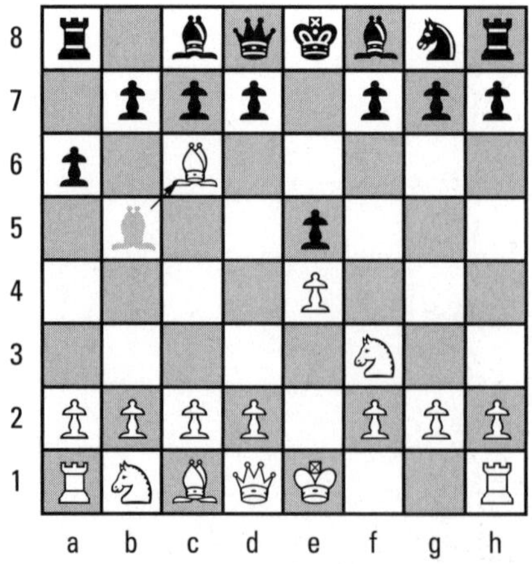

Figure 6-6:
The white bishop captures the black knight on c6.

Now, black can capture the white bishop with one of two pawns. Black decides to capture the bishop with its pawn from d7, so the notation is written like so:

4. ... dxc6

Take a peek at Figure 6-7 to see the result of all this action.

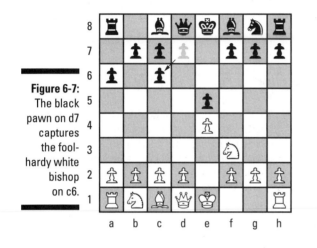

Figure 6-7: The black pawn on d7 captures the fool-hardy white bishop on c6.

Suppose, however, that black decides to take the bishop with his pawn from the b7 square instead. Back up one step as I show you this variation.

If black captures the bishop with the pawn on b7, the notation reads like this:

4. ... bxc6

Figure 6-8 illustrates this setback for the white bishop.

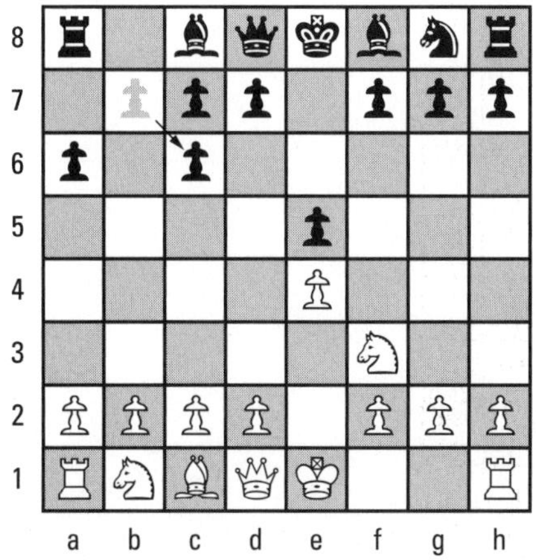

Figure 6-8: The black pawn on b7 captures the white bishop on c6.

White's next move may be to castle on the kingside (see Chapter 5 for castling details). The notation for castling on the kingside is 0-0, but the notation for castling on the queenside is 0-0-0. White's action (see Figure 6-9), then, is written like this:

5. 0-0

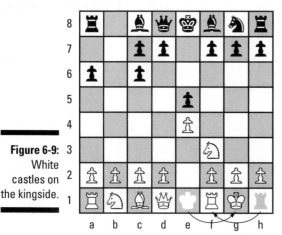

Figure 6-9: White castles on the kingside.

If you don't need a chessboard to follow the preceding notation, you may be ready for blindfold chess, where you play a game without sight of the board just by calling out the notation!

Recording a pawn promotion

You may play lots of games without ever promoting a pawn (see Chapter 5 for this special move), but if you do end up doing it, you'll need to be able to write the move down correctly.

Notation accounts for the promotion of a pawn by adding the piece designation to the move. For example:

✔ If on your 40th move you play your pawn to the eighth rank on the b-file and promote it to a queen, you write 40. b8Q.

✔ If on your 40th move you promote to a bishop on the eighth rank of the b-file, you write 40. b8B.

Accounting for Ambiguities (Which Knight, for Pete's Sake?)

What if two pieces can capture on, or move to, the same square? Chess play-ers solve that potential dilemma by adding the file to the piece designation with a slash. In Figure 6-10, for example, you see that two knights can move to the same square, d2. The notation of N/bd2 means that the knight standing on the b-file is the one that moves to d2.

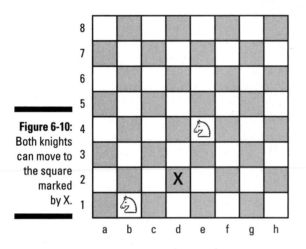

Figure 6-10: Both knights can move to the square marked by X.

So what do you write if two knights on the b-file can move to d2 (as in Figure 6-11)? To indicate which knight moves in that case, write the entire designation of the originating square: N/b3d2. Or, for clarity's sake, you can add a hyphen: N/b3-d2. This notation means that the knight on b3 moves to d2. (Don't worry, this situation doesn't happen all that often! But when it does, the pesky knights are usually the culprits.)

When capturing en passant (see Chapter 5), you may have two pawns that can make the same capture. This situation isn't ambiguous, however, because you always indicate the originating file that the capturing pawn is on (exd, for example). Very, very rarely, however, it's possible to have two pawns on a file, one that can capture en passant and one that can capture normally. This case is handled by adding the abbreviation e.p. to the notation, as in exd e.p. The lack of the trailing e.p. indicates that the other pawn on that file made the capture.

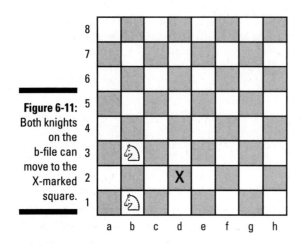

Figure 6-11:
Both knights on the b-file can move to the X-marked square.

Commenting on a Game after the Fact

Some notation marks don't apply when you're writing down your moves *during* a game, but you can use them to *annotate* a game (that is to say, to comment about a game that has been played previously). These annotations, which usually include symbols, were made to enhance the reader's ability to understand a game and are used in chess books, magazines, and newspaper columns. See Table 6-2 for the most commonly used annotations and their definitions.

Table 6-2	Chess Annotations
Annotation	*Definition*
!	A good move
!!	A very good move
?	A bad move
??	A very bad move
1-0	White won the game
0-1	Black won the game
½	The game was a draw
+/	White has a winning advantage
/+	Black has a winning advantage
+/=	White has a slight advantage
=/+	Black has a slight advantage
=	The positions of black and white are considered equal
+	Check
#	Checkmate

Nowadays, software exists to help you place these symbols after moves that deserve special mention, but you can always write on your score sheet the old-fashioned way. You wouldn't call attention to a normal move, such as 1. e4, but you may want to give 1. Na3 a question mark because it's a dubious way to open a chess game. The ten games in Chapter 18 are annotated and use symbols.

Keeping score during a tournament

In a tournament game, both players are required to write down all the moves (called "keeping a game score"). This scorekeeping helps the director settle potential disputes. For example, if one player claims a draw because the same position has occurred three times (a draw according to the rules), the director uses the players' score sheets to decide whether this is actually the case. This written record is also used to determine whether players have made the minimum number of moves in a given time period, which is called the *time limit* and is specified at the start of every competition.

Some grandmasters are notorious for their poor handwriting, and making heads or tails of their score sheets is impossible (just check out the example here to see what I mean!). Tournament officials usually rely on the opponent's score sheet in order to reconstruct the game.

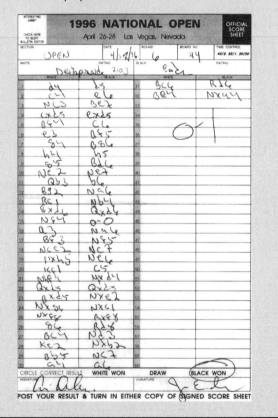

Part II
Gaining Chess Know-How

The 5th Wave — By Rich Tennant

Cowboy Chess

"And I'm sayin' no one has 3 bishops on the board unless he's a slimy, no account chess cheat!"

In this part . . .

In this part, I demonstrate how to use chess tactics and how to create combinations to increase your chances of winning. This hand-to-hand combat is the part of a chess game that holds the most aesthetic appeal for most people. I cover what it means to make a sacrifice and why doing so is sometimes necessary, even if the idea of letting your opponent capture your piece is counterintuitive. I also discuss the general importance of pattern recognition and cover specific mating patterns, which lead to checkmate, along with pawn formations.

Chapter 7

Trying Out Tactics and Combinations in Hand-to-Hand Combat

In This Chapter

▶ Maneuvering your pieces to accomplish a short-range objective

▶ Surprising your opponent with a carefully planned combination

*L*et the mortal combat begin. When pieces engage one another, either at close quarters or from a long range, tactics rule the day. In fact, tactics — sometimes even elementary ones — are the deciding factor for most chess games. So becoming familiar with the most basic examples and looking for them throughout the game are critical. You can make 40 great moves and still lose the game by overlooking your opponent's tricks on the 41st!

Combinations, which are based on tactics, are great techniques, too. Everything leading up to a combination may feel like mere plot development, because combinations are the car-chase scenes of chess. A combination can appear like a bolt out of the blue, but despite this almost inevitable element of surprise, a combination is most often the result of careful planning.

In this chapter, I help you avoid the disastrous blunder of making lots of great moves and losing the game by missing your opponent's one great tactic. I also give you the lowdown on combinations, discussing the most common tactical devices that serve as building blocks — after you familiarize yourself with these combination themes, you'll be able to recognize them in play and respond accordingly. Knowing the names of combinational themes isn't as important as understanding how and why they work, so I answer such questions for you here.

Knowing Your Tactical Game Plan

A *tactic* is a move or a series of moves designed to bring about benefits in the short term, and it usually leads to an advantage in one or more of the elements of chess. (See Chapter 3 for a discussion of the elements of chess.) Studying the basic types of tactics in the following sections can lead to an immediate improvement in your results. Of course, you won't find a shortcut to chess mastery, but by becoming a strong tactician, you can pocket many a point along the way.

Don't make a move in the hopes that your opponent won't see your threat. Instead, stick to the basic principles of play.

Bullying two guys at once: The fork

One of the most basic of chess tactics, the *fork* is a simultaneous attack on two or more pieces by a single piece (for the sake of brevity, I call the pawn a *piece* here). Either knights or pawns usually do those down-and-dirty forks, although any piece can get in on the action (the knight, however, is the ideal forking piece). During a successful fork, your opponent can't protect all the threatened pieces at once and, as a result, must risk the loss of one.

A variation of the *Vienna game* (an opening sequence of moves that became popular after a tournament in Vienna) provides a good example of both knight and pawn forks. Some people call this variation the *Frankenstein-Dracula* or *Monster* variation because the tactics are so scary. Almost every move in this opening contains a threat, which is the essence of chess tactics.

Chess players call an opening that has many tactical possibilities *sharp*. This Vienna game variation, featuring multiple forks, is one of the sharpest in all of chess.

The Vienna game begins with both sides advancing the pawns in front of their kings two squares, as shown in Figure 7-1a (in chess notation, the move is written 1. e4 e5; see Chapter 6 for all you need to know about reading the notation that I provide throughout this chapter). On the next turn, both sides bring out one of their knights, as you can see in Figure 7-1b (2. Nc3 Nf6).

Next, white *develops* (brings out) the bishop (3. Bc4), as Figure 7-2a shows, and the black knight captures the white pawn on e4 (3. ... Nxe4), as shown in Figure 7-2b, with the intent of employing a pawn fork in the near future.

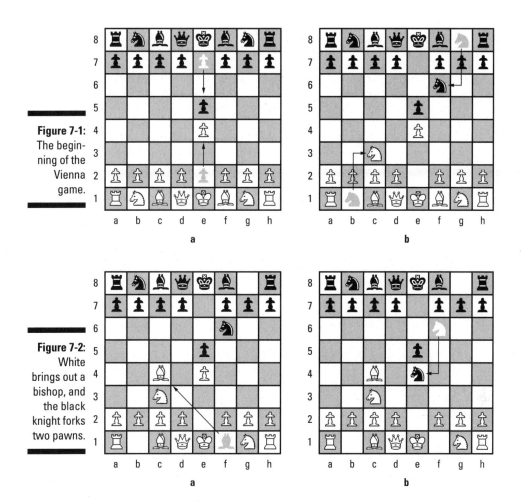

Figure 7-1: The beginning of the Vienna game.

Figure 7-2: White brings out a bishop, and the black knight forks two pawns.

The pawn fork

If the white knight on c3 captures the black knight on e4 (4. Nxe4), as Figure 7-3a shows, then a black pawn can fork the bishop and knight by moving to d5 (4. ... d5), as you see in Figure 7-3b. In other words, the pawn threatens to capture one of the pieces on its next move. In this way, black regains the lost piece and has a *free game* (meaning that the development of the rest of the pieces will be relatively easy). White can, of course, take the offending black pawn on d5 with its bishop (5. Bxd5), but the black queen would then swoop down upon the white bishop (5. ... Qxd5). Notice how white can save either the bishop or the knight, but not both, from capture.

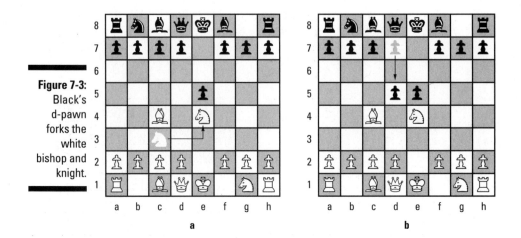

a   **b**

Usually, white avoids the pawn fork in the preceding section by making a counterthreat before the pawn fork can develop. Instead of capturing the black knight with the white knight (as shown in Figure 7-3), white brings out its queen to h5, with the immediate threat of checkmate (4. Qh5); see Figure 7-4a.

If black doesn't respond well, then white can capture the black pawn on f7 with the queen (5. Qxf7#) and announce the cry of victory: "Checkmate!" (I explain checkmate in Chapter 4.) However, because it's black's turn to move, black retreats the knight to d6 (4. ... Nd6). The knight now guards against the threat of checkmate and simultaneously *attacks* (threatens) white's bishop (Figure 7-4b).

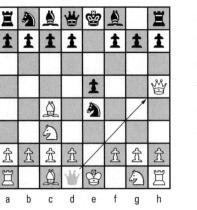
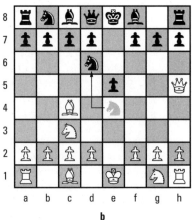

a   **b**

In one of the main variations of this opening, white chooses to retreat the bishop away from the attacking black knight by moving to b3 (5. Bb3), as Figure 7-5a shows. Black now chooses to develop the other knight to c6 in order to defend the king's pawn on e5 (5. ... Nc6); see Figure 7-5b.

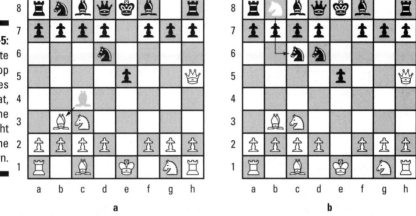

Figure 7-5:
The white bishop escapes the threat, and the black knight defends the king's pawn.

White now takes advantage of the fact that one of black's knights is tied down to defend against the threatened checkmate, and white attacks the defender by moving the knight on c3 to b5 (6. Nb5), as Figure 7-6a shows. *Removing the defender* is a tactical theme that you see over and over again in chess.

Black can't capture the cheeky white knight because of the threat of checkmate. Black also can't ignore the threat of its knight being taken by white's knight. This loss would put the black king in *check* (meaning, black's king is attacked; see Chapter 4 for more about check) and allow white to deliver checkmate with the next move. Instead, black moves the pawn on g7 forward one square (6. ... g6) in order to defend the checkmate and to attack the white queen at the same time (see Figure 7-6b).

A move that defends and attacks simultaneously is almost always a good one!

Now white's queen must retreat, but she heads to a square that keeps the threat to black alive, f3 (7. Qf3); see Figure 7-7a. Defense and attack at the same time! Black has the same problem as before — the king and the f-pawn are feeling the pressure — and advances the f-pawn two squares (7. ... f5), as Figure 7-7b shows). This move once again blocks the threatened checkmate, because the queen is no longer attacking the f7 square.

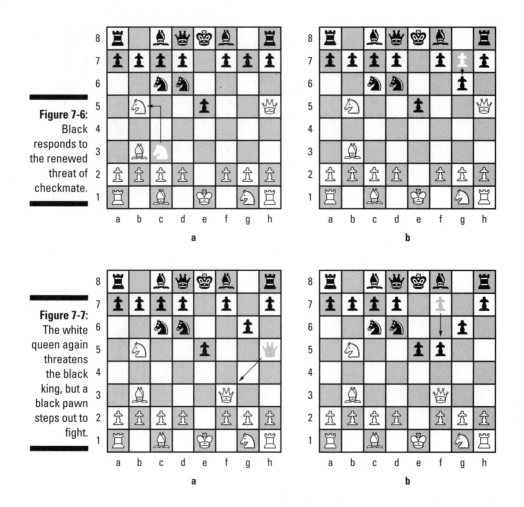

Figure 7-6:
Black responds to the renewed threat of checkmate.

Figure 7-7:
The white queen again threatens the black king, but a black pawn steps out to fight.

Black once again threatens to simply take the advanced white knight on b5, which is left hanging (lacking protection) — or *en prise* in chess terms. So white finds still another way to renew the threat of checkmate by again moving the queen, this time to d5 (8. Qd5); see Figure 7-8a. Black is out of defensive pawn moves and is forced to move out her queen to defend against the checkmate (8. ... Qe7), as Figure 7-8b shows.

The knight fork

Finally — time for the *knight fork!* The white knight captures the black pawn on c7 (9. Nxc7+), thereby putting the black king in check and simultaneously attacking the black rook in the corner (see Figure 7-9). Black must move the king out of check and allow white to capture the rook.

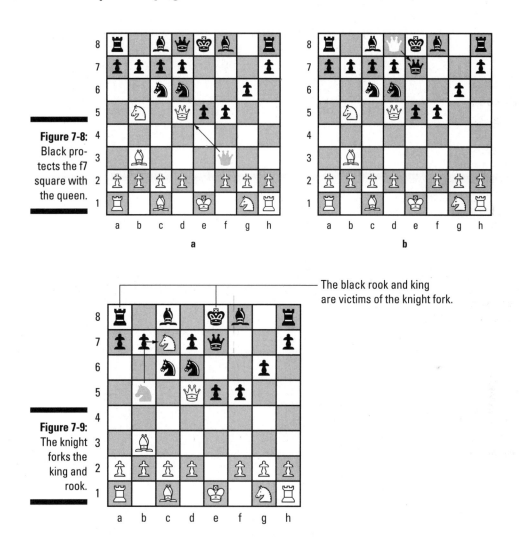

Figure 7-8: Black protects the f7 square with the queen.

a

b

The black rook and king are victims of the knight fork.

Figure 7-9: The knight forks the king and rook.

Going after the bodyguard: The pin

The pin is the most frequently used chess tactic. If patent lawyers were around before chess came about, somebody would've become a millionaire many times over by patenting this maneuver.

To achieve the *pin,* the pinning piece attacks one of two enemy pieces lined up along a rank, file, or diagonal (see Chapter 1 for information on ranks, files, and diagonals). The pinned piece is the one between the attacker and the other piece. Usually, the pinned piece is of lesser value than the other — so that if it were to move, the more important piece would be subject to capture.

Only queens, rooks, and bishops can pin an enemy piece, because they're the pieces that can attack multiple squares along a rank, file, or diagonal. Of the three, the bishop is most commonly used to establish a pin because it's more likely to find pieces of greater value than itself to attack.

Pinned pieces can move (although you may not want them to!) except when they're pinned to the king. Exposing the king to capture is illegal, so pinned pieces in cases involving the king are *really* nailed down.

In Figure 7-10a, the black knight on c6 is attacked by the white bishop on b5 but isn't pinned. In Figure 7-10b, however, when black moves her d7 pawn to d6, the white bishop pins the knight to the king, so the knight can't move.

Figure 7-10:
The knight becomes pinned when the d-pawn moves.

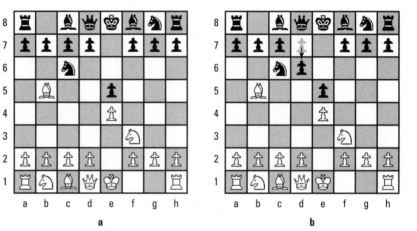

One very powerful type of pin can occur whenever the queen and king are lined up on a rank, file, or diagonal. When this positioning occurs, a bishop or rook may be able to pin the queen to the king. Be careful whenever your king and queen are on a line together, and be alert for the chance to pin when your opponent's are.

You can break a pin in four ways:

- ✔ **Capture the pinning piece.** You aren't really in much of a pin if you can take the pinning piece away, so capturing the pinning piece isn't often an option.

- ✔ **Attack the pinning piece and force it to capture or retreat.** This attack is called *putting the question to* the pinning piece.

- ✔ **Place a less valuable piece or pawn in the path between the pinned piece and the more valuable one.** This move is called *interposing*.

- ✔ **Remove the more valuable piece from the pinning path.** This strategy is appropriately called *running away*.

Pinning during the Nimzo-Indian opening

One of the chess openings popularized by Aaron Nimzowitsch still bears a portion of his name. (And just to confuse you, his name is spelled in various ways; you may also see it as Aron Nimzowitsch or Aaron Nimzovich.) The Nimzo-Indian belongs to a class of openings that are referred to as *Indian Defenses* (see Chapter 13). These openings are usually characterized by the development of a bishop on the flank, called *fianchetto*. The word is a diminutive of the Italian *fianco*, a flank.

In the Nimzo-Indian, the player often fianchettoes the queen's bishop. The player uses the king's bishop to establish an early pin. Here are the opening moves of the Nimzo-Indian: 1. d4 Nf6, 2. c4 e6, 3. Nc3 Bb4 (see the following figures).

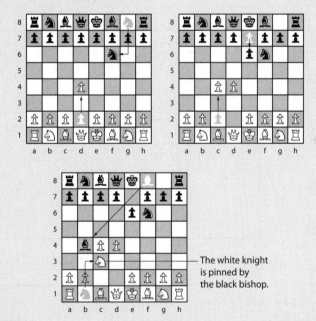

The white knight is pinned by the black bishop.

Black establishes a pin on the third move. The knight on c3 is pinned to the white king and can't move. Chess masters have tried all sorts of strategies in this position, but it has proven to be one of the most effective defenses in all of chess. Black is ready to castle and can then safely counterattack white's setup. (If you don't understand castling, see Chapter 5 for an explanation of this special move.) The pin proves to be more than just a minor annoyance for white. Sometimes the pin is mightier than the sword!

Forcing your opponent to move it or lose it: The skewer

The pin's cousin is the skewer, because it also exploits the positioning of two enemy pieces along a rank, file, or diagonal. The *skewer* is an attack on a piece that must move or be lost. In this case, the more valuable piece is attacked first. After the threatened piece moves, it exposes a second piece to capture. The bishop is the ideal skewer, and the king and queen are its frequent targets.

Can you find an opportunity for the skewer in Figure 7-11? It's white's move. (With a black queen against a white bishop, black has an overwhelming material advantage, but white can even the score by making use of the skewer.)

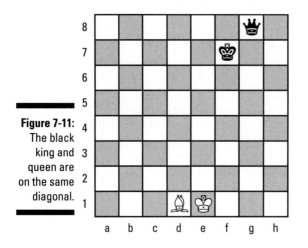

Figure 7-11: The black king and queen are on the same diagonal.

Figure 7-12 shows the skewer in action:

- ✔ In Figure 7-12a, white moves the bishop to b3 (1. Bb3+) in order to put the black king in check.

- ✔ Figure 7-12b shows that the black king is forced to move out of check (1. ... Kg7). Now the white bishop can simply capture the black queen!

The skewer can also take place in another way, when the attacking piece is between the two defenders. This type of skewer is illustrated in Figure 7-13. In this case, the white bishop attacks the two enemy pieces on either end of the diagonal. Think of a shish kebab — if black decides to move her king, then the white bishop takes the queen. If black decides to take the white bishop with her queen, black loses her queen to the white king. In any case, black has let a chance to win slip away and now must accept a draw — no one can win!

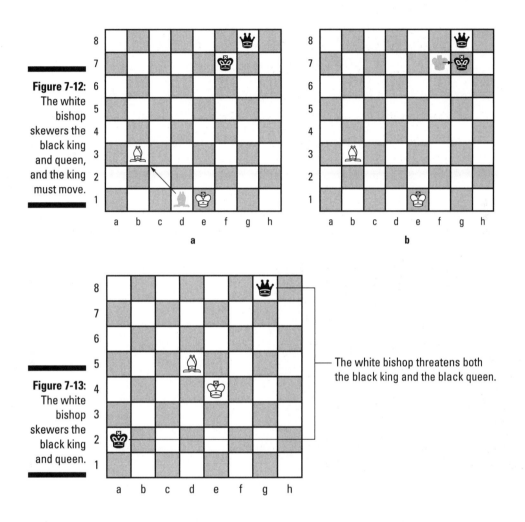

Figure 7-12:
The white bishop skewers the black king and queen, and the king must move.

Figure 7-13:
The white bishop skewers the black king and queen.

The white bishop threatens both the black king and the black queen.

In practice, the skewer doesn't occur as often as the fork or pin, but the move is so powerful that when it does occur, it usually decides the game. So be alert for the possibility of a skewer at any time, especially when the king and queen are exposed along a rank, file, or diagonal.

Stealing the show: The discovered attack

A *discovered attack* is the movement of a piece or pawn resulting in an attack by a piece that you didn't move. When you move a piece and expose an attack by a second stationary piece, the moving piece is free to create some mischief of its own. If the moving piece also attacks a piece of value, the situation is called a discovered *double attack.* The victim of a double attack can usually defend against one threat or the other, but not both.

A famous discovered attack occurred in the game Legall–St. Brie Paris, 1750. The term *Legall's mate* refers to the type of mating pattern seen in that game, which I depict in the following figures.

In Figure 7-14, the black bishop on g4 is pinning the white knight on f3 to the queen — the knight can't move without subjecting the queen to capture. (I describe pinning earlier in this chapter.) However, if the white knight's move results in a forced checkmate, who cares about the queen?

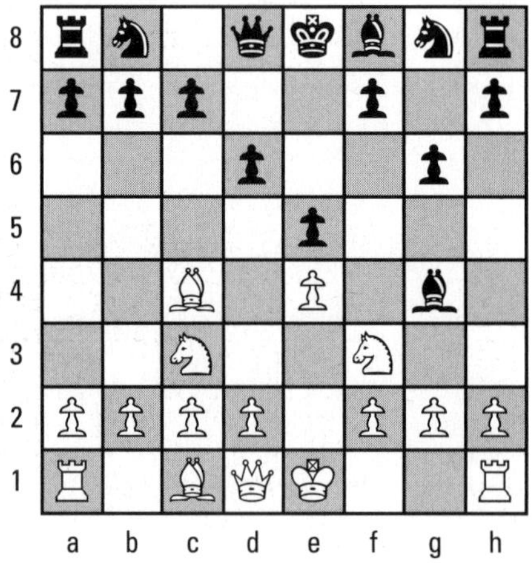

Figure 7-14:
The knight on f3 is pinned to its queen by the black bishop on g4.

Figure 7-15a shows that the white knight on f3 captures the black pawn on e5 (1. Nxe5). Now, the white bishop on c4 and the white knight on e5 are both attacking the black pawn on f7. The smart thing for black to do is capture the knight. However, the knight move has also exposed (discovered) an attack on the black bishop by the white queen. If black captures the white knight (1. ... dxe5), then white captures the black bishop (2. Qxg4) and pockets the captured e-pawn. In the actual game, Legall's opponent couldn't resist capturing white's queen with the bishop (1. ... Bxd1), as shown in Figure 7-15b, and was checkmated quickly.

Legall brought home the bacon by capturing the black pawn on f7 with his white bishop (2. Bxf7+); see Figure 7-16a. The black king is now in check, and his only escape is to move to e7 (2. ... Ke7), which he does in Figure 7-16b.

In Figure 7-17, the white knight on c3 moves to d5 (3. Nd5#), checking the king and cutting off the king's escape square on f6. The result is checkmate!

When you find yourself surprised by a discovered attack — and you will be surprised — the best course of action is to reduce your losses. In the Legall–St. Brie Paris game, black found himself in checkmate, but he could have kept his loss to a single pawn. Always choose the lesser of two evils.

Figure 7-15:
A double attack on f7.

a

b

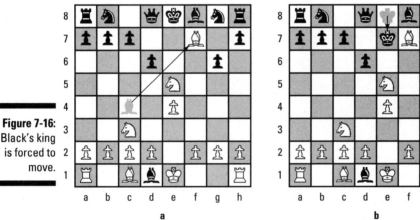

Figure 7-16:
Black's king is forced to move.

a

b

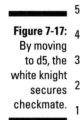

Figure 7-17:
By moving to d5, the white knight secures checkmate.

Making the king sweat: The discovered check and the double check

The term *discovered check* refers to the movement of a piece or pawn that produces a check by a different, unmoved piece. A *double check* occurs when the moving piece also checks the king. The only way to escape a double check is to move the king.

The game Réti-Tartakower Vienna, 1910, is perhaps the most famous example of a double check. I should point out that it wasn't a regular tournament game but a rather quick one, or what chess players refer to as a *blitz game*. The finish is amazing nevertheless. At one point in the game, the board looked like the one in Figure 7-18. Notice the queen-bishop-rook queue on the d-file. At first glance, it doesn't appear to be dangerous.

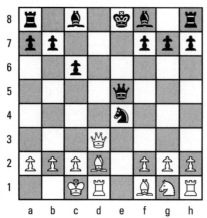

Figure 7-18: The board at one point in the Réti-Tartakower Vienna, 1910 game.

From this starting point, white delivers checkmate in three moves. The first move is a queen sacrifice (1. Qd8+), as shown in Figure 7-19a, which must have come as a rude shock to Saviely Tartakower. Because check can't be ignored, black must capture the white queen with the king (1. ... Kxd8), as Figure 7-19b shows.

The white bishop then moves from d2 to g5 (2. Bg5++) and checks the black king (see Figure 7-20). This move also discovers a check from the white rook on d1, creating a double check that seals black's fate. White will deliver checkmate on d8 no matter what black does:

- ✔ If black's king moves to c7 (2. ... Kc7), then the white bishop will move to d8 (3. Bd8#).

- ✔ If, on the other hand, the black king moves to e8 (2. ... Ke8), then the white rook will move to d8 (3. Rd8#).

In either case, the result is checkmate. This type of checkmate is now known as *Réti's mate*.

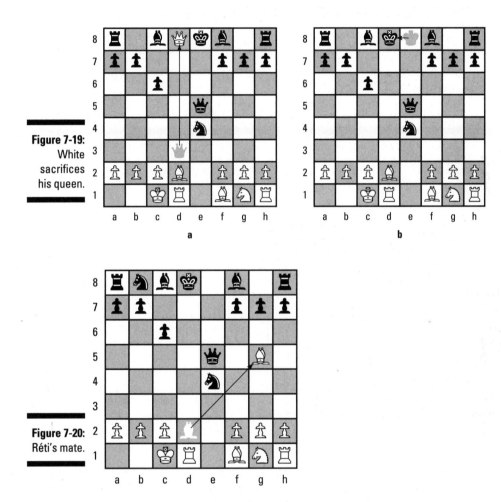

Figure 7-19: White sacrifices his queen.

a

b

Figure 7-20: Réti's mate.

One of the important aspects of the double-check tactic is that the king must move — you have no other way to escape a double check. If the king has nowhere to go, checkmate! Discovered and double checks are very powerful tactics. As with most tactics, it's better to give than receive. Be alert for your chances to use them, and be especially alert to your opponent's chances.

Combining Moves to Speed Your Progress

If you combine tactical threats when you initiate a sequence of moves with a specific goal in mind, you're making a *combination*. By combining threats, you force your opponent to choose among bad moves. Combinations often involve a sacrifice (see Chapter 8), but the idea is to derive some tangible benefit after the forced sequence is complete. This benefit can be anything from a small improvement in position to checkmate. Although any phase of a chess game can have a combination, the technique is most frequently found in the middlegame (see Chapter 14).

Combinations consist of tactics, including mating patterns (see Chapter 11 for more on mating patterns), so you can't spot one unless you can see the underlying tactics that make it work (and the only way you'll notice them in a game is to get really familiar with them, so read the preceding section and Chapter 11 over and over until you have them down pat). Certain themes of combinations are documented in chess literature; these themes may occur in your own games, but they may go unnoticed unless you're trained to look for them (and if you're not, you may sit there scratching your head when you lose).

Combinations happen to you when you assume something to be true that isn't. A rook may seem to be guarding a pawn, but it really isn't if it also has to guard a queen. A piece may seem to be safe, but it really isn't if your opponent can deflect it to a more dangerous square. Things aren't always the way they seem in chess, and combinations reveal deeper truths.

All the moves in a type of combination won't be the same every time. Your opponent is going to make a choice — called a *variation* — about how to react to the moves of your combination. (That's fine, as long as your opponent's countermoves don't work!) If your combination produces your desired result, it's considered *sound,* but if one of your opponent's responses makes your combination go awry, the combination is considered *unsound.*

Combinations are really the only way for a weaker player to defeat a stronger one. This triumph can happen when the stronger player is lulled to sleep and is expecting a certain sequence of moves, only to be surprised when a combination initiates a different sequence than she expected. So if you're the underdog, use the combinative themes in this section to pull the rug out from under the enemy.

Sacrificing a piece to clear a path

You'll undoubtedly face times when you want to play a certain move but can't because one of your own pieces is in the way; this scenario frequently happens when you want to employ a combination. The solution may be to sacrifice that piece, called making a *clearance* sacrifice (because you're clearing a path for another piece; see Chapter 8 for more on sacrifices). You do this in order to set up any of the basic tactics or mating patterns.

Some players don't even consider making such sacrifices, because surrendering their own material is counterintuitive. But you need to recognize the importance of surprise in the game of chess. If you're willing to consider and be on the lookout for clearance sacrifices when your opponent isn't, you stand a good chance of catching her off-guard and gaining a significant advantage (or even victory).

One example of a clearance sacrifice combination is Damiano's mate (see Chapter 11 for more on Damiano's mate including a queen and a pawn). In that case, white sacrificed both rooks to get them out of the way so that the queen could deliver checkmate. Figure 7-21 shows the starting position for a different clearance sacrifice combination that occurred in the Karpov-Chom game in 1977. The key to this combination is spotting the mating pattern of the rook and queen (see Chapter 11 for more about mating patterns). If the white queen could move to the square g7, she'd put the black king in checkmate — but how can she get there?

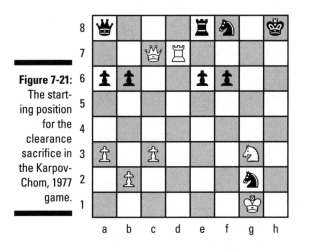

Figure 7-21: The starting position for the clearance sacrifice in the Karpov-Chom, 1977 game.

Karpov (white) wanted to move his queen, on c7, to h2 in order to check the black king and eventually put black in checkmate (by ultimately getting his queen to g7). However, his knight on g3 was in the queen's way. His solution was to move the knight to f5 (1. Nf5), as illustrated in Figure 7-22, in order to clear the way for the queen, even though black's e-pawn could then capture the knight.

The black pawn on e6 can capture the knight (1. ... exf5), as indicated in Figure 7-23a. When the white queen moves down the diagonal to h2 (2. Qh2+), however, she attacks the black king along the h-file, as shown in Figure 7-23b.

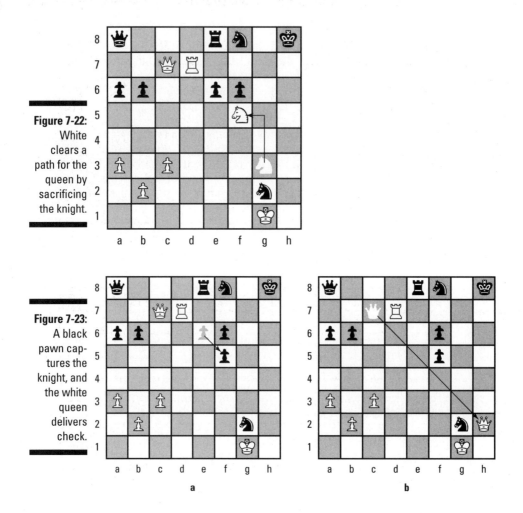

Figure 7-22: White clears a path for the queen by sacrificing the knight.

Figure 7-23: A black pawn captures the knight, and the white queen delivers check.

a

b

The king can escape the check by moving to g8 (2. ... Kg8), as Figure 7-24a shows, but the queen isn't through yet. Figure 7-24b shows her next attack, a simple move to g3 (3. Qg3+) to reinstate check.

Black can again escape the check by moving back to h8 (3. ... Kh8), as shown in Figure 7-25a, but checkmate is unavoidable. The queen simply moves straight ahead to g7 (4. Qg7#) and announces checkmate with a cry of victory (see Figure 7-25b).

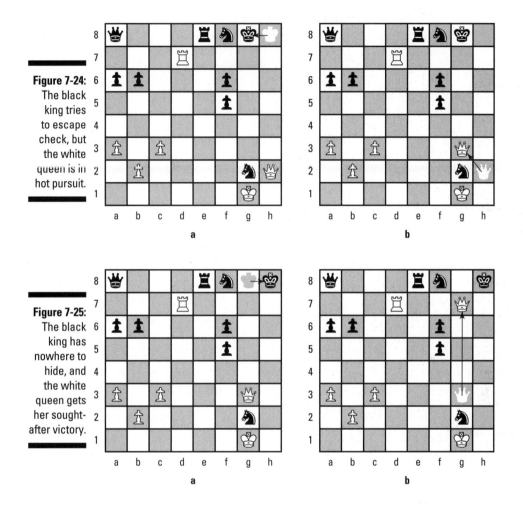

Figure 7-24:
The black king tries to escape check, but the white queen is in hot pursuit.

a

b

Figure 7-25:
The black king has nowhere to hide, and the white queen gets her sought-after victory.

a

b

Going back to black's potential capture of the white knight with a pawn, as the situation stands in Figure 7-22, black didn't necessarily have to capture the knight. Instead, by playing a different move, he would've seen another variation of white's combination. All the possible variations, however, would have ended in black being checkmated. White, after 1. Nf5, could have unleashed a new threat by performing another clearance sacrifice with the rook, moving it to h7, when the black knight on f8 would have been forced to capture the rook because black can't ignore check (2. Rh7+ Nxh7). The queen would have then moved to g7 to deliver checkmate (3. Qg7#). No black move could prevent the dual threats posed by the two clearance sacrifices. Therefore, all the variations lead to victory for white. Karpov's clearance sacrifice combination is considered sound.

Luring your opponent with a decoy

A *decoy* is used to entice your opponent's piece onto a square or *line* (meaning a file, rank, or diagonal) with fatal consequences. The decoy piece sacrifices itself for the greater good; the enticed piece may win a victory by capturing the decoy but will be doomed in the end. Decoy opportunities can happen at any time, but like most combinations, they most frequently occur in the middlegame (see Chapter 14). The objective is usually to win material, but if the combination results in checkmate, all the better!

The position in Figure 7-26 is set up for white to use a decoy to win material (see Chapter 3 for more on material). Although the material is even, the black king and queen are on the same rank, which often spells trouble. Whenever the king and queen are lined up on the same rank, file, or diagonal, look for a tactic, such as a pin or skewer (which I describe earlier in this chapter), to exploit the position. If a straightforward tactic isn't available, a combination, where you generally sacrifice a piece to allow for a tactic, may be.

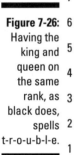
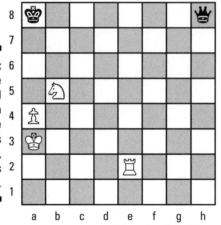

Figure 7-26: Having the king and queen on the same rank, as black does, spells t-r-o-u-b-l-e.

White exploits the positioning of black's king and queen by moving the rook to e8 to use it as a decoy (1. Re8+), in an effort to lure the queen from her perch to her impending doom, as shown in Figure 7-27a. Black has no real choice but to accept the decoy and capture the rook with the queen (1. … Qxe8), as demonstrated in Figure 7-27b — if the king moves out of check, the white rook will simply capture the queen.

Black is now set up for a fork (see the fork tactic discussion earlier in this chapter), where the white knight moves to a position where it threatens both black's king and queen, c7 (2. Nc7+); see Figure 7-28. The knight will capture the black queen on white's next turn, because black must respond to the check by moving the king.

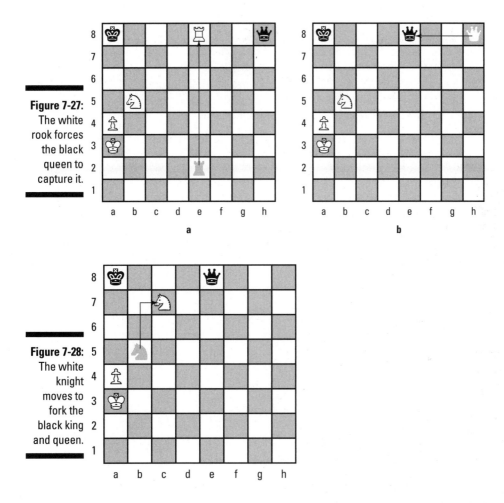

Figure 7-27:
The white rook forces the black queen to capture it.

a

b

Figure 7-28:
The white knight moves to fork the black king and queen.

Deflecting your opponent's piece off a key square

The combination involving a deflection is similar to the decoy that I describe in the preceding section. Instead of luring your opponent's piece to a place where it meets its end, however, a *deflection sacrifice* causes an opponent's piece to abandon a key square, rank, file, or diagonal. You're then free to use this key square, rank, file, or diagonal to your advantage.

At first glance, the position in Figure 7-29a appears to be a certain *draw* (where neither side is capable of winning). Material is even, and no back rank mate possibilities exist (see Chapter 3 for a list of piece values and Chapter 11 for more on the back-rank mate). However, the black rook is defending the black queen, and if white can entice the rook to move off of the d-file, then black will lose her queen.

The white rook can deflect the black rook from the defense of the black queen by moving to e8 and putting the black king in check (1. Re8+); see Figure 7-29b.

If black's rook captures white's (1. ... Rxe8), as shown in Figure 7-30a, then the black queen is left undefended. White can then capture her with her own queen (2. Qxd2), as shown in Figure 7-30b, leaving white with a clear material gain.

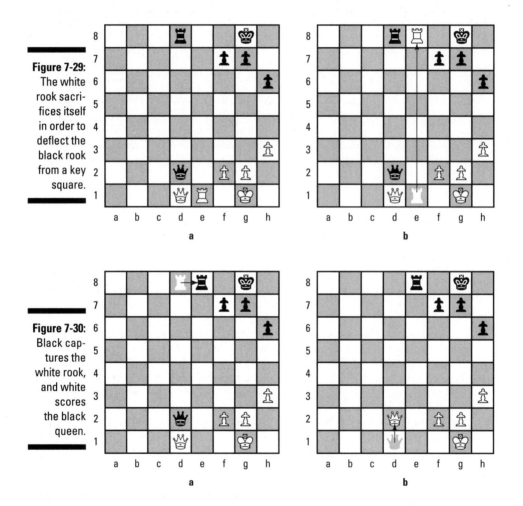

Figure 7-29: The white rook sacrifices itself in order to deflect the black rook from a key square.

Figure 7-30: Black captures the white rook, and white scores the black queen.

Black can choose not to take the offered rook, but that variation is also bad. If the black king simply moves out of check (1. ... Kh7), as in Figure 7-31a, then the white rook captures black's rook (2. Rxe8), as shown in Figure 7-31b. Do you see how white's rook move makes use of both deflection and double attack? The white rook and queen then protect one another, even though the black queen is between them — the black queen can't capture either piece without being captured in return. Because both variations are bad for black, the decoy combination is sound for white.

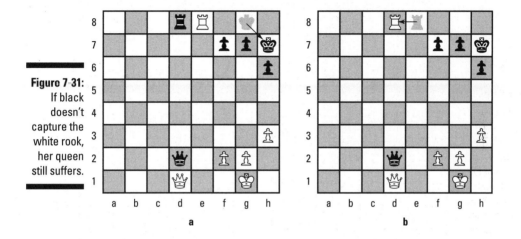

Figure 7-31:
If black doesn't capture the white rook, her queen still suffers.

a

b

Destroying the guard

Sometimes a single piece is guarding against disaster, and eliminating that piece may trigger a chess apocalypse. If you're the attacker, it may well be worth a significant material sacrifice in order to eliminate the key defender, or as chess players say, *destroy the guard*.

In Figure 7-32, the black rook on d8 is guarding against a back-rank mate (see Chapter 11 for more on the back-rank mate). The rook is all that stands between black and disaster. The white queen on g5 is attacking the black rook, which the black knight on c6 is defending. However, because the knight moves in an "L" shape, it can't guard the back rank if it takes the rook's place.

In Figure 7-33a, the white queen sacrifices herself by moving to d8 (1. Qxd8) in order to destroy the guard (the rook). The black knight then replaces the black rook by capturing the white queen (1. … Nxd8), as shown in Figure 7-33b, but is unable to perform the rook's guard duty.

Even though white lost a queen for a rook, the chance to deliver a back-rank checkmate by moving the white rook to e8 (2. Re8+), as shown in Figure 7-34, makes the sacrifice in material worthwhile.

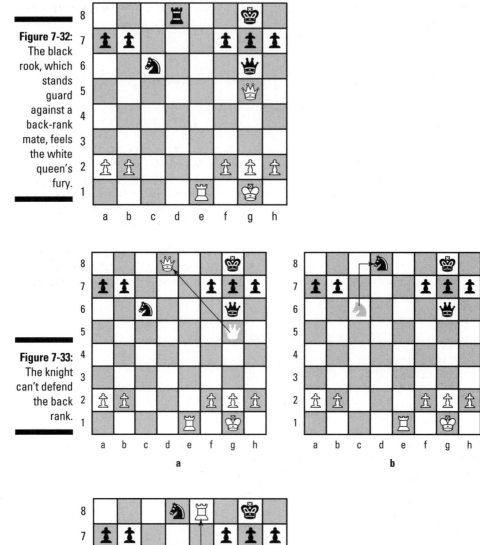

Figure 7-32: The black rook, which stands guard against a back-rank mate, feels the white queen's fury.

Figure 7-33: The knight can't defend the back rank.

a

b

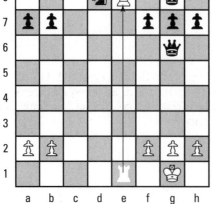

Figure 7-34: Checkmate! The white rook delivers the back-rank mate.

When your opponent has a piece performing a critical function — as black's rook was — look for a way to eliminate it. Don't be afraid to consider any possibility, even the loss of your queen.

Overloading one piece to make another piece vulnerable

Sometimes a piece or pawn has too much on its hands to do everything asked of it and must choose which responsibility to fulfill. In this case, the piece is said to be *overloaded,* and the combination is called *overloading.* When your opponent's piece is overloaded, it's just asking for trouble — and for you to put a combination into action to exploit that piece. If one piece has two critical tasks to perform (defending two different pieces, perhaps), you may be able to cause it to choose one at the expense of the other.

In Figure 7-35, the black rook on d7 is overloaded: It's charged with defending the black queen on d6 (which is under attack from the white queen on a3) and the black pawn on f7 (which is under attack by the white bishop and rook).

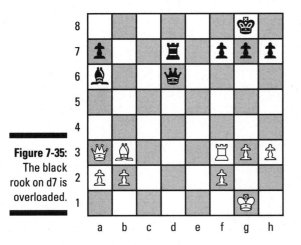

Figure 7-35: The black rook on d7 is overloaded.

If white captures the black queen with her own queen (1. Qxd6), as shown in Figure 7-36a, then the black rook is forced to abandon its defense of the black pawn on f7. The rook must capture the white queen (1. ... Rxd6), as in Figure 7-36b, to restore material balance.

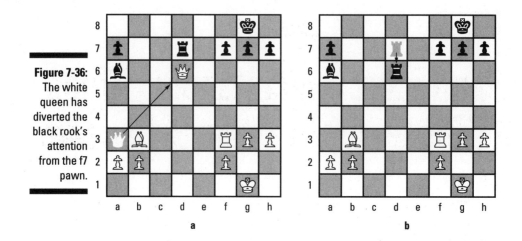

Figure 7-36: The white queen has diverted the black rook's attention from the f7 pawn.

With the black rook now on d6, no one is left to guard the f7 pawn, and white is free to capture it. Either the white rook on f3 or the bishop on b3 can do the dirty work (2. Rxf7 or 2. Bxf7+), as Figure 7-37 shows. Notice that 2. Rxf7 threatens a discovered check, and so offers a much more powerful follow-up. But either move nets the pawn.

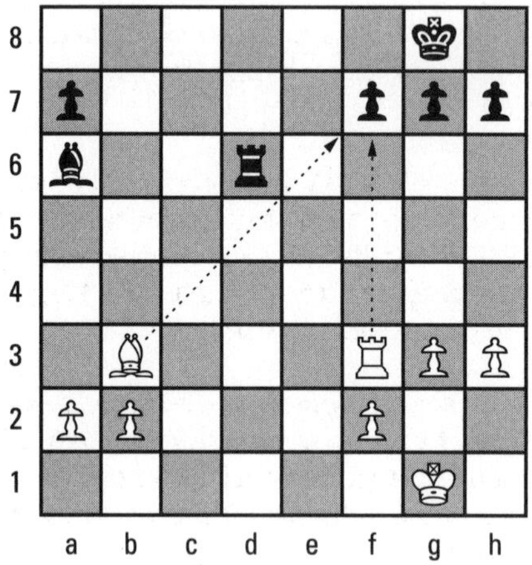

Figure 7-37: White can capture the black pawn with either the bishop or the rook.

Chapter 8

Sacrifices: Understanding When It's Better to Give than to Receive

*I*f you were a single king or queen working two jobs just to send your little pawns to college, you'd undoubtedly consider yourself to be making a significant sacrifice. On the chessboard, however, a *sacrifice* (real or otherwise) is simply an intentional loss of a valuable piece. (An *unintentional* loss of something of value is technically called a *blunder.*)

Note: Sometimes, you may think you're making a sacrifice, but you really aren't. For example, if you win your opponent's queen at the cost of your knight, it may seem like a plain old sacrifice. However, that assumption isn't quite correct. You may feel as though you're sacrificing the knight, but really you're simply trading it for a piece of higher value.

One of the odd things about chess is that every move involves both an advantage and a disadvantage. You must give up something, whether it be material or space, to get something, such as a lead in development (see Chapter 3 for more on these elements of chess). So, in the broadest terms, every move in a chess game involves some sacrifice.

Although speaking of a sacrifice in any one of the elements in chess is technically correct, the most common sacrifice by far is that of material. Specific — and planned — sacrifices of certain pieces at the right time can help players gain an advantage. Knights may impale themselves on spears so that other pieces can infiltrate behind enemy lines, pawns may throw themselves under the cavalry's hooves to slow an enemy advance, or the queen may take an arrow meant for the king — all so that other pieces on the board may someday be better off (that is, on the winning side). The greatest thrill is to sacrifice the queen, because she's the most powerful piece of all. Chess players tend toward a flair for the dramatic, and if any chess player can give up a queen and still beat you, well, just expect a great deal of teasing.

In this chapter, I discuss the intentional sacrifice of a pawn or piece, either temporary or permanent, that a player performs in the hope of capitalizing on some other advantage — and ultimately winning the game.

No true chess aficionado can deny that sacrifices rank among the most dramatic events in a chess game. Sacrifices introduce an imbalance among positions and often act as the proverbial bolt from the blue, just as combinations do (see Chapter 7 for more on combinations, which often involve sacrifices). If your opponent makes a sacrifice that you haven't considered, that move can be quite unnerving. The best thing to do in this situation is to take a few moments to compose yourself and then calmly try to figure out what's going on and how best to proceed. The rule of thumb is that the only way to refute a sacrifice is to accept it! If you don't know what to do, take the material.

Sacrificing for an Edge in Development: The Gambit

In trying to make chess seem difficult and mysterious, chess players have long called a common type of sacrifice by a different term entirely. We refer to sacrifices that occur in the opening phase of the game as *gambits*. Gambits almost always involve the sacrifice of material for a positional advantage. In other words, you trade a piece (or more often just a pawn) for a gain in *development* (the element of time; see Chapter 3 for details). The reasoning is simple: If you can get more pieces out into attacking formation much more quickly than your opponent can, you can conceivably win back the sacrificed material — and then some — while your opponent is scrambling to catch up.

Gambits are very popular, but you should always keep in mind that they can be very dangerous. If you don't secure some compensating advantage, you'll be stuck with a long-term material deficit.

One of the oldest gambits in chess is the *King's Gambit,* where white's f-pawn is the object of sacrifice. A player enters into this type of move by using the common double king pawn opening (1. e4 e5), where both white and black advance the king's pawn two squares (see Figure 8-1). (If you aren't familiar with the chess notation I just provided, flip to Chapter 6 for details.)

White's next move is to advance his king's bishop pawn by two squares (2. f4), where the white pawn threatens and is itself threatened by the black e-pawn (as shown in Figure 8-2a). Black can accept the gambit and win material by capturing the offered white f-pawn (2. ... exf4); see Figure 8-2b. White can't immediately *recapture* the pawn, meaning that he can't get even by capturing the black pawn that just took his pawn.

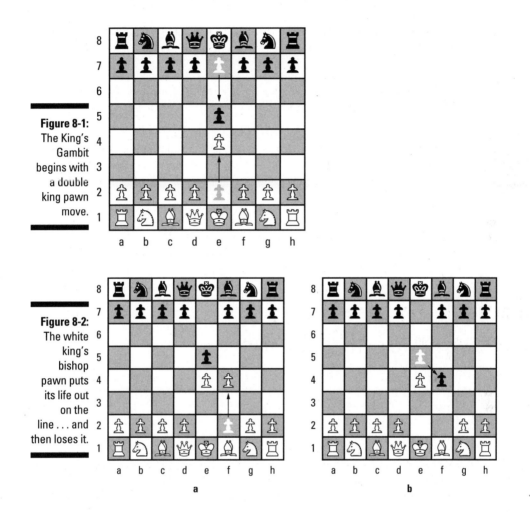

Figure 8-1: The King's Gambit begins with a double king pawn move.

Figure 8-2: The white king's bishop pawn puts its life out on the line . . . and then loses it.

a

b

White was willing to gambit a pawn in the hopes of securing an advantage in space by controlling the center (if black's e-pawn captures white's f-pawn, he no longer contests the d4 square). Is the element of material (white will have one less pawn) more important than the element of space (white will have more control of the center)? In chess, this type of question has no definitive answer — that's why you play the game and see how various situations play out.

Many chess players have differences of opinion about the effectiveness of the King's Gambit, as they do about most gambits. Some players like it, and some don't. The King's Gambit is rarely played at the highest levels of chess, so that tells you that the best players don't think it's the best opening choice. However, this gambit is still dangerous at lower levels, where a single mistake by black can give white the upper hand.

Is a gambit a gamble?

A certain amount of risk is involved in playing a gambit, but the term didn't derive from the word "gamble." It comes from the Italian word *gambetta,* which was a wrestling term for tripping up your opponent by the heels. The gambit was first used in its chess sense by Ruy Lopez, a Spanish priest and a renowned chess player, in 1561.

Setting Up an Attack on the Enemy King: The Classic Bishop Sacrifice

One of the earliest recorded sacrifices appears in Gioacchino Greco's infamous chess handbook of 1619. This move, called a classic bishop sacrifice, has been used prominently ever since then, and I advise the serious chess student to become intimately aware of this type of sacrifice. Nearly every experienced player knows this sacrifice, because it occurs in practice relatively often. By that, I mean the sacrificial theme occurs in several standard opening variations.

A bishop sacrifice is especially powerful if a player uses the move to expose the enemy king to attack. Sometimes this sacrifice can lead directly to checkmate, as in the following example, but often the move just wins back the material — with interest.

In Greco's *classic bishop sacrifice,* one player sacrifices a bishop to expose the enemy king to a brutal attack by the queen on d1 and the knight on f3. The white bishop on d3 has access to the black king via the black pawn on h7. Meanwhile, the white queen on d1, along with her knight on f3, is prepared to quickly enter the fray. Figure 8-3 shows the basic setup for the classic bishop sacrifice.

To initiate the sacrifice, the white bishop captures the black pawn on h7 (1. Bxh7+), putting the enemy king in check (see Figure 8-4a). Of course, the black king can escape the check by moving right one square to h8, but if he doesn't capture the white bishop, then he'll have lost a pawn for nothing (see the king's capture in Figure 8-4b).

White is now behind in material, having traded a bishop for a pawn, or three points for one. (Consult Chapter 3 for the relative value of pieces.) However, this loss in material is meaningless if white can deliver checkmate.

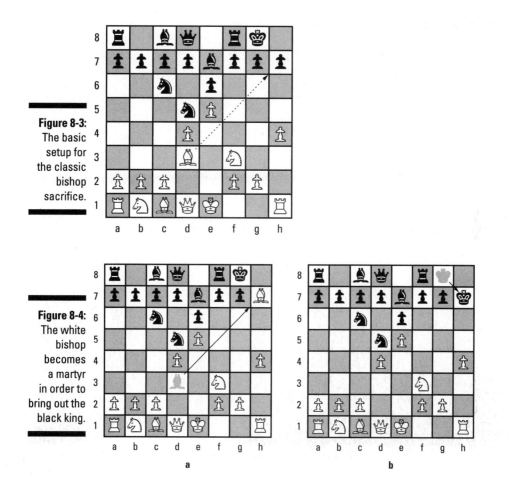

Figure 8-3:
The basic setup for the classic bishop sacrifice.

Figure 8-4:
The white bishop becomes a martyr in order to bring out the black king.

Next, the white knight from f3 jumps into the arena by moving to g5 (2. Ng5+), putting the black king in check (see Figure 8-5a). The black bishop on e7 can capture the marauding white knight on g5, but if it does, its fate is sealed. White could capture the black bishop with the pawn on h4, and the white rook on h1 would attack the black king with a discovered check. The white queen would then join the attack on the next move by moving to the h-file, and the lights would go out for the black king.

Jumping back to the situation at hand, black avoids this fate by moving his king back to g8 (2. ... Kg8), as shown in Figure 8-5b.

Even though black sidestepped one scenario ending in checkmate, he's still foiled once again by the relentless advance of the white queen to h5 (3. Qh5), as shown in Figure 8-6. Checkmate is next no matter what black does, because white will move the queen to h7. For example, if black moves the f-pawn forward to f6 (3. ... f6), then the white queen's next move to h7 (4. Qh7#) would be checkmate.

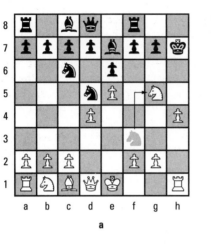

Figure 8-5:
The white knight checks the black king, so the king gets the heck out of the way.

a

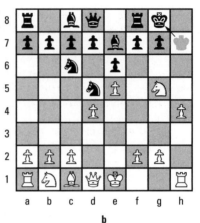

b

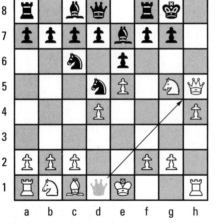

Figure 8-6:
The black king senses the smell of death as the white queen hunts him down.

Immediate Gratification: The Temporary Sacrifice

Chess players call sacrifices that lead directly to the win of more material *pseudo-sacrifices* or, more commonly, *temporary sacrifices.* This type of sacrifice involves an initial loss of material but is followed by its immediate, or near immediate, recovery.

The following example demonstrates a temporary sacrifice in practice. The position is pretty similar to the one in Figure 8-3 in the preceding section on the classic bishop sacrifice, but in this case, white merely wins material and doesn't press on to checkmate. (See Figure 8-7 for the setup, which has a few subtle differences from the one in the preceding section — namely, the absence of the knight's firepower reduces white's attacking ability.)

As in the classic bishop sacrifice, white sacrifices its light-squared bishop by capturing the black pawn on h7 (1. Bxh7+), putting the black king in check (see Figure 8-8a). The black king then must capture the bishop (1. ... Kxh7) or else suffer the uncompensated loss of a pawn (see Figure 8-8b).

White then brings out the queen to h5 (2. Qh5+); in doing so, the queen executes a double attack — checking the black king and simultaneously threatening the unprotected knight on d5 (see Figure 8-9a). The black king is forced to retreat to g8 (2. ... Kg8) on the back rank (see Figure 8-9b).

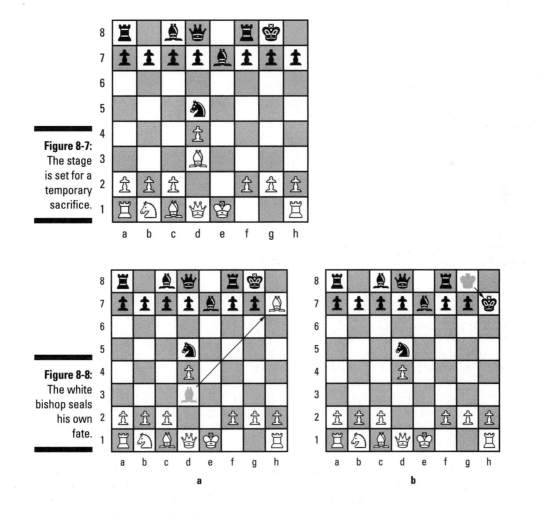

Figure 8-7: The stage is set for a temporary sacrifice.

Figure 8-8: The white bishop seals his own fate.

a

b

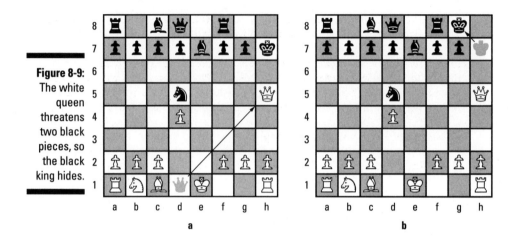

Figure 8-9:
The white queen threatens two black pieces, so the black king hides.

The black king's retreat enables the white queen to capture the black knight on d5 (3. Qxd5), as shown in Figure 8-10. White thus wins a knight and a pawn in exchange for temporarily sacrificing the bishop.

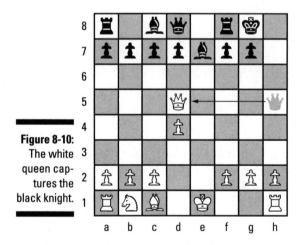

Figure 8-10:
The white queen captures the black knight.

A Strategic Move for the Patient: The Permanent Sacrifice

A *permanent sacrifice* is one where the material isn't immediately recovered. Usually, the goal in making this type of sacrifice is a strategic one. One side gives up material in order to secure a lasting advantage in another area, such as space or development (see Chapter 3 for more about these elements of chess). You can't calculate these types of sacrifices; instead, they're products of intuition and imagination — and are what elevate chess play to artistry.

In the classic example of a permanent sacrifice, white gives up a pawn to disrupt black's development. In this case, white isn't simply trading a pawn for a quick lead in development, as it may do with a gambit (which I describe earlier in this chapter), but rather for a lasting advantage based on black's difficulty in getting its pieces coordinated. The following example gives you an idea of how such a sacrifice may work.

Check out the starting position (which is from a variation of the Caro-Kahn Defense) in Figure 8-11. White is about to permanently sacrifice the e-pawn.

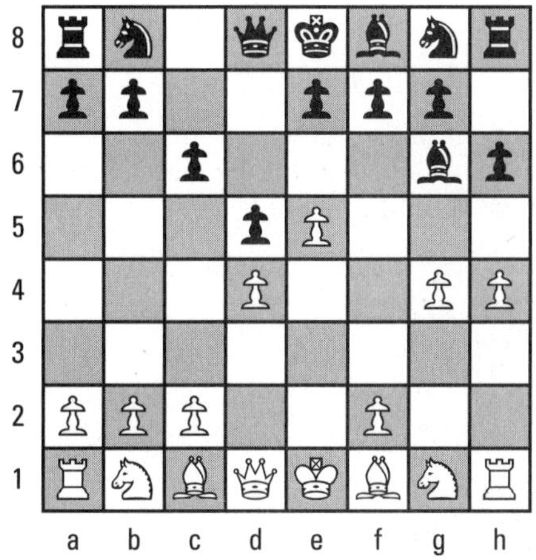

Figure 8-11:
The board right before white makes a permanent sacrifice.

To initiate the sacrifice, white advances his pawn on e5 to e6 (1. e6) and exposes it to capture (see Figure 8-12a). The black pawn on f7 then takes out the white pawn (1. ... fxe6); see Figure 8-12b.

In response to his sacrifice, white doesn't try to regain the pawn. White simply continues to develop his pieces by moving out the kingside knight to f3 (2. Nf3); see Figure 8-13. But has the white pawn's valor gone unnoticed? By no means. Black's position is now disorganized thanks to white's sacrifice, and getting his pieces out to good squares is now going to be difficult. In particular, black has doubled e-pawns — the pawn on e7 can't move until the one on e6 does (see Chapter 3 for more on doubled pawns). So none of black's pieces can move onto or through the e7 square until both e-pawns are moved. White may need to make many additional moves to take advantage of the scrambling on black's end. It's not clear when, or even if, the lost pawn will ever be recovered, which is why the sacrifice is called a permanent one.

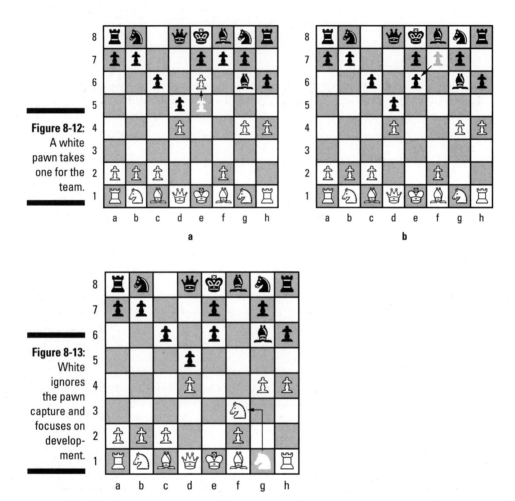

Figure 8-12: A white pawn takes one for the team.

a

b

Figure 8-13: White ignores the pawn capture and focuses on development.

The king of sacrifice, Mikhail Tal

A grandmaster from Riga, Latvia, Mikhail Tal (1936–1992) became world chess champion in 1960. Tal was widely popular for his brilliant sacrificial play. Describing the details of his brilliancy would take way more page space than this book allows, so I recommend that you check out *The Magic of Mikhail Tal* by Joe Gallagher (Everyman Chess) to see what I mean.

Tal was so taken with chess that he supposedly kept sneaking out of the hospital after having a

kidney removed, just to play in the local chess club. He was also famous for his intimidating stare. Combined with his ability to seemingly summon sacrifices out of the air in positions where no one else would even consider them, this stare gave Tal an almost mystical aura. One grandmaster even went so far as to wear sunglasses during a game to avoid Tal's "evil eye."

Chapter 9

Building Pattern Recognition

*O*ne of the great myths surrounding the game of chess is that you must be a human calculating machine to play the game. A certain amount of calculation is involved in any chess game, of course, but chess players primarily rely on *pattern recognition* (the ability to spot similar configurations of pieces and pawns) and on intuition to choose their moves. They rarely tell you this fact, because most of the time the process is subconscious. If you ask them why they played this move instead of that one, they often reply, "I just knew what the right move was" — or something equally unenlightening.

If you're unfamiliar with chess, all positions on the chessboard probably appear equally chaotic to you. If, however, you've seen scores and scores of games, the significance of many relative positions among chess pieces is understandable at a glance. Some chess aficionados have likened this building up of a store of recognizable patterns to a sort of chess vocabulary. The words of any non-native language seem unfamiliar to you at first exposure, but after you build your vocabulary, you understand many words, terms, and concepts in the language without any conscious thought at all. That general idea is pretty much the same in chess.

In this chapter, I explain how chess is all about pattern recognition. As you become familiar with such tactics as the pin or the fork (see Chapter 7), you're actually learning to recognize a pattern. If you can remember the ins and outs of a few patterns of pawn structures (covered in this chapter and in Chapter 10), your play in the opening and early middlegame will become much more coherent and pointed. Finally, by developing your technique in the endgame, you add the last piece to the puzzle of playing a well-rounded game of chess. (Also, as you study mating patterns in Chapter 11, you build up a store of knowledge that can help you during play. You suddenly foresee possible moves much earlier in the game, and you play that much better.)

Analyzing Chess Positions and Looking Ahead

Strong players can quickly evaluate many types of positions because they've seen similar positions before. Of course, most positions in chess have their own quirks or involve other variables that require specific calculations to truly understand them, but chess players start from a base of common knowledge about the game and work out the variations from there. Therefore, by zeroing in on a few moves to study seriously, you can greatly reduce the amount of actual calculating you have to do.

Processing and analyzing chess positions seem to be one of those left-brain–right-brain things. People who are good at spatial relationships seem able to absorb the patterns in chess a bit easier than those who aren't so good in this area. Spatially oriented players build up their chess vocabularies more rapidly and become fluent in the language of chess somewhat earlier than do their nonspatially oriented brethren. True pattern recognition skills, however, come mostly from experience with the game. After you see enough different positions on the chessboard, you begin to just know what kinds of moves you should consider, almost without conscious thought, and you don't bother looking at all the alternatives.

Almost every chess master has heard this question: "How many moves can you see ahead?" One master answered, "Only one. The best one." This statement contains at least a kernel of truth. I always answer, "It depends." If you want to know whether I calculate all the possibilities in any given position, the answer is a definite no. If you want to know how many moves ahead I can see in any one particular sequence, the answer is that in some cases, I can see quite far, and in other cases, I can see only a very few moves ahead. If the position is of a *forcing nature,* which means that my opponent's moves are highly predictable, and I recognize the pattern, then I can calculate about a dozen moves ahead, sometimes more. The more patterns I recognize, the farther ahead I can calculate my moves.

Picking Up on Pawn Formations

The easiest patterns to recognize, besides mating patterns (head to Chapter 11), are pawn formations, which are often referred to as the pawn structure. When I speak of *pawn formations,* I mean the positioning of the white pawns in relationship to the black pawns, and vice versa. Most masters can come across a game in progress and make an educated guess as to how that game began simply by looking at the current pawn structure. They can do this because pawns are relatively immobile, and radically altering their positioning from one phase of the game to the next is difficult.

Branching out: The tree of analysis and candidate moves

Alexander Kotov (1913–1981), a former Soviet champion, wrote a very famous book called *Think Like a Grandmaster.* (Well, the book is familiar to most chess players, at least.) In the English translation, Kotov introduces players to the concepts of the tree of analysis and candidate moves.

You can't climb the *tree of analysis,* but you can understand its roots. You can meet each move that your opponent makes with one of several replies, and your opponent may in turn respond to each reply with any of several other moves. The alternative moves available to you and your opponent branch out and quickly mask the forest for all the trees.

Kotov taught that in order to reduce the bushiness of the tree and see farther ahead in your moves (as well as anticipate an opponent's moves), you first need to settle on which moves are the candidate moves. *Candidate moves* are those moves that you intend to examine closely based on your intuition. First you look around and use your intuition to figure out which moves are the important ones, and only then do you begin to calculate concrete variations. You must, according to Kotov, examine each candidate before making your final selection.

Candidate moves are chosen by a combination of intuition and judgment. The choices you make in determining these moves get better with experience. The calculation of concrete variations is more like work, but it, too, gets better with practice. The more you practice these aspects of your game (as well as all others), the better you get as a chess player.

By virtue of their relatively fixed nature, the pawns tell you where to put your pieces, where to attack, and where to guard against attack. Because the pawns can't be as easily repositioned as the pieces, much of the middlegame's strategy, where the bulk of the battle occurs, revolves around pawn formations. Furthermore, the many slightly differing endings that arise from these formations are tied together by common threads. So understanding pawn formations is pretty darned important to your game.

I learned about pawn structures from a book by the great American champion Reuben Fine (1914–1994) called *The Ideas Behind the Chess Openings.* It may be hard to find nowadays, but it remains an excellent resource.

Studying the pawn formations that are common to a few opening systems gives you the knowledge of a general strategy that guides you in selecting specific moves at every turn. Because learning every opening in chess is impossible, most players concentrate on one or two openings to use when playing white and then a couple more when playing black. If you familiarize yourself with the formations, you can usually choose good moves — if not always the very best moves. (I cover the basics on pawn formations in the following sections, but more advanced formations are in Chapter 10.)

Testing pattern recall ability

Researchers have conducted experiments to demonstrate the notion of chess as language, using a sampling of people of widely different chess strengths. The scientists involved in these experiments exposed players to several different chess setups consisting of both random positions and actual gamelike positions. Each exposure lasted for only a few seconds at a time. The researchers then asked the players to reconstruct the various positions as the players remembered them. The stronger players scored much better in reconstructing the actual gamelike positions than did the weaker players, but this advantage on the part of the better players virtually disappeared when they attempted to reconstruct the random positions. The conclusion? If you take away a player's knowledge base about chess by removing any resemblance to actual game positions, you also take away that player's apparent superiority in recall.

The French Defense and pawn chains

The pawn formation that I understand best arises from an opening called the *French Defense.* The French Defense, or simply the *French,* gained its modern name in 1834, when a Paris team used the opening to defeat a London team in a correspondence match.

Figure 9-1a shows the starting position for the French Defense. White (the English) opens the game by moving out the king's pawn on e2 two squares to e4 (1. e4). Black (the French) responds by moving out her king's pawn on e7 one square to e6 (1. ... e6). (If you're unfamiliar with the chess notation I just used, flip to Chapter 6.) The idea behind the French Defense is to strike back at white's center pawn in order to contest white's control of the center. The first move provides support for the intended second move.

After white advances the other center pawn on d2 two squares to d4 (2. d4), black follows suit, moving the d7 pawn to d5 (2. ... d5); see Figure 9-1b. Black has now established a *pawn chain* — which is the way chess players refer to two or more pawns that are linked together — on the squares f7, e6, and d5.

Now many alternatives are available to white, but one variation in particular provides the best opportunity to discuss pawn formations. By advancing the pawn on e4 to e5 (3. e5), white butts heads with black and creates a pawn chain on squares d4 and e5, as shown in Figure 9-2a.

Pawn chains occur in many games, and the ability to correctly manage such chains is one of the keys to playing chess well. Aaron Nimzowitsch, a great expert in the French Defense, taught chess players to attack a pawn chain at its base. If the base is destroyed, the entire chain is weakened.

Armed with Nimzowitsch's insight, you can easily predict the most usual response by black, an advance of the pawn on c7 (3. ... c5) to attack the white pawn on d4, the base of the chain — see Figure 9-2b.

TIP

Attacking an advanced pawn chain aggressively, early, and often is vital. If you don't attack the chain this way, your opponent gains an advantage in space — the white e5 pawn is advanced and uses that advantage to mount an attack. Then you're too *cramped,* meaning your pieces don't have enough maneuvering room, to meet the attack unless you first go about chipping away at the chain.

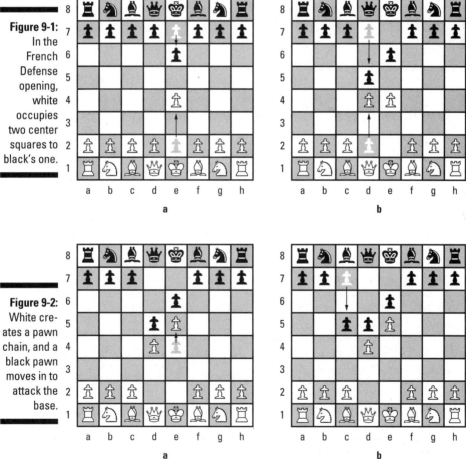

Figure 9-1: In the French Defense opening, white occupies two center squares to black's one.

Figure 9-2: White creates a pawn chain, and a black pawn moves in to attack the base.

White's next move is easy to understand if you think in terms of the strength of pawn chains (see Figure 9-3a). When the white pawn on c2 moves out to c3 (4. c3), white establishes an even longer pawn chain, the base of which lies deep in white territory and thus is very difficult to attack. Black's strategy is to now move the knight on b8 out to c6 (4. ... Nc6), with the intent of continuing to attack white's center pawn on d4 and trying to break the chain apart, as shown in Figure 9-3b.

White knows exactly what black is trying to accomplish and brings up reinforcements, in the form of its own knight (5. Nf3), to protect the threatened center pawn on d4 (see Figure 9-4a).

Black's next move may seem strange unless you understand the strategy involved. Once again, the goal is to attack a vulnerable point in the chain, the same point that the black pawn and black knight are attacking and that the white pawn and white knight are defending (in this case, d4). The strategy in the French Defense revolves around the attack and defense of this point. To continue the attack, the black queen on d8 moves to b6 (5. ... Qb6), a position that further supports the attack on this point (see Figure 9-4b). The queen attacks this strategic point by throwing her weight behind the black pawn.

At this point, white's options are many, but they all revolve around the attack and defense of the pawn chain. If white secures the chain, then this success will lead to a white advantage in space, because the chain is so advanced (see Chapter 3 for a discussion of space). As a result of this space advantage, white's pieces will have more options than black's, and — unless black is very resourceful — white may be able to make threats that black will be unable to defend against.

Figure 9-3:
White extends the pawn chain, and a black knight attempts to break it apart.

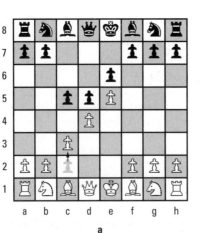

a

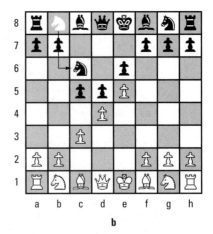

b

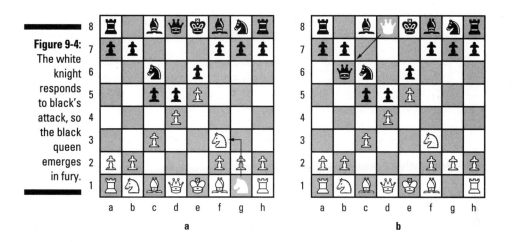

Figure 9-4: The white knight responds to black's attack, so the black queen emerges in fury.

Black, on the other hand, will continue to try to undermine white's pawn chain. If the pawn chain is weakened — for example, if the base is easily attacked — then white's pieces will be forced to defend it. These defending pieces may then become passive (doing little else but guard duty). Passive pieces generally become less powerful than active ones, and if black is successful in making white's pieces take up passive positions, it will soon be black's turn to become aggressive and launch an attack.

This back-and-forth tug-of-war over key points is what fills a chess game with tension. Whoever achieves the short-term goal of securing (or undermining) the pawn chain is then able to turn her attention to a long-term goal, such as winning material.

Typical pawn formations after the French Defense

From the early opening on, a wide variety of options are open to both players regarding pawn play. The players can choose to

- ✔ Exchange pawns
- ✔ Attack pawns with pieces or with other pawns
- ✔ Protect pawns with pieces or other pawns

Regardless of these choices, however, the resulting pawn formations always boil down to a manageable size. After you become familiar with these formations, the best thing to do is to take a look at some master games that include them. You may begin to appreciate some moves the masters make that previously may have mystified you. Soon you'll have a handle on how to play these formations no matter what choices your opponent makes, and no move any opponent can make will ever freak you out!

Note: In the following sections, I use the figures to show you only the pawns to best draw attention to the formations themselves. Of course, the pieces are still an important part of the strategy, but I've taken them out of the pictures just to help you see these formations clearly.

Abandoning the head of the chain

The first of the typical pawn formations that stem from the French Defense opening and the one that I want you to consider in this section is the most basic one. In the basic position in Figure 9-5, play revolves around the attack and defense of the white pawn on d4. Sometimes, white abandons the point by capturing the black pawn on c5 with the d4 pawn (1. dxc5) to whip up a speedy attack. Black then captures the white pawn on c5 with a piece (which, for the sake of these pawn illustrations, is still invisible).

The resulting pawn formation is shown in Figure 9-6. Black could then begin an attack on white's advanced pawn on e5, which is suddenly shorn of its protector, forcing white to find a new way to defend it.

White needs to use a piece to defend the advanced e-pawn (and keep in mind that pieces don't like guard duty — they'd rather be off attacking something) or bring up another pawn, f4, to serve as a defender. If white takes the latter course, the resulting formation may look like the one shown in Figure 9-7a. Black may then strike at the head of the pawn chain by moving the f-pawn to f6, creating a structure that looks like the one shown in Figure 9-7b.

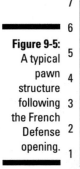

Figure 9-5:
A typical pawn structure following the French Defense opening.

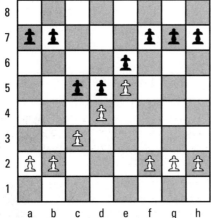

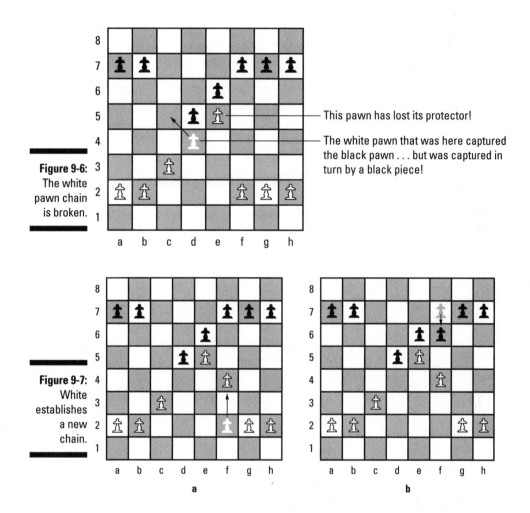

Figure 9-6: The white pawn chain is broken.

This pawn has lost its protector!

The white pawn that was here captured the black pawn . . . but was captured in turn by a black piece!

Figure 9-7: White establishes a new chain.

a

b

The pawns may or may not capture one another, but two different types of formations can result if they do:

- If the white pawn on e5 captures the black pawn on f6 (exf6), and a black piece captures the white pawn on f6 on black's next turn, then the structure will look like the one in Figure 9-8 (but keep in mind that the pieces on this series of boards are still invisible).

- If, on the other hand, white doesn't choose to capture the black pawn on f6 and makes some other move instead (which I haven't shown for the sake of keeping the focus on the pawn formation only), another situation is possible. The black pawn on f6 can capture the white pawn on e5 (fxe5), and the white pawn on f4 can capture back (or as chess players say, *recapture*). The structure would look like the one in Figure 9-9.

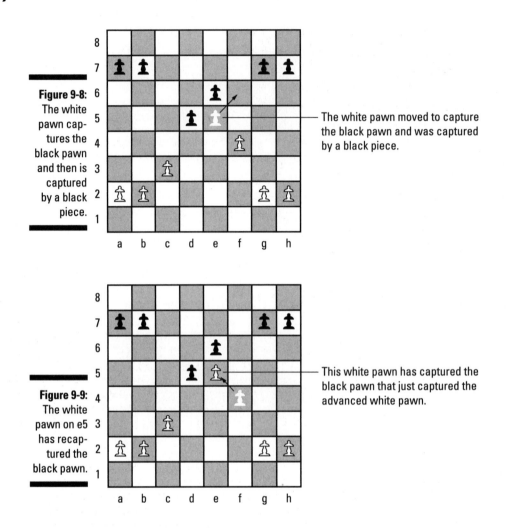

Figure 9-8: The white pawn captures the black pawn and then is captured by a black piece.

The white pawn moved to capture the black pawn and was captured by a black piece.

Figure 9-9: The white pawn on e5 has recaptured the black pawn.

This white pawn has captured the black pawn that just captured the advanced white pawn.

Defending the head of the chain

Of course, white can employ a whole different strategy, going all the way back to Figure 9-5. White doesn't have to abandon the chain with the capture of the black pawn on c5. If white decides not to capture the black pawn on c5, black may *exchange* pawns (the black pawn on c5 captures the white pawn on d4, cxd4, and the white pawn also captures the black pawn on d4, cxd4). The base of the chain would then be on d4. The formation could then look like the one shown in Figure 9-10.

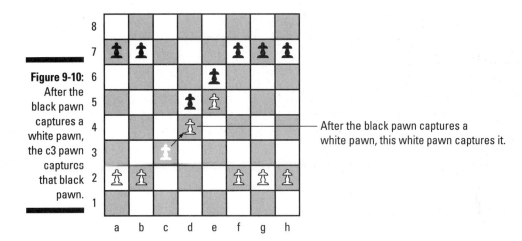

Figure 9-10: After the black pawn captures a white pawn, the c3 pawn captures that black pawn.

After the black pawn captures a white pawn, this white pawn captures it.

Eyeing Endgame Patterns

Certain types of endings will be won, lost, stalemated, or drawn depending both on how they objectively should play out and on your ability to recognize certain endgame patterns as they appear. You can try to figure out which endgame patterns work — and which don't — right at the chessboard as you play . . . or you can find out about these patterns beforehand in the privacy of your own home. (I recommend the latter.) After you add a number of these patterns to your repertoire, expect to notice a big jump in your playing strength.

Endgame patterns are an important, but often neglected, area of chess — an area that all players need to understand. Inexperienced players, however, may simply think that they can worry about the end of the game when — and if — they get there. Such thinking is flawed for many reasons, primarily because of the enormous difficulty involved in inventing (or more precisely, reinventing) the correct line of play as you reach that portion of the game — which you're likely to need to do if you've neglected to study your endgames. And, of course, most players find extremely helpful the ability to determine whether a certain endgame pattern is likely to end in a win, a draw, or a loss *before* going into it. Many of the decisions you make in your middlegame are likely to depend on your knowledge of these patterns. (For example, should I trade queens and go into the ending, or keep the queens on the board and go for an attack?)

The good news, however, is that you don't have to study all the various endgame patterns that are available — especially if all you want is to enjoy playing chess. If, however, your goal is to become a chess master, you need to master the endgame.

Note: Endgame patterns are not to be confused with mating patterns — mating patterns can occur in either the middlegame or the endgame. I discuss mating patterns in detail in Chapter 11.

The endgame pattern known as *Lucena's position* was first recorded in the oldest surviving book on chess, written in 1497 by Luis Lucena. This pattern, with its two methods of play, is only one of many such endgame patterns you can use to strengthen your game. Building your chess vocabulary with this and other endgame patterns, however, requires a great deal of study. And as is true of study in any other field, mastering the subject matter takes work.

Figure 9-11 shows the starting lineup for Lucena's position. In this endgame pattern, white is trying to *queen its pawn* on d7 (which means advancing the pawn to the last rank and converting it to a new queen; see Chapter 5 for this special move known as *pawn promotion*), and black is trying to prevent that from happening. If black can keep the pawn from queening, then the game ends in a draw, because that is the only decisive advantage either side has. If white can force the black rook on c2 to sacrifice itself to prevent the pawn from queening, white can then use the king and rook to force checkmate, using a mating pattern described in Chapter 11.

Lucena demonstrated two methods to force a win for white in this position. The first method is probably the easiest, but you really need to know both methods because a peculiar arrangement of pieces sometimes forces you to use one instead of the other. I explain both methods in this section.

Looking for additional information on endgame patterns? An outstanding introduction is *Chess Endings: Essential Knowledge* by Yuri Averbakh (Everyman Chess).

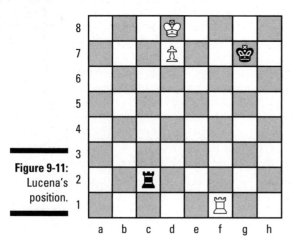

Figure 9-11: Lucena's position.

Transferring the rook

The first idea is for white to transfer the rook on f1 to the eighth rank (specifically to c8) in two steps in order to support the advance of the d7 pawn to d8. The first step in the transfer is shown in Figure 9-12a, when the white rook slides left to a1 (1. Ra1). Black responds by bringing the king on g7 closer to the pawn, to f7 (1. ... Kf7); see Figure 9-12b.

White now transfers the rook on a1 to the eighth rank (2. Ra8); see Figure 9-13a. Black marks time with the rook because there is nothing better to do, moving it down to c1 (2. ... Rc1); see Figure 9-13b.

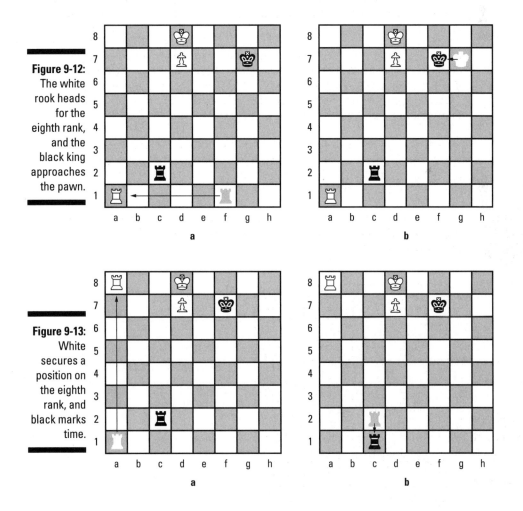

Figure 9-12: The white rook heads for the eighth rank, and the black king approaches the pawn.

Figure 9-13: White secures a position on the eighth rank, and black marks time.

Notice that if black uses her king to attack the white pawn by moving him to e6, then the black king actually serves as a shield for white's king. The white king could then move in front of the black king to e8, allowing the white pawn to queen on the next move (note that the black king would block the black rook from checking the white king).

White attacks the black rook by moving the rook on a8 to c8 (3. Rc8), as shown in Figure 9-14a, forcing the black rook to move off the c-file. The black rook, therefore, has nothing better to do than attack the white pawn, so it moves to d1 (3. … Rd1); see Figure 9-14b. This strategy creates an escape route for the white king, because white is now in control of the c-file.

The white king moves to c7 (4. Kc7), which the black rook no longer attacks, and in turn clears the way for the advance of the d7 pawn to the last rank; see Figure 9-15a. Black must now check the white king to prevent the pawn from queening, so the d1 rook moves to c1 (4. … Rc1+); see Figure 9-15b.

If, instead, the black king were to approach the white pawn again by moving to e6 (4. … Ke6), white could win by checking the black king with the rook, supported by the pawn. This move would force the king to retreat anywhere, allow the white pawn to queen, and force black to give up the rook for the pawn, leaving white with rook and king versus rook. The mate with king and rook versus king is demonstrated in Chapter 4.

The white king approaches the black rook by moving to b6 and out of check (5. Kb6), as shown in Figure 9-16. Black can continue checking the white king with the rook — but only until the king advances far enough to attack the rook. At that point, black must surrender the rook for the pawn and eventually get checkmated.

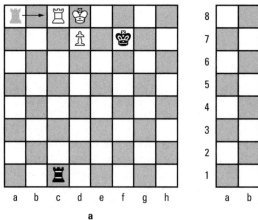
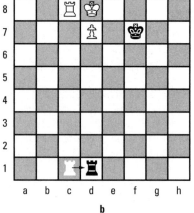

Figure 9-14:
The white rook forces the black rook to move.

a

b

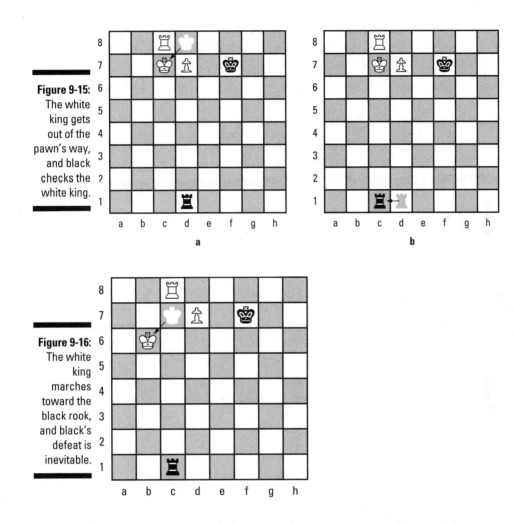

Figure 9-15:
The white king gets out of the pawn's way, and black checks the white king.

Figure 9-16:
The white king marches toward the black rook, and black's defeat is inevitable.

Building a bridge

The second winning method using Lucena's position is often called *building a bridge*. In this method, white uses the rook to shield the king from checks by the black rook. The starting pattern for building a bridge is the Lucena position (refer to Figure 9-11). From there, the first step is for white to move the rook to the fourth rank (1. Rf4), as shown in Figure 9-17a. (The reason for this move becomes clear by the end of this example.) Because the black rook has nothing better to do, it can only mark time in one of several ways (in this case, 1. ... Rc1; see Figure 9-17b), none of which affect the outcome.

White's king now comes out from under the cover of the pawn by moving to e7 (2. Ke7), as Figure 9-18a illustrates. The best defense available to black is to constantly harass the white king, so black then checks the white king by moving the rook to the e-file (Re1+); see Figure 9-18b.

The white king moves onto the same file as the white pawn (3. Kd6), as shown in Figure 9-19a. Black checks the white king again by moving the rook to d1 (3. ... Rd1+); see Figure 9-19b.

White moves the king away to e6 (4. Ke6) and still protects the pawn (see Figure 9-20a). Black checks the white king again by moving the rook to e1 (4. ... Re1+), as Figure 9-20b shows.

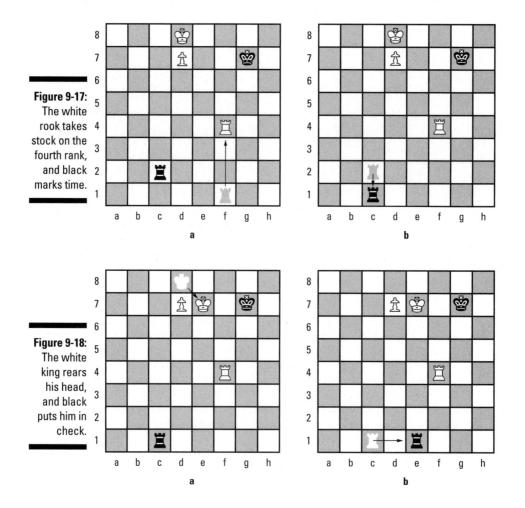

Figure 9-17: The white rook takes stock on the fourth rank, and black marks time.

a

b

Figure 9-18: The white king rears his head, and black puts him in check.

a

b

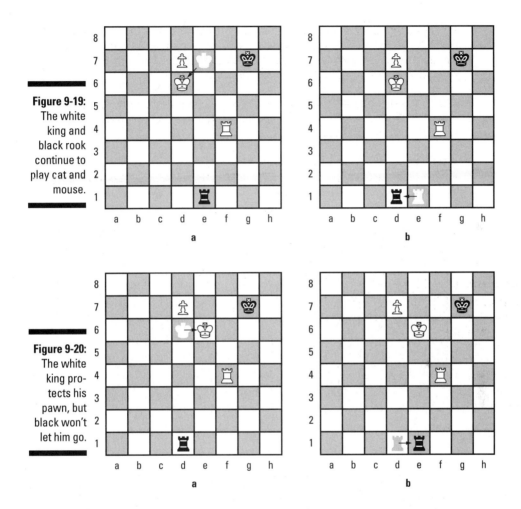

Figure 9-19: The white king and black rook continue to play cat and mouse.

Figure 9-20: The white king protects his pawn, but black won't let him go.

White advances the king toward the black rook (5. Kd5), again moving out of check (see Figure 9-21a). Black gives check with the rook one last time by moving to d1 (5. ... Rd1+); see Figure 9-21b.

White then builds the bridge — a phrase coined by chess expert Aaron Nimzowitsch — by covering the king with the rook (6. Rd4); see Figure 9-22. Now the reason why white moved the rook to the fourth rank back in Figure 9-17 is clear: The rook can now shield the king from further checks.

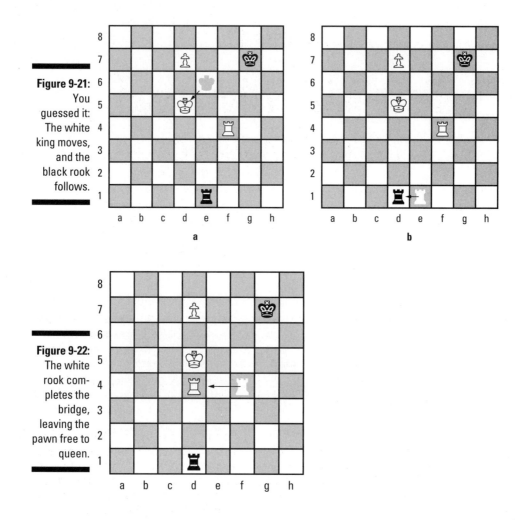

Figure 9-21:
You guessed it: The white king moves, and the black rook follows.

a

b

Figure 9-22:
The white rook completes the bridge, leaving the pawn free to queen.

Chapter 10

Recognizing Advanced Pawn Formations

In This Chapter

▶ Understanding why pawn formations matter

▶ Identifying the strengths and weaknesses of certain pawn formations

*W*hen you first start to play chess, it may seem as though the pawns are just in the way of the real pieces. You may move them only because you have to in order to get the big guys (and gal) involved. You may also be thinking that those pesky pawns move about the board rather stuffily — after all, they're allowed only to move forward and often only one square at a time. Be that as it may, they still have a huge influence on the game. (See more about their influence and structure in Chapter 3.)

In Chapter 9, I introduce you to the fundamentals of pawn formations; in this chapter, you explore several tried-and-true pawn formations that you can use to your advantage. After you understand where the pieces ought to go to complement these different pawn formations, you're well on your way to playing a good game of chess. *Note:* Some pawn formations are specific to an opening or a defense, but they can theoretically occur for either white or black.

Exploring the Powers of Pawn Formations

A *pawn formation,* which is a group of pawns working together, can make a big difference in the way a game plays out. Experienced players can often look at a game in progress and correctly identify the game's opening moves because some openings regularly produce the same types of pawn formations. In large part, these formations determine what the optimal piece placement should be in the game, providing, in effect, a guide for subsequent play.

Didn't know that pawns had such power? The good news is that you don't have to figure out where the pawns go all by yourself. Some specific formations stand the test of time (like the ones in Chapter 9 and in this chapter).

The bad news is that you can't always choose the formation you want. Your opponent has some say in the matter, too, because how he plays affects the choices you have. For that reason, you should at least be somewhat familiar with multiple types of pawn formations.

In the following sections, I describe several main powers of pawn formations: their ability to limit your opponent's mobility, enhance your strengths, and minimize your weaknesses.

Restricting your opponent's mobility

Because pawns are more stationary than the rest of the chess pieces — they can't back up, and they normally stay in the same place for a while — recovering from a mistaken pawn move is difficult. So deciding when and where to move them is important. When you know where the pawns go to create formations, you have a good idea of where the other pieces should go to complement them. You also have insight into which pieces you want to keep and which ones you want to get rid of.

Figure 10-1 shows a typical position in the advanced variation of the French Defense (see Chapter 9 for the basics on that opening) after the opening pawn moves (1. e5 e6 2. d4 d5; flip to Chapter 6 if you need help deciphering the notation in this chapter). The chain of black pawns on light squares greatly restricts the mobility of the black light-squared bishop, which makes that piece less valuable.

These pawns block black's
light-squared bishop.

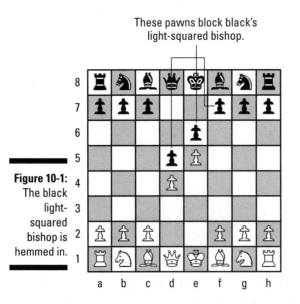

Figure 10-1: The black light-squared bishop is hemmed in.

You can already see why the pawn formation is important. A piece's power is based on its mobility, and white's light-squared bishop is much more mobile than black's, which is hemmed in behind its own pawns. Black should try to *trade* the two bishops, eliminating both, to free up some mobility, but white should try to avoid such an exchange. Why give up a strong (more mobile) piece for a weaker one?

Beginners sometimes check their opponents as soon as possible, but doing so is often a mistake. For example, white can give a check by moving its light-squared bishop to b5 (3. Bb5+), as demonstrated in Figure 10-2a, but that move is weak. Figure 10-2b shows why. If the black light-squared bishop moves out (3. … Bd7), white has to either retreat, which is a waste of time, or allow the bishops to be traded. With white's center pawns on dark squares, white should try to keep its light-squared bishop on the board.

Figure 10-2:
Checking an opponent too soon in a game is foolish.

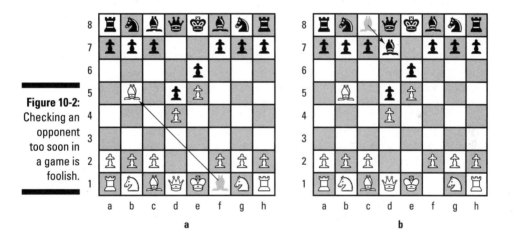

Why, you ask? The mobility of white's light-squared bishop is unimpeded by the pawns, and it can guard squares that the pawns can't. The mobility of black's light-squared bishop is severely limited and guards the same squares as black's pawns on light squares. White's bishop is relatively strong, and black's is relatively weak. You should try to keep your strong pieces and seek to trade your weak ones.

Playing up your strengths and minimizing your weaknesses

Recognizing pawn formations goes a long way toward identifying the best course of action to take in any given game. Understanding the strengths and weaknesses of particular formations guides you as to where to place your pieces. It also helps you identify the appropriate plan to accentuate strengths in your position and minimize weaknesses. Pawns may not be as powerful as the other pieces on the board, but they are big variables in any chess equation.

One of the advantages of moving first is that establishing a pawn formation, such as the Nimzo-Botvinnik or Closed English (see upcoming sections for a lowdown on these formations), is easier. Part of the struggle in a game of chess is over which pawn formation arises:

- ✔ **Closed:** Some people like closed pawn formations, such as the Stonewall (which I discuss later in this chapter). A closed pawn formation is one that restricts piece movement.

- ✔ **Open:** Others prefer open formations, where the pieces have free reign (I go into closed and open formations in more detail in Chapter 12).

The game can turn into a real contest of wills if one player is trying to keep the formation closed and the other is trying to open it.

The key to understanding any kind of pawn formation is to evaluate its strengths and weaknesses. Some formations cause certain pieces to become more valuable than others, as demonstrated earlier in Figure 10-2b. Many different types of pawn formations exist, and they may change during the course of a game. A closed formation may suddenly open, for example, if enough pawn exchanges take place.

No matter what the pawn formation is, you can learn something from it. The formation may tell you which pieces to keep and which ones to get rid of. It may dictate whether you should attack on one side of the board or the other. Just remember that pawn formations offer a lot of information, and it pays to listen carefully to what they have to say.

Involving the Bishop with the Fianchetto

Fianchetto (pronounced fyan-*ket*-toe; plural, *fianchetti*) is a diminutive of an Italian word that means "on the flank." In chess terms, the word applies to a particular pawn and bishop formation and is a common feature of many openings. The fianchetto pawn formation would be weak without the presence of the bishop, because the pawns control squares of one color only, not both.

In Figure 10-3a, the light squares around black's queenside pawns, a6 and b7, are undefended and weak; so are the light squares around white's kingside pawns, such as h3. Each side's bishop thus comes in to guard the squares that the pawns don't, creating a black queenside fianchetto and a white kingside fianchetto, as shown in Figure 10-3b. ***Note:*** In order to clearly depict the formation, I've stripped the pieces that are unessential to this formation from the figures.

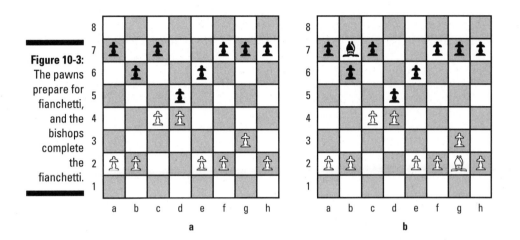

Figure 10-3: The pawns prepare for fianchetti, and the bishops complete the fianchetti.

Looking at the fianchetto's strengths

In chess history, the fianchetto took a while to catch on. Classical theory considered it important to centralize pieces, and obviously, the fianchetto bishop is developed on the flank. The fianchetto became popular in the 20th century, when players learned that occupation and control of the center weren't necessarily one and the same. Another maxim was to minimize pawn moves around your king, so castling behind a fianchetto formation didn't seem safe. (See Chapter 5 for the scoop on castling.)

However, it turns out that the fianchetto is a tough nut to crack, because all the squares are covered either by the pawns or the bishop. Attacking isn't easy when your opponent's lineup doesn't have a weakness.

Another strength of the fianchetto formation is that the bishop is placed on the longest diagonal possible. This placement potentially maximizes its mobility. Lastly, this diagonal cuts through the center of the board, so the bishop really is centralized in a manner of speaking, but from a safe distance.

Watching out for the fianchetto's weaknesses

If you can manage to eliminate the fianchetto bishop, the surrounding squares will be weakened (refer to Figure 10-3a). You may be able to maneuver your pieces onto those weakened squares, in which case your opponent will have a difficult time driving them away.

Figure 10-4 illustrates one way you may accomplish this position. In Figure 10-4a, the white queen supports the white bishop's impending invasion of h6. After the bishop moves to h6 (1. Bh6), as shown in Figure 10-4b, it can capture black's fianchettoed bishop on g7 (2. Bxg7). Even though black can restore material balance by recapturing the white bishop with the king (2. ... Kxg7), the dark squares on black's kingside will have lost their primary defender.

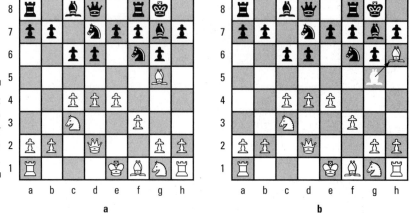

Figure 10-4: One way to maneuver around the fianchetto.

Varying the Sicilian with the Dragon

The Dragon, which is the name of a variation of the Sicilian Defense (see Chapter 13 for more on that opening), features a kingside fianchetto (see the preceding section). It was named after the constellation Draco, the Dragon, and arises after the following opening moves:

1. e4   c5
2. Nf3   d6
3. d4   cxd4
4. Nxd4   Nf6
5. Nc3   g6

By looking at just the Dragon's pawn formation (see Figure 10-5), you can make an educated guess as to where some of black's pieces belong. White's d-pawn has been eliminated (as shown in Figure 10-6), so it can't be used in the fight to control the d4 and e5 squares. Black will use pawns and pieces to control those squares. Black also wants to use the long diagonal (a1–h8) to attack deep into white's position. So black's dark-squared bishop will be ideally posted along this diagonal.

Black usually castles behind the Dragon formation (see Chapter 5 for details on castling), and the knights move to their optimal squares, c6 and f6, as illustrated in Figure 10-6.

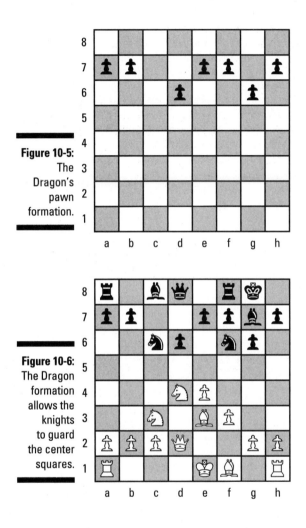

Figure 10-5: The Dragon's pawn formation.

Figure 10-6: The Dragon formation allows the knights to guard the center squares.

Clawing your way through the Dragon's pros

Black's dark-squared bishop is one of the strengths of the Dragon formation. White's d-pawn has already been eliminated (refer to Figure 10-6), so the bishop usually has a clear path all the way from black's kingside to white's queenside. In addition, it's natural for black to move at least one rook onto the c-file because black's c-pawn is gone. The combined pressure from the bishop on the long diagonal and a rook on the c-file can force white into a defensive posture.

The Dragon is at its best when black is attacking aggressively and white has been reduced to passive defense.

Getting past the Dragon's drawbacks

The Dragon was once very popular, but a variety of attacking systems for white have been developed over the years, and most of its fangs have been pulled. It's still playable, but its glory days may be over.

One drawback of the Dragon is that you can't always play it. If white doesn't allow the d-pawn to be captured by black's c-pawn, then black won't have the Dragon formation. It may have something close, but these seemingly trivial differences are actually quite important, because they may mean you should put your pieces on entirely different squares.

If black does get the Dragon formation, white will try to capture black's dark-squared bishop. The elimination of that bishop seriously weakens the Dragon formation. White also has an edge in space (see Chapter 3 for more on that element), which can be used to develop an attack in the center or on the kingside.

The Dragon is often considered double-edged, because both sides are trying to be as aggressive as possible. Black attacks primarily on the queenside, and white attacks in the center and on the kingside.

Exercising Your Pawns' Flexibility with the Scheveningen

The Scheveningen, which is named after the Dutch city, is a variation of the Sicilian Defense (see Chapter 13), just like the Dragon (see the preceding section). This opening features a very flexible pawn formation, giving you multiple and equally effective ways to position your pieces and multiple ways to respond to various white maneuvers. Many of the world's best players employ the Scheveningen because it has proven to be resilient in withstanding the various attacks that white has dreamt up over the years. It arises from the following moves:

1. e4   c5
2. Nf3   e6
3. d4   cxd4
4. Nxd4   Nf6
5. Nc3   d6

With the Scheveningen, black usually ends up with an extra center pawn and active play on the queenside. White retains a spatial advantage and opportunities for attack in the center and on the kingside. Figure 10-7a shows the Scheveningen pawn formation, while Figure 10-7b shows a typical piece configuration.

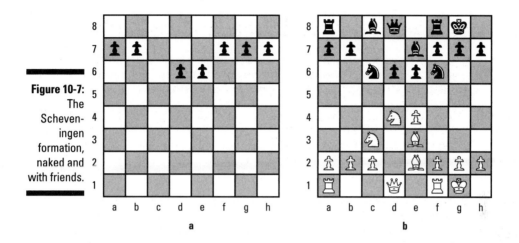

Figure 10-7: The Scheveningen formation, naked and with friends.

Note that in Figure 10-7b, the bishop on e7 is developed in a more classical manner in the Scheveningen than in the Dragon (see the preceding section), where it's developed on the flank. From e7, the bishop can help protect the black d-pawn. Meanwhile, white retains an advantage in space, because his center pawn (e4) is on the fourth rank, whereas black's center pawns are on only their third.

Assessing the advantages

Similar to the Dragon, the Scheveningen is a defense against a king pawn opening. Achieving the Scheveningen pawn formation may not be possible unless white cooperates. Obviously, 1. e4 isn't a mandatory move.

The Scheveningen seeks to establish a safe haven for the black king. The kingside minor pieces are well posted defensively, remaining close by the king but also available for action in the center. The black d- and e-pawns are positioned to prevent white's pieces from penetrating into black territory. With a strongly defended kingside castle, black is free to initiate action on the queenside.

Black often advances the remaining queenside pawns, partly to drive away white pieces and partly to acquire more space. Black can choose to develop the light-squared bishop on either the d7 or b7 square, while black's major pieces (queen and rooks) will gravitate toward the half-open c-file.

Looking at the downside

Aside from the fact that white may not allow black to set up the Scheveningen, the only real drawback is that the formation cedes white a spatial advantage. White often seeks to capitalize on this advantage by attacking in the center and on the kingside.

A typical move against this formation is for white to advance his f2 pawn to f4. Black then has to guard against further pawn advances, which threatens to break down the kingside defenses.

Building the Stonewall

The idea behind the Stonewall is to keep the center blocked and launch an attack on the wing. Its fairly rigid pawn formation may leave little operating room for the pieces. Either side may try to erect the Stonewall, as white has done in Figure 10-8a. Note that the pawns on d4 and f4 are well protected and are used to prevent any attempted central advance by black. Figure 10-8b illustrates how little choice white has about where to place his pieces, so transferring the queenside pieces to the kingside is difficult. The square e5 is white's only central invasion point.

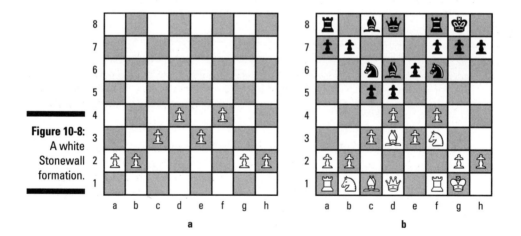

Figure 10-8: A white Stonewall formation.

Note: The Stonewall is more popular with inexperienced players, because they can be fairly certain that they're moving their pieces to the proper squares. More experienced players prefer to have more flexibility than this formation allows.

Relying on the Stonewall's strengths

The Stonewall formation usually results in a closed center, which makes maneuvering pieces from one side of the board to the other quite difficult.

If you can launch an attack on one side of the board, the defender may have a tough time bringing up reinforcements. For example, because the white f-pawn has already been advanced in the Stonewall (refer to Figure 10-8a), white should attack on the kingside. You generally try to attack where you have an advantage in space.

Coping with the Stonewall's weaknesses

The main drawback to the Stonewall formation (from white's perspective), besides its rigidity, is the weakness of the e4 square — with all of white's center pawns on dark squares, the light squares are weakened. Notice that no white pawn can ever guard e4. Therefore, that square may become a haven for black's pieces. Allowing your opponent such a nice perch in your own territory is seldom a good idea. This drawback is one reason why strong players rarely play the Stonewall.

Matching Color to Center Squares with the Closed English

In the Closed English formation, white tries to control the light squares in the center with a combination of pieces and pawns. Unless black tries to challenge white's control over the light squares, the center may remain closed for quite some time. White usually expands on the queenside, and black on the kingside.

A typical Closed English pawn formation is illustrated in Figure 10-9a. Note that white would be willing to trade the c-pawn for black's d-pawn. Otherwise, white uses the c-pawn to attack the light square in black's center. See Figure 10-9b for a common piece placement — after the following opening moves:

1. c4   e5

2. Nc3   Nc6

3. g3   g6

4. Bg2   Bg7

5. d3   d6

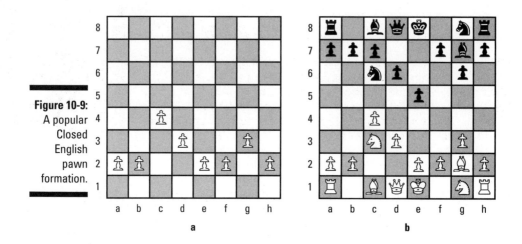

Figure 10-9:
A popular
Closed
English
pawn
formation.

a   b

Notice how white's c- and d-pawns, queenside knight, and kingside bishop all attack the light squares in the center (d5 and e4). Black also uses both pawns and pieces to control the dark center squares. Both players control half the center and concede the other half.

Players who are uncomfortable with the opening moves of a pawn to e4 or d4 often play a pawn to c4, which is called the English Opening. Although the move to c4 isn't as popular as the ones to e4 and d4, it's still considered mainstream. In other words, you see it at all levels of play.

The fianchetto formation in Figures 10-9a and 10-9b, created by the f-, g-, and h-pawns, tells you where white's light-squared bishop belongs (g2). I discuss the fianchetto in detail earlier in this chapter.

Eyeing the benefits

White has a natural advantage on the queenside due to the advanced c-pawn. Also notice the uninterrupted path of the white fianchetto bishop (on g2) all the way from the kingside to black's queenside. White will castle kingside and advance pawns on the queenside in order to grab even more space (flip to Chapter 5 for the scoop on castling).

Coming to terms with the pitfalls

While white is grabbing space on the queenside, black is doing the same on the kingside; in Figure 10-9b, black's pawn on e5 secures an edge in space on the kingside. This hustle can be a little dicey because the kings are usually castled on the kingside. If you're uncomfortable allowing your opponent more space on the side of the board your king is on, the Closed English may not be the best choice for you.

Winging It with the Nimzo-Botvinnik

The Nimzo-Botvinnik formation is characterized by pawns on c4 and e4 as well as a kingside fianchetto (described earlier in this chapter), as shown in Figure 10-10a. White piles up pressure on the light center squares, creating a strong, closed center, and prepares for an attack on either wing. Figure 10-10b illustrates a typical piece placement associated with this pawn formation — after the following opening moves:

1. c4   c5
2. Nc3   Nc6
3. g3   g6
4. Bg2   Bg7
5. e4

Figure 10-10: In the Nimzo-Botvinnik, two pawns guard the center, and a fianchetto marks a wing.

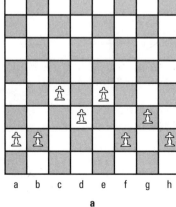

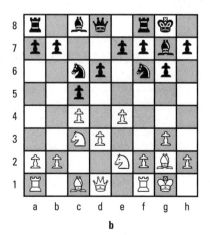

This formation comes about most frequently from the English Opening (and is a variation of the Closed English formation that I describe in the preceding section). It's a very solid setup that also retains a good amount of flexibility.

In Figure 10-10b, the white knight is developed on e2 for these reasons:

- ✔ It doesn't interfere with the fianchetto bishop or the possible advance of white's f-pawn.
- ✔ It's able to take the other white knight's place, should that piece move or be captured.

Discovering the advantages

One big advantage of the Nimzo-Botvinnik formation is that white has a secure hold on the light squares in the center and can expand on either wing. White can choose to advance on the queenside or the kingside, so this pawn formation provides a little more flexibility than the Closed English.

Weeding out the weaknesses

The primary weakness of the Nimzo-Botvinnik is the lack of control over the d4 square. If black tries to establish as firm a grip on the dark center squares as white has on the light ones, white may have to contest it. Also, with so many of white's pawns on light squares, activating white's light-squared bishop may be difficult.

Chapter 11

Mastering Mating Patterns

*T*o my knowledge, Dr. Ruth has never seriously studied mating patterns in chess, but I think that everyone interested in the game should engage most seriously in such a study. In case you're wondering, procreation isn't involved; in chess, *mating* means to combine the pieces' powers to end up with *checkmate,* the position that signals victory (*mate,* in turn, is short for checkmate; see Chapter 4 for an introduction to checkmate). One of the best ways to become familiar with the powers of each piece on the chessboard is to try to checkmate a lone king with each of them in turn. You quickly discover that, even with the help of the king, neither the knight nor the bishop can accomplish checkmate without the aid of another piece, but the rook and the queen can (as long as the king helps them, of course).

Some mates occur frequently or are otherwise well known in chess literature, and these are generally referred to as *mating patterns.* Most strong players have committed a slew of mating patterns to memory. Memorizing such patterns makes calculating your moves much easier, so I highly recommend that you become familiar with at least some of the patterns described in this chapter. These patterns occur again and again in chess, and nothing is quite like the feeling of seeing one pop up in one of your own games. You're either ecstatic to spot a way to checkmate your foe or downcast when you realize that you're the one caught in the net. Knowing patterns also allows you to play proactively by instigating a particular pattern setup.

For more information on mating and mating patterns, I recommend *The Art of Attack in Chess* by Vladimir Vukovic (Everyman Chess). Most of what I know about the subject I learned from that book.

Trapping the King: Back-Rank Mates

The first mating pattern — and by far the most common — is the *back-rank mate,* which involves an unprotected back rank and a trapped king on that rank. Rooks and queens are always on the lookout for an unprotected back rank. After the king castles (see Chapter 5 for details on castling), he's often under the protection of three pawns positioned directly in front of him. Sometimes, however, these protectors become turncoats — the pawns protect their king but also trap him (see Figure 11-1). The difference in the two sides' positions in Figure 11-1 is that the white rook is protecting the white back rank, but the black rook isn't protecting its own back rank.

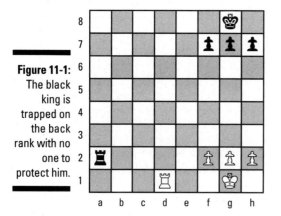

Figure 11-1:
The black king is trapped on the back rank with no one to protect him.

White takes advantage of black's unprotected back rank by moving its rook to d8 and checkmating the black king (1. Rd8#); see Figure 11-2. (Flip to Chapter 6 if you're unfamiliar with the chess notation I just used.) If the turn to move had been black's, black could have avoided the checkmate by moving any of the pawns forward, giving the black king some room to move.

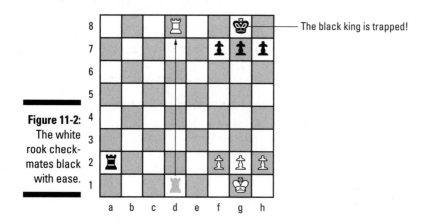

The black king is trapped!

Figure 11-2:
The white rook checkmates black with ease.

Beware the scholar's mate

Beginners are frequently seduced by the power of the queen and move her early and often. This tendency is unfortunately reinforced in their minds when they find out about the *scholar's mate* (*mate* is shorthand for checkmate). The scholar's mate is one of the shortest mates possible, but you can easily defend against it. First, both players advance the pawns in front of their kings (1. e4 e5). Next, they both develop their bishops to a centralized square (2. Bc4 Bc5). See the following two figures for the illustration.

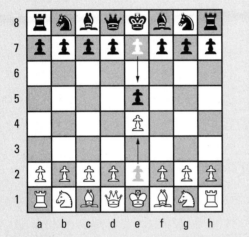
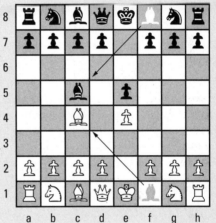

Third, white brings out its queen to attack several black pawns (3. Qh5), and black's knight (3. ... Nc6) defends the pawn in the center of the board — which is the wrong pawn to defend! Observe the suspenseful scenario in the following two figures.

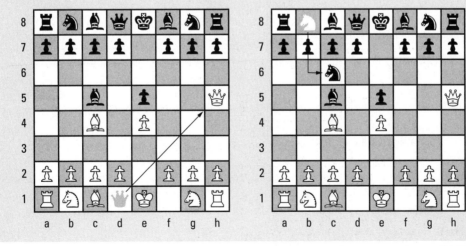

(continued)

(continued)

White delivers checkmate with her queen (4. Qxf7#)! Black's king is trapped, with nowhere to move and no one to help him. See the following figure.

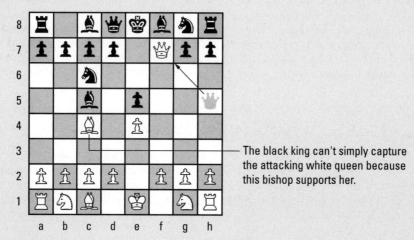

The black king can't simply capture the attacking white queen because this bishop supports her.

The scholar's mate isn't a dangerous strategy. Here's just one idea that prevents white from executing her plan. By moving the knight out before the bishop, black not only takes away the queen's move, but also threatens the advanced white pawn (see the following figure). White would be frustrated on the second move!

The white queen would be captured (by the black knight) if placed here.

Pairing the Heavy and the Light: Queen and Pawn Mates

The queen can't deliver checkmate without help but can do so with the aid of even a single pawn. Many chess games have been decided by a variation of this theme. In the following sections, I show you the simplest form of the queen and pawn mate, and then I explain a more complicated — but common — version.

A simple queen and pawn mate

The position in Figure 11-3 illustrates a typical queen and pawn mating pattern. White is a queen ahead in this scenario and should win in any case, but the point is to concentrate forces on the cluster around the black king. The black king can't escape and can't avoid white's threat to deliver checkmate.

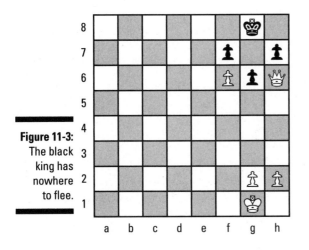

Figure 11-3: The black king has nowhere to flee.

Because it's white's turn, the queen moves to g7 and puts black in check (1. Qg7#); see Figure 11-4. Black has no open squares to move to, and because the white pawn on f6 is protecting the queen, the black king can't capture the queen — checkmate!

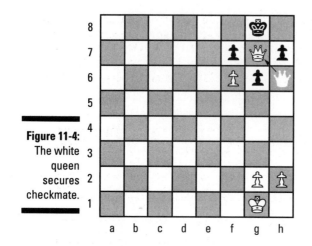

Figure 11-4:
The white queen secures checkmate.

Note: The pattern in Figures 11-3 and 11-4 also occurs where the advanced white pawn is on h6 and the queen is on f6. The queen can still deliver check-mate on g7.

A complicated queen and pawn mate

Now for the more complicated version: In 1512, a Portuguese apothecary named Damiano published a study of the queen and pawn mating pattern. The study concludes with a classic queen and pawn mate that's known as *Damiano's mate.*

The mating pattern is essentially the same as in the example in the preceding section — the black king is trapped behind a combination of white and black pawns (see Figure 11-5).

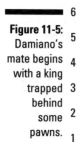

Figure 11-5:
Damiano's mate begins with a king trapped behind some pawns.

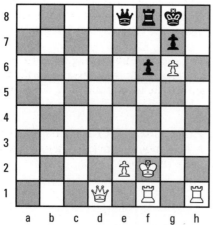

After white recognizes the mating pattern, finding the rather shocking *rook sacrifice* (where the rook sacrifices his life for the greater good; see Chapter 7) is easy. In Figure 11-6a, white sacrifices the rook on h1 by moving it to h8 (1. Rh8+), putting the enemy king in check. Because the black king has no other legal move, he's forced to capture the white rook (1. ... Kxh8) in order to escape the check; see Figure 11-6b.

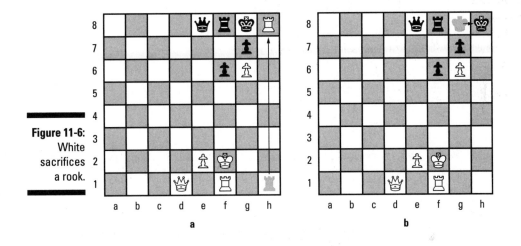

Figure 11-6:
White sacrifices a rook.

The idea behind this particular rook sacrifice is that the white rook can't deliver checkmate from h7, but the white queen can. (The white pawn on g6 would protect the white queen on h7. The trick is figuring out how to get her there.) This idea leads white to consider how best to get the queen into position without giving black any time to ready a countermove. The concept of clearing the rooks out of the way to enable the queen to deliver checkmate is now a chess standard. Chess players now call such moves *clearance sacrifices* (see Chapter 7 for more on the combination involving the clearance sacrifice).

In Figure 11-7a, white checks the black king by moving the rook on f1 to h1 (2. Rh1+). Black has only one move in order to escape the check and moves back to g8 (2. ... Kg8), where it was before the rook capture (see Figure 11-7b).

Now white performs another rook sacrifice by moving the rook to h8 (3. Rh8+), as in Figure 11-6, to clear the path for the queen along the first rank; see Figure 11-8a. Black must capture the white rook (3. ... Kxh8), just as before; see Figure 11-8b.

Now the white queen can move to the h-file (4. Qh1+) and put the black king in check, as Figure 11-9a shows. In response, black's king must move back to where he came from, g8 (4. ... Kg8); see Figure 11-9b.

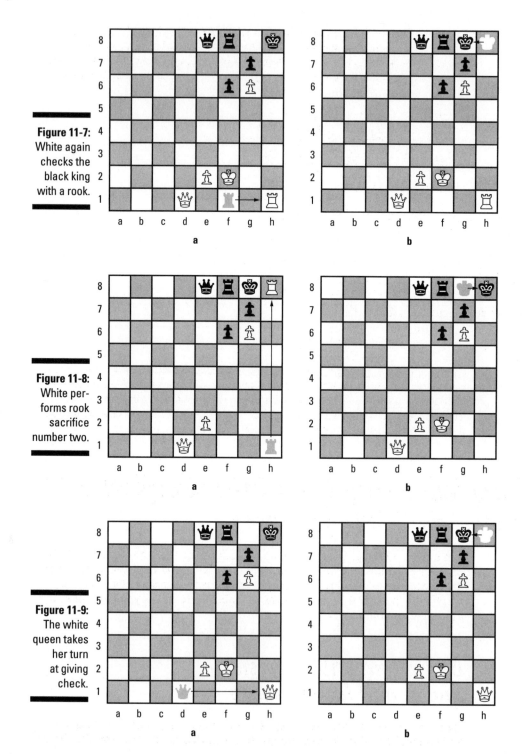

Figure 11-7: White again checks the black king with a rook.

Figure 11-8: White performs rook sacrifice number two.

Figure 11-9: The white queen takes her turn at giving check.

After all this shuffling around, what has white accomplished? For starters, white has lost two rooks! However, in this case, material doesn't matter. White's next move is to advance the queen to h7 (5. Qh7#), which is under the protection of the white pawn on g6, and declare checkmate — see Figure 11-10.

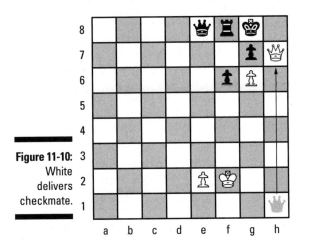

Figure 11-10: White delivers checkmate.

Queen and pawn mates occur infrequently at the higher levels of chess competitions because both sides know them so well. At lower-level competitions, however, queen and pawn mating patterns may not be well known at all. Therefore, Damiano's mate can be an important weapon to have in your arsenal as you begin your chess adventures!

Complementing Each Other Perfectly: Queen and Knight Mates

The queen and knight are especially powerful in mating combinations. This capability has something to do with the fact that the knight has powers that the queen doesn't, and the two pieces are perfect complements — so they join forces in several ways to produce mating patterns, as you find out in the following sections.

Beginning with a basic queen and knight mate

Figure 11-11a shows the beginning of a common mating pattern with queen and knight. The white knight and queen are both attacking h7, and the threat is checkmate on white's next move of the queen to h7 (1. Qh7#). Notice that moving either pawn wouldn't help black, because the queen's move to h7 would still be checkmate. Black's only chance to escape checkmate is to move the suffocating rook away to c8 (1. ... Rc8), as shown in Figure 11-11b.

The rook retreat only prolongs the agony, however, as white still delivers check by moving the queen to h7 (2. Qh7+), as shown in Figure 11-12a. The black king is forced to move to f8 (2. ... Kf8) to escape check; see Figure 11-12b.

Note that the role of the white knight is primarily to support the white queen's incursion into the black king's position by defending h7.

The black king is stuck on the eighth rank, so the white queen now delivers checkmate by moving to h8 (3. Qh8#); see Figure 11-13.

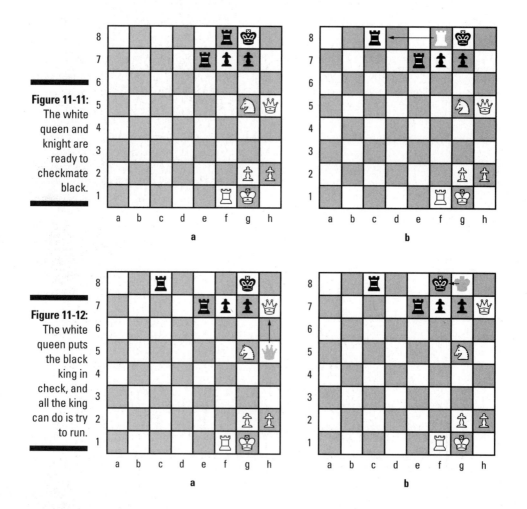

Figure 11-11: The white queen and knight are ready to checkmate black.

a

b

Figure 11-12: The white queen puts the black king in check, and all the king can do is try to run.

a

b

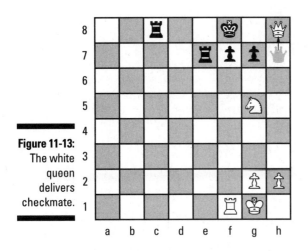

Figure 11-13: The white queen delivers checkmate.

Surveying the smothered mate

The queen and knight can combine to deliver checkmate in other ways as well. One combination in particular is known as the *smothered mate*, where one poor king's own pieces help trap him.

In Figure 11-14a, the white queen on c4 is putting the black king on g8 in check, so the king must move. If the black king moves one square to the left, next to the black rook, white's queen could deliver checkmate at once by moving the queen to f7, directly in front of the black king. Note how in that event, the white knight (on g5) would be supporting the queen. So black tries to escape the threat by moving the king into the corner on square h8 (1. ... Kh8), as Figure 11-14b shows.

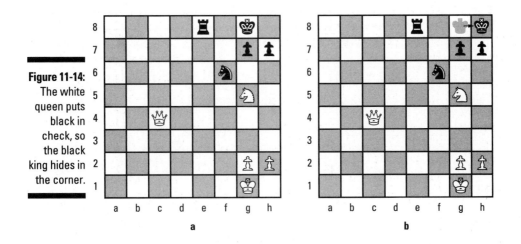

Figure 11-14: The white queen puts black in check, so the black king hides in the corner.

a   b

The white knight jumps to f7 (2. Nf7+), as shown in Figure 11-15a, putting the black king in check and forcing him back to where he started (2. ... Kg8); see Figure 11-15b.

The white knight then moves to h6 (3. Nh6++), delivering double check. (*Double check* is a form of discovered check that occurs if the king is attacked by two pieces at once, in this case, the white queen and knight — see Figure 11-16a.) This type of check is very powerful, because it forces the king to move. Black has no way to block both checks or capture both checking pieces. The king finds himself forced back into the corner (3. ... Kh8), as shown in Figure 11-16b.

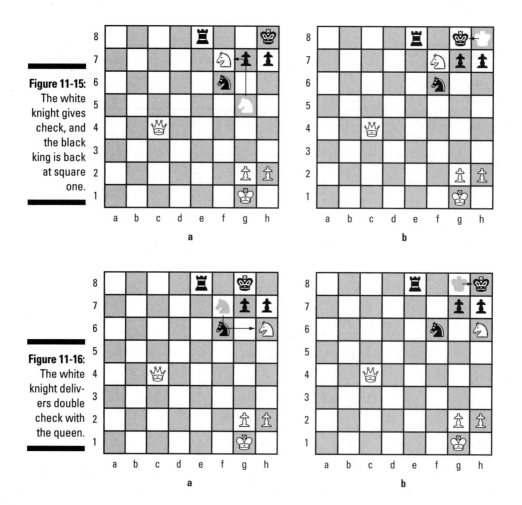

Figure 11-15: The white knight gives check, and the black king is back at square one.

Figure 11-16: The white knight delivers double check with the queen.

Now white's next move may seem quite bizarre if you don't know the smothered mate pattern — the white queen sacrifices herself by moving to g8 (4. Qg8+), as shown in Figure 11-17a. In doing so, however, the queen allows the knight to eventually deliver checkmate. The white knight guards the queen on g8, so the black king can't capture her. The piece that black does use to capture the queen — the knight or the rook — doesn't matter, because checkmate follows in either case. In this example, black takes the queen with the rook (4. ... Rxg8); see Figure 11-17b.

The white knight then trots to f7 (5. Nf7#), declaring checkmate, as shown in Figure 11-18.

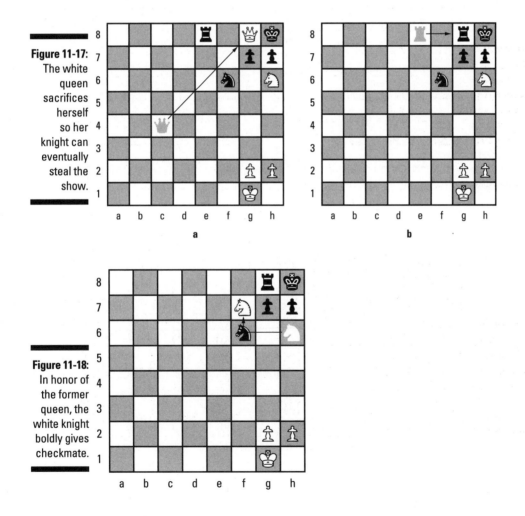

Figure 11-17: The white queen sacrifices herself so her knight can eventually steal the show.

Figure 11-18: In honor of the former queen, the white knight boldly gives checkmate.

The smothered mate is a bit rarer in practice than other queen and knight mates but is still worth knowing. If you get a chance to deliver checkmate in this way, consider yourself to be extremely cool.

Creating a Steamroller: Bishop and Rook Mates

In addition to the queen and knight (see the preceding section), the other two powerful pieces — the rook and bishop — make a great mating combo. The two pieces complement one another because the rook controls files and ranks while the bishop controls diagonals.

Morphy's mate, named after Paul Morphy, is an example of the bishop and rook working well together in a mating pattern. Morphy was one of the greatest attacking players of all time. He played some of the most beautiful games in chess history and introduced chess mavens to more than one mating pattern. (Find out more about him in the nearby sidebar "Paul Morphy: The pride and sorrow of chess.")

The starting position for this mating pattern is shown in Figure 11-19; the white bishop and rook may look harmless enough, but they're anything but harmless. Don't worry about the piece count in this example; just concentrate on the mating pattern of the bishop and rook.

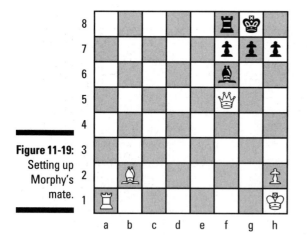

Figure 11-19: Setting up Morphy's mate.

From the starting position, white makes a surprising move to inevitably produce checkmate. By capturing the black bishop on f6 with the queen (1. Qxf6),
as shown in Figure 11-20a, white forces the black pawn on g7 to capture the
queen (1. ... gxf6); see Figure 11-20b. Otherwise, the white queen could take
that pawn, which is protecting the black king, on the next move. (Note how the
white bishop on b2 is providing support along that long diagonal.)

This move by black creates a line to the black king along the now open g-file.
The white rook on a1 heads for g1 (2. Rg1+) to put the black king in check
(see Figure 11-21a), forcing the black king into the corner (2. ... Kh8); see
Figure 11-21b.

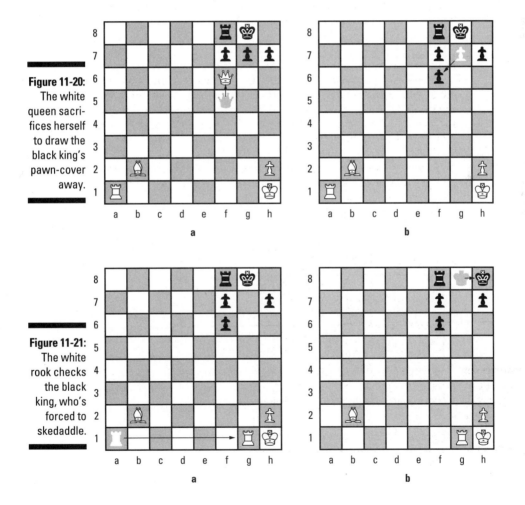

Figure 11-20:
The white
queen sacri-
fices herself
to draw the
black king's
pawn-cover
away.

Figure 11-21:
The white
rook checks
the black
king, who's
forced to
skedaddle.

With the rook guarding the g-file, white then delivers checkmate by capturing the black pawn on f6 with the bishop (3. Bxf6#), leaving no chance of escape for the black king — see Figure 11-22.

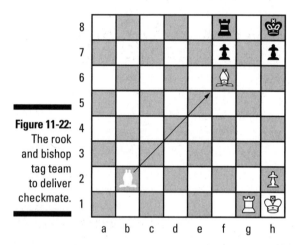

Figure 11-22: The rook and bishop tag team to deliver checkmate.

Paul Morphy: The pride and sorrow of chess

Born in New Orleans, Paul Morphy (1837–1884) had a truly meteoric chess career. At a young age, he burst upon the international scene and defeated all comers in scintillating fashion. His games were models of rapid development and attack.

Morphy was gifted in other fields as well. He earned his law degree before the age of 21 but was too young to practice — he believed that he was simply marking time playing chess until he became old enough to practice law. In regard to his talents, his memory was so great that he could recite much of the Civil Code of Louisiana verbatim.

Sadly, however, Morphy's descent from the top was as abrupt as his rise. At the height of his powers and fame, he abandoned the game and grew increasingly withdrawn. He was said to have suffered from a persecution complex and died a lonely death. Myths have been built up surrounding the chess great to account for his behavior, including unrequited love and bitterness at being snubbed by an elder champion. Unfortunately, the truth is more likely a prosaic, if sad, case of mental illness.

Part III

Game Time: Putting Your Chess Foot Forward

The 5th Wave   By Rich Tennant

BAD CHESS OPENING

©RICHTENNANT

What's a nice pawn like you doing in a chess match like this?

In this part . . .

*I*n this part, I help you get your game going. From choosing a strategy that works to diving headfirst into the opening of the game, everything you need to know to get started is in these chapters. I also discuss the middle-game, where combat is at its most fierce, and the end-game, so you can make sure you finish a winner.

Chapter 12

Selecting Your Strategy: The Principles of Play

In This Chapter

▶ Picking the right type of game

▶ Centralizing your game

▶ Trading your pieces for your opponent's

▶ Taking control of key squares

▶ Preventing your opponent's pawns from moving forward

Sometime after I first started playing tournament chess, a friend of mine occasionally walked up to me during his own tournament game and lamented, "I have the position I wanted, but I just can't do anything!" Everyone who's ever played chess has felt this way at one time or another during a game.

The question is what do you do if you can't pin and win, use a fork, or find a mating pattern? The answer becomes clearer as you develop your knowledge of positional play. Even if no specific tactics (see Chapter 7) are currently available to you, you can always develop a strategy.

In fact, tactics don't simply materialize out of thin air, especially if you're engaged at higher levels of play. Tactics spring from a well-developed plan — a *strategy*. And in reality, the long-range planning efforts are what set up these tactical skirmishes so that one side has more opportunity for success than the other. The great attacking master Rudolf Spielmann (1883–1942) was said to have claimed that he could make sacrifices just as well as Alexander Alekhine (who was world champion at the time) could — but just couldn't reach the same positions!

Entire volumes have been written about planning in chess. (One of the best guides, by the way, was written by former world champion Max Euwe and is called *Judgment and Planning in Chess* — Random House published it.) This chapter, therefore, can serve only as an introduction to the topic. But I hope that the chapter, brief as it must be, impresses one thing onto the chess-playing nodes of your brain: Employing even a little bit of strategy is better than having no strategy at all up your sleeve — or, as we chess enthusiasts often say, even a bad plan is better than no plan at all. As you continue to progress, you'll find that chess has even deeper subtleties than you've ever imagined. This endless process of discovery is at the heart of the game's appeal.

Examining Different Types of Games and Choosing Which Type Is Right for You

Chess games are often sorted into classifications called *types*. The two main types are open and closed, although variations of these types exist:

- ✔ **Open:** The type of game that features free and easy movement of the pieces is referred to as an *open* game.

- ✔ **Closed:** If the pieces have difficulty moving from one side of the board, the type of game is called *closed*.

Wondering what determines whether a game is open, closed, or somewhere in-between? The short answer is "pawns"!

- ✔ An early exchange of center pawns generally leads to open lines for the pieces to move along.

- ✔ When center pawns are not exchanged and just butt heads with each other, the game is likely to require extensive piece maneuvering before enemy forces come into conflict.

The following list describes in more detail the two main types of chess games (open and closed, as noted earlier), along with a few variations:

- ✔ **Open games:** Open games feature the starting moves 1.e4 e5 (see Figure 12-1, and check out Chapter 6 if you're unfamiliar with the chess notation I just used). Lines have already been opened for the queen and king's bishops. Central pawn exchanges are likely, which will open even more lines for a variety of pieces to move along.

- ✔ **Semi-open games:** Games that begin with 1.e4 and any reply other than 1... e5 are called *semi-open* games (see Figure 12-2, which depicts the Sicilian Defense covered in Chapter 13). These types of games tend to have fewer open lines, but still provide lots of potential for good piece mobility.

- ✔ **Closed games:** The type of game referred to as closed begins with the moves 1.d4 d5 (see Figure 12-3). Closed games require more strategic planning and feature fewer tactical battles in the early stages of the game.

✔ **Semi-closed games:** *Semi-closed* games begin with any black response to 1.d4 other than 1... d5 (see Figure 12-4). These games can quickly turn into pitched battles, where black allows white to establish pawns in the center of the board with the intention of attacking and destroying them later on.

✔ **Flank openings:** Games that begin with moves other than 1.e4 or 1.d4 are called *flank openings.* The most common flank opening is the English opening established by playing 1.c4 (see Figure 12-5). Flank openings allow you to be pretty flexible in how you respond to your opponent's moves and usually postpone direct confrontation until later in the game. There's no predicting how open or closed a flank opening will be.

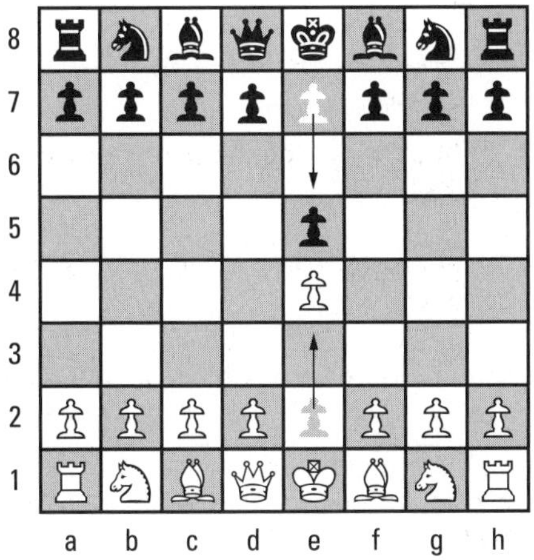

Figure 12-1:
Games that begin with the moves 1.e4 e5 are called open games.

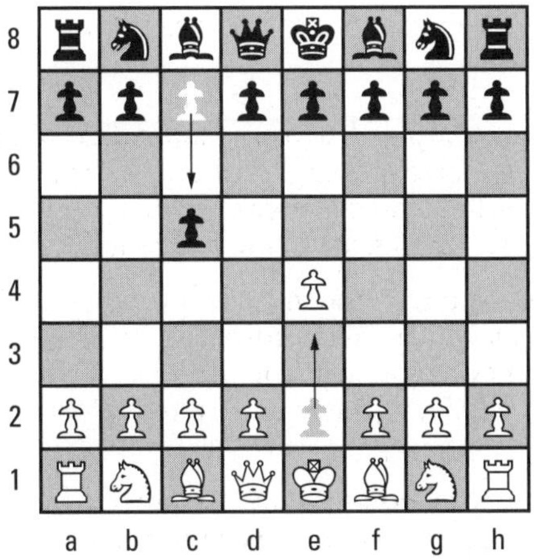

Figure 12-2:
The Sicilian Defense occurs after the moves 1.e4 c5 and is the most popular of the semi-open games.

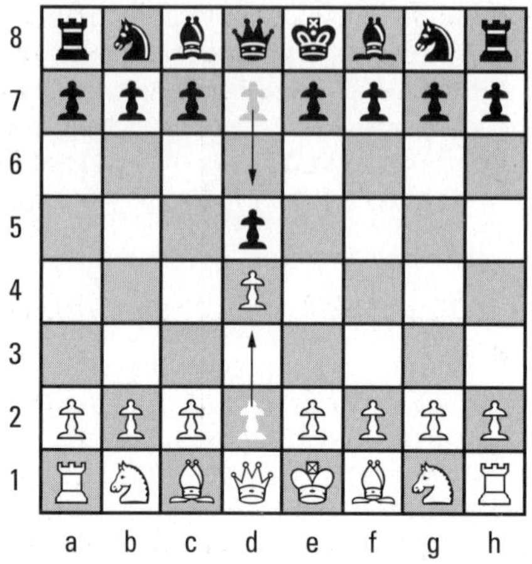

Figure 12-3:
Games that begin with the moves 1.d4 d5 are referred to as closed games.

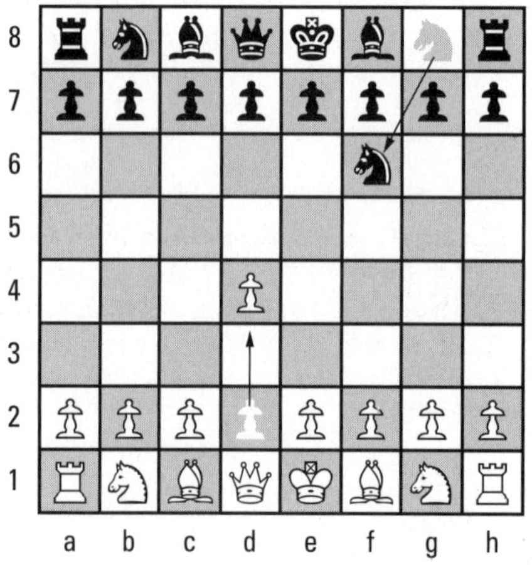

Figure 12-4:
The moves 1.d4 Nf6 fall into the category of semi-closed games.

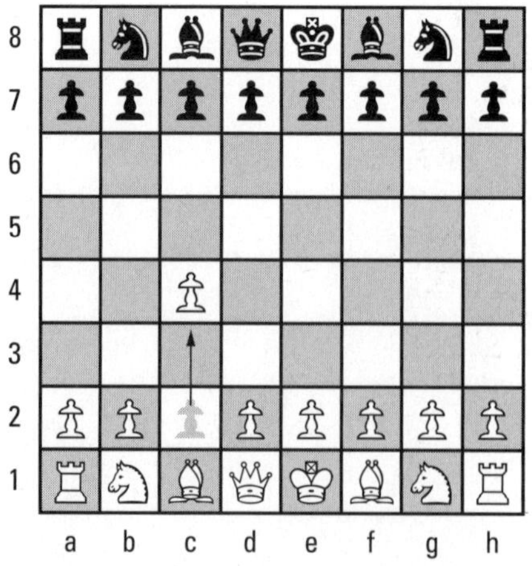

Figure 12-5:
The move 1.c4 establishes a flank opening called the English.

The preceding classification scheme is a fairly crude way of sorting complicated games along similar lines; open games can become closed, and closed games can open up. Many a game has twisted and turned around one player trying to open up a closed game, while the other is trying to keep it closed! However, understanding what type of game you're most comfortable with is still useful. Armed with that knowledge, you can try to steer your games accordingly:

✔ If you like to attack and are undeterred by early tactical skirmishes, you may prefer to play open games.

✔ If you prefer to play a more strategic and more slowly developing game, you may be more comfortable with closed types of games.

There's no right or wrong when it comes to choosing a type of game to play. The question is almost entirely one of personal preference. Whatever type you choose, you'll find that all types have one thing in common: a need to control the center of the board. (Read on to find out what I'm talking about.)

Aiming for the Center

Not all squares on the chessboard were created equal. The four central squares — d4, e4, d5, and e5 — are the most important in chess (see Figure 12-6). The squares next to them are the next most important, and so on. Logically, therefore, the player who controls the center of the board controls the game.

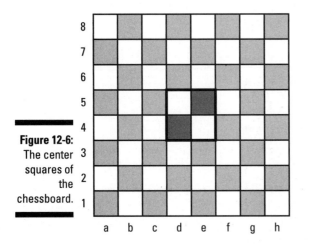

Figure 12-6:
The center squares of the chessboard.

Pieces generally increase in power as they come into contact with the center. Rooks, queens, and bishops can control squares from a distance, but pawns and knights must move closer to the action in order to be effective. Bringing pieces to bear on the center is called *centralization*.

The struggle for the center is the primary theme behind most games' openings. I could use just about any opening sequence to demonstrate this concept, but in the following sections, I draw your attention to an opening known as the *Queen's Gambit* (see Chapter 8 for more about gambits, although the Queen's Gambit isn't a true gambit).

Starting the game with center pawns

In the Queen's Gambit, both sides open by advancing the pawns in front of their queens (1. d4 d5), as shown in Figures 12-7a and 12-7b; as you find out in the previous section, these moves start off a closed game.

White advances the queen's bishop pawn (2. c4) to attack the black center pawn, a move that characterizes the Queen's Gambit (see Figure 12-8a). Black can accept the Queen's Gambit and capture the pawn, but doing so means abandoning the center, because white would then be able to play the e2 pawn to e4.

If black captures the pawn, the opening is called the *Queen's Gambit accepted*. This results in perfectly playable positions, but the *Queen's Gambit declined*, when black doesn't capture the pawn, is the more usual choice, because it allows black to retain a foothold in the center. In the Queen's Gambit declined, black uses another pawn to support the queen's pawn and maintain his share of the center (2. … e6); see Figure 12-8b.

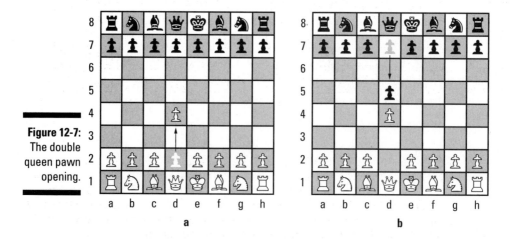

Figure 12-7: The double queen pawn opening.

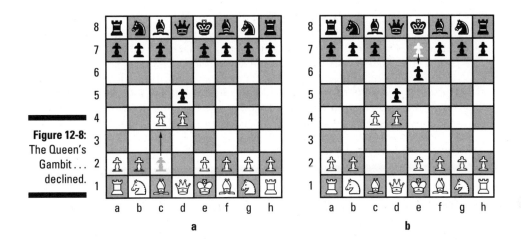

Figure 12-8:
The Queen's Gambit . . . declined.

Developing the knights and bishops

White chooses to develop a knight toward the center (3. Nc3), as shown in Figure 12-9a. Notice how the knight is now also attacking the black center pawn. Black, in turn, also develops a knight toward the center in defense of the attacked pawn (3. ... Nf6); see Figure 12-9b.

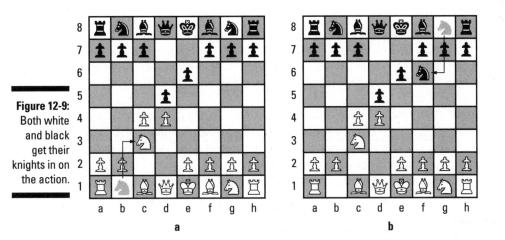

Figure 12-9:
Both white and black get their knights in on the action.

White develops another piece, this time moving the queen's bishop out to attack black's knight (4. Bg5), as Figure 12-10a shows. The white bishop now pins the black knight to its current position (see Chapter 7 for info on pinning); otherwise, the black queen would be exposed to attack by the foraging bishop. Because the move by white attacks one of the center pawn's defenders (the black knight), it indirectly influences the center.

In Figure 12-10b, black breaks the pin by developing the king's bishop (4. ... Be7), which now shields the queen. This move enables the black knight to again concentrate solely on defending the queen's pawn, although a slight difference in position is already evident: The white bishop is still attacking, and the black bishop is now defending. These positions mean that the white bishop is more aggressively posted and can still influence the center by capturing the knight — but the black bishop has no such option.

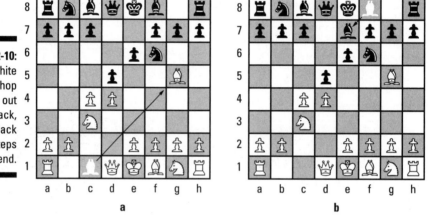

Figure 12-10: The white bishop moves out to attack, so the black bishop steps in to defend.

a   b

Looking for control of the center

In the next series of figures, the two sides move with an eye toward controlling the center. White advances a pawn (5. e3), paving the way to centralize the king's bishop — see Figure 12-11a. Black develops the remaining knight in support of the one under attack (5. ... Nd7), as shown in Figure 12-11b).

If white now chooses to capture the black knight with the queen's bishop, the other black knight can in turn capture the white bishop, taking its twin's place as a defender of the queen's pawn — so white would accomplish nothing by exchanging pieces. (I discuss exchanging pieces in more detail later in this chapter.)

White develops the remaining knight toward the center (6. Nf3); see Figure 12-12a. Black responds by castling (6. ... 0-0), as shown in Figure 12-12b. Castling safeguards the black king and prepares the way for the rook to move toward the center. (For details on castling, jump to Chapter 5, where I explain some special chess moves.)

White develops the king's bishop (7. Bd3) and prepares to castle the king with the king's rook — see Figure 12-13a. Black advances the queen's bishop pawn to support the center pawn once more (7. ... c6); see Figure 12-13b.

Figure 12-11:
The white pawn makes way for the bishop, but the black knight defends its twin.

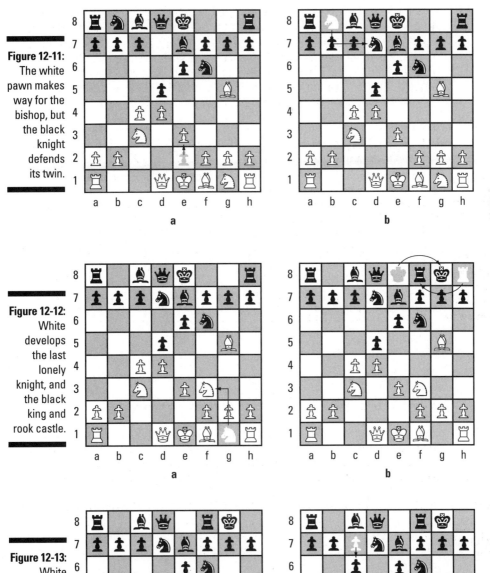

a

b

Figure 12-12:
White develops the last lonely knight, and the black king and rook castle.

a

b

Figure 12-13:
White prepares to castle, while black loads up the support for its center pawn.

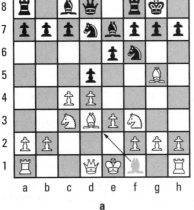

a

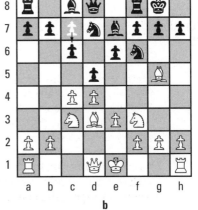

b

Understanding initiative, positional advantage, and what happens next

The placement of pieces on the board in Figure 12-13 reflects a classic position in the Queen's Gambit declined:

- ✔ Black has staked out a foothold in the center and has developed several pieces with the aim of maintaining this hold on the center.

- ✔ White has developed pieces more aggressively by attacking the black center. This *initiative* (white attacking, and black defending against white's attack) comes from having the first move and from making each move an aggressive one.

White enjoys a greater control of the center than black does because of the better arrangement of the white pieces. (In chess terms, these pieces are *more centralized* than black's.) This centralization has already left its mark on the position. Notice how white's light-squared bishop has much more freedom than black's light-squared bishop; it can move to a greater number of squares. This additional freedom of movement is a *positional advantage*. A positional advantage isn't the same as a material advantage or an advantage in pawn structure. (See Chapter 3 for a discussion of chess elements.) This type of advantage provides a player with a more subtle edge than other advantages and can evaporate quickly as a result of inexact play. White can't force the win of material or ruin black's pawn structure and must now think in terms of forming a strategic plan that can maintain and even increase the positional advantage.

White normally continues by castling and then by centralizing the queen and rooks. Black wants to centralize these pieces, too, but has a more difficult time doing so because of the cramped position of his pieces. White then typically tries to create a weakness, such as a backward pawn (see Chapter 3), in the black position and exploit that weakness.

Exchanging Pieces

If one player captures a piece and the other player then captures the piece that first attacked, the pieces are said to have been *exchanged*. Knowing exactly when to exchange and when not to exchange pieces is often difficult, even for seasoned veterans. *Positional understanding* (the strategic knowledge in chess as opposed to the tactical knowledge) gives you the ability to determine whether an exchange is advantageous to you. Just remember not to exchange pieces simply because you can. Exchange only if you have a good reason.

As your positional sense develops, you come to better understand that you shouldn't exchange bishops for knights — unless you have a good reason to do so (such as winning material, time, or a key square). Two bishops together can cover the entire board, but one alone can cover only half the board. Bishops may also become more powerful as the endgame approaches because they can cover more of a relatively clear board than a knight can.

Yet, in many master games, one player does, in fact, trade a bishop for a knight. Why this seeming contradiction? Although exchanging a bishop for a knight for no reason is a mistake, many valid reasons actually may exist for making the exchange.

✔ It wins material or cripples the pawn structure (see Chapter 3 for details about pawn structure).

✔ The knight is occupying a key square, so removing the piece is necessary. (See the next section for more information about key squares.)

✔ The exchange results in a lead in development in your favor (meaning a gain in time).

Generally, the cramped side seeks exchanges, and the freer side seeks to avoid them. Exchanges ease the burden of defense, because such exchanges leave fewer attacking pieces on the board and decrease the likelihood of defending pieces tripping over one another.

The Exchange

An odd custom in chess refers to a certain trade of pieces as *The Exchange*. The Exchange occurs whenever one side trades a knight or a bishop for a rook. In case you're wondering, this swap is considered odd because chess players usually speak of exchanging pieces of equal value (see Chapter 3 for a table of piece values). You hear people say things such as, "I'll be okay if I can force the exchange of queens." The rook, however, is worth far more than either the bishop or knight; thus The Exchange represents a material gain for one side and a loss for the other side, depending on who captures whose rook.

Nevertheless, this seeming uneven exchange occurs so often in chess that players routinely call this trade *The Exchange* even though the term doesn't seem to make sense. (Interestingly, in other languages, this unequal trade is known by different terms. Germans, for example, talk of losing or gaining "The Quality.") You may hear players say, "I lost (or won) The Exchange." All experienced chess players know what that statement means. If you intentionally give up a rook for a bishop or knight, for whatever reason, you're justified in saying, "I sacrificed The Exchange," or as experienced players more typically phrase it, "I sacked The Exchange."

Controlling Key Squares to Lock Up an Advantage

Sometimes the positional struggle in chess revolves around what chess players call a *key square* (generally an outpost for further invasion). The location of a key square can be anywhere on the board. The attacker desires control of this square, and the defender disputes that control.

The control and eventual occupation of the key square by the attacking side generally leads to a superior placement of the attacking pieces. The defender drifts into passivity by merely guarding against the opponent's threats. Eventually the defender may not be able to successfully counter the attacker's maneuvers.

Chess players often refer to a key square as a *strategic outpost*. Knights love to occupy these outposts. Many games have been won by creating an outpost in enemy territory and then sinking a knight onto that square!

You should almost always use pieces rather than pawns to occupy key squares. Generally, the pawn isn't mobile enough to exploit its advantageous position.

The pawn structure depicted in the following example may arise out of the Sicilian Defense (see Chapter 13) and is characterized by a fight for the key square, which is marked by an X in Figure 12-14. Black has a backward pawn on d6 (see Chapter 3 for more on the backward pawn) and wants to advance and exchange it for a white pawn. White wants to place a piece on the key square and block black's potential pawn advance.

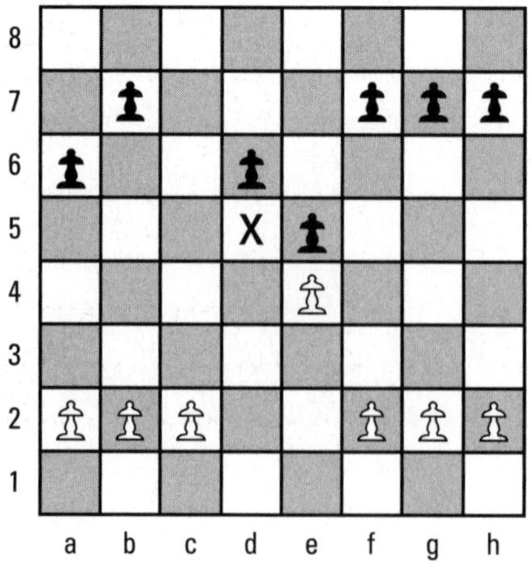

Figure 12-14:
The X marks the key square.

Now I add a knight on d5 for white (see Figure 12-15) in order to show how a piece may be used to occupy and secure a key square. Notice how the knight adds to white's control of the key square. If black can't dispute the point with a piece of equal value to the knight, white moves the knight to the key square, and that piece becomes a bone in black's throat for the rest of the game.

In Figure 12-16a, black now has a bishop in play, but the bishop is on the wrong-colored square. Black's bishop, therefore, can never contest the key square and can't support the advance of black's backward pawn. The pawn will remain a roadblock in the bishop's way for the foreseeable future. If black had a light-squared bishop, however, black could move that bishop into position to fight for the key square (see Figure 12-16b).

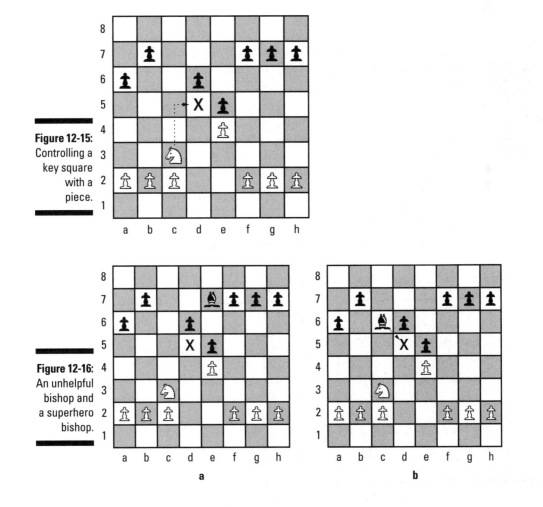

Figure 12-15: Controlling a key square with a piece.

Figure 12-16: An unhelpful bishop and a superhero bishop.

a

b

Now, if white occupies the key square with his knight, black can simply capture the white knight with his own bishop. White then captures the black bishop (exd5) with his own pawn, and the value of the key square drops because of the white pawn's restricted mobility (see Figure 12-17).

If you add both sides' queens to the equation, however, you can see that this setup, too, may change matters (see Figure 12-18). As long as white can keep a piece on the key square, the backward black pawn will be a weakness. Now white can move his knight to the key square, and should black capture the white knight with his own bishop, white can recapture that square with his queen instead of his pawn (1. Nd5 Bxd5 2. Qxd5). By keeping control of the key square, white thus preserves a slight advantage in position.

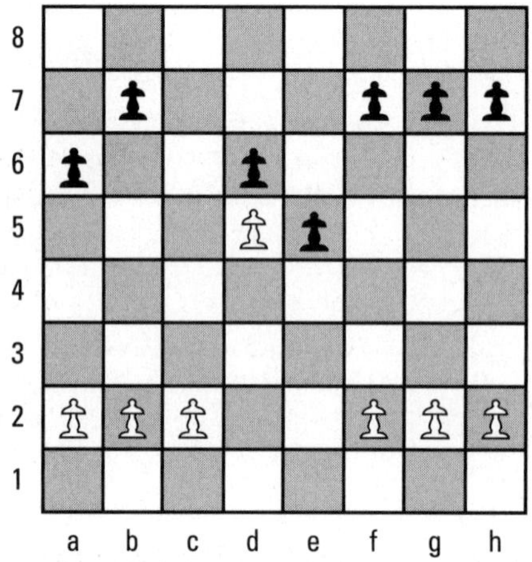

Figure 12-17:
The white pawn occupies the key square, and the square's value plummets.

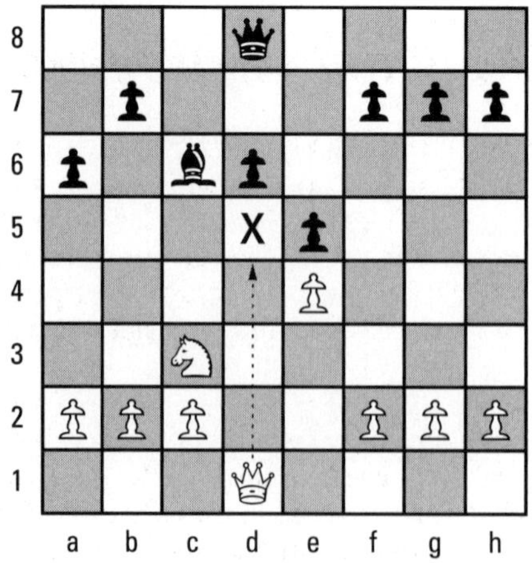

Figure 12-18:
Pieces, not pawns, belong on key squares.

CHESS MASTER

Good knight versus bad bishop

A well-executed strategy may result in only a very subtle advantage. One way of exploiting a positional advantage, for example, may be to enter an ending with the better (more aggressive) minor piece or with the superior (more aggressive) king position. The classic example of a superior piece ending is that of the "good knight" versus the "bad bishop." (I like this ending because it's counterintuitive.)

Bishops and knights are generally considered equal in value through most of the game, but bishops are quite often more powerful than knights in the endgame. This advantage comes because bishops may effortlessly roam the board from side to side, while knights must furiously hop around here and there to accomplish the same thing.

Chess masters can often sense whether one or the other piece is better suited to a particular endgame. Although masters may prefer the bishop, all things being even (which, of course, they never are), cases may exist where the same players would opt for the knight if given the choice. If, for example, the bishop is constrained from moving freely by pawns on the same colored squares, that piece may have less mobility than the knight. The knight, able to hop from white squares to black and back again with ease, taunts the poor bishop who remains in chains.

The "good" knight in such a case can almost always outplay the "bad" bishop and force the win of material. Often the player with the bad bishop runs out of good moves and is forced to play a bad one (as chess doesn't allow a player to pass but requires a move on every turn). If compelled to make a move when all moves are bad, the player faces what chess players call by the German word *Zugzwang*. (There we go showing off our worldliness again.) Experienced chess players derive a peculiar joy from putting their opponents in Zugzwang. The situation is one of the few times you can be happy that it isn't your turn to move!

Holding Back Pawns with a Blockade

If you know even a little bit about chess, you know that pawns are valuable little soldiers. One strategy you can employ is to restrain pawn advances, which you can do well by blocking them with pieces. (This move is called a *blockade*.) Contrary to what you may first think, these pieces aren't wasting time keeping a lowly pawn in check, because such blockading pieces often find themselves well posted for future attacks and unassailable from enemy counterattacks.

Figure 12-19 shows a passed pawn on d5. An isolated pawn (which may or may not be passed) may be weak because that pawn lacks the support of its peers. (Passed and isolated pawns are covered in more detail in Chapter 3.) Therefore, the strategically correct way of combating an isolated pawn is to blockade it.

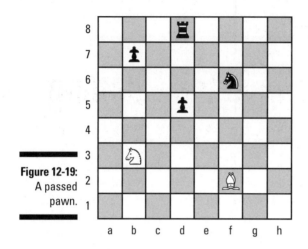

Figure 12-19: A passed pawn.

According to conventional wisdom since Nimzowitsch (1886–1935), simply controlling the square in front of the pawn isn't enough; rather, you must occupy that square. This occupation of the square in front of the pawn is the difference between merely *restraining* a pawn's advance (by controlling the square with pieces) and *blockading* the pawn (physically preventing it from moving). The white knight is the ideal blockader, because that piece retains its powers even while doing guard duty and can't easily be driven off. The correct move (1. Nd4), in which white moves the knight to occupy the square in front of the black pawn, is now easy to understand (see Figure 12-20).

Notice how the mobility of the knight on d4 is unimpaired. The pawn's mobility, on the other hand, has been brought to a screeching halt. If you can impair your opponent's mobility without reducing your own, your chances of eventually outmaneuvering your opponent increase.

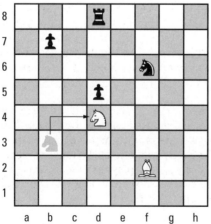

Figure 12-20: The black pawn on d5 can't advance — it's in jail and not merely under police watch!

Chapter 13

Coming on Strong in the Opening

*I*n chess, quicker isn't necessarily better. If you're trying to checkmate your opponent as fast as possible, you're almost certain to make inferior moves in the opening phase of the game. If you reach for the brass ring too early, you're bound to fall off your knight . . . er, horse. Rather, if you use your opening moves to rapidly deploy your pieces to good squares, your ultimate goal of checkmate eventually will come within your grasp.

At the highest levels of chess, knowing tons of opening variations is extremely important. Entire volumes are available describing even some of the most obscure chess openings. Rest assured, however, that for the vast majority of chess players, such intense knowledge isn't at all necessary to compete — and to compete well.

Instead of simply memorizing the opening moves or suggestions of masters (which is referred to as *opening theory*), you need to understand some general principles of opening play, which I name and describe for you in this chapter. After you grasp these principles, you can play reasonably well in this phase of the game. (If you're interested in the nitty-gritty of chess openings, I provide much more extensive examination in my book *Chess Openings For Dummies* (John Wiley & Sons, Inc.)

If you start in one opening but then find yourself in another, you've *transposed* into the second opening, which may or may not be a good thing. Many opening systems offer such possibilities, and transposing from one opening to another is a subtle nuance that you often find at the higher levels of play. Good chess players may try to fool you into playing an inferior variation of one opening by transposing into it from another. Transposing isn't all that important, however, for recreational players.

Certainly, on occasion, you're still going to make mistakes or get caught in inferior positions, which chess players call *traps,* but making errors is how you gain experience in the game. No one attains master status in chess without getting plenty of bloody noses. You make far more progress by figuring out *why* you got the worst of a particular opening than by spending hours of study time beforehand hoping to avoid that fate.

Developing Your Pieces

The first lesson you must learn on the road to improving your game is to get your priorities straight. Not only should you *not* try to checkmate your opponent in the opening, but also you shouldn't even try to win material (see Chapter 3 for more on material). Save both objectives for later in the game. Instead, the primary objective of the opening is the rapid deployment of your pieces to their optimal posts. You shouldn't put a piece on a good square, however, if that piece can easily be driven away by your opponent's pieces, so getting your pieces not only on good squares, but also on *safe* squares, is critical to your opening game. (For details on controlling key squares, see Chapter 12.)

The rapid mobilization of pieces is called *development.* Development, for either side, isn't considered complete until the knights, bishops, queens, and rooks are moved off their original squares. Normally, getting the knights, bishops, and queen off the back rank is important as well. Rooks may be effective in fighting from their starting rank, but the other pieces usually increase in power only as they move toward the center.

In the following sections, I explain two basic concepts behind development: controlling the center of the board as fast as you can and interfering with your opponent's development. I also list some basic development principles for you to try.

Controlling the center as efficiently as possible

As I describe in Chapters 3 and 12, control of the center and centralization of your pieces are critical objectives in a chess game. The pieces generally increase in power as you move them closer to the center. In the opening phase, you want to maximize the power of the pieces in a minimal amount of time.

Moving one piece three times to position it on the best square doesn't help much if, in the meantime, your other pieces languish on their original squares. So the key is focusing on not just one piece, but deploying all of them sensibly.

Watching your opponent

Just as important as developing quickly is preventing your opponent's development. Some otherwise strange-looking moves can be explained only in this way. If you waste two moves to force your opponent to waste three, well, those moves weren't wasted after all!

Don't get so caught up in your plans that you forget about your opponent's moves. Just as you are, your opponent is trying to interfere with your development while developing her own pieces — at your expense.

Following basic development principles

As you become familiar with the game, you begin to pick up on a few basic principles of opening play, not only from your own experiences but also from those of other players:

- ✔ Place the pieces where they can develop their greatest power, and do so as efficiently as possible.
- ✔ Don't move an already developed piece when other pieces remain undeveloped unless you have a strong reason for doing so.
- ✔ Avoid putting pieces on squares where they can be driven off by moves that also contribute to the development of enemy pieces and pawns.
- ✔ Keep pawn moves in the opening game to a minimum; they serve only as an aid to the development of your pieces and as a means of fighting for the center.

Many principles are just guidelines — don't think you're bound by them. If, for example, your opponent slips up and gives you the opportunity to deliver checkmate, do so! Don't worry that such a move develops your queen too early!

Attacking Your Opponent's Pieces

After you discover what it means to develop your pieces (see the preceding section), the question that naturally follows is "What's the big deal about having a lead in development?" How can you translate a lead in development into a more permanent advantage, such as a material edge or a superior pawn structure?

The simple answer is — attack! If you have a lead in development and fail to attack, you're almost certainly going to see your advantage slip through your fingers.

If you enjoy a lead in development, open up the game. You want open files and diagonals leading to your opponent's vulnerable points. You want to use these open lines to move your pieces to increasingly aggressive locations. Ideally, you want to combine your development with strong threats to your opponent, such as an attack on an undefended piece. If you can develop a piece and simultaneously threaten an enemy piece (or pieces!), your opponent may lose additional time scurrying to defend against your attack. Your pieces become increasingly threatening, and the defender's pieces become increasingly passive. Then comes the time, usually in the middlegame (covered in Chapter 14), to try to win material or play for checkmate.

The player who's ahead in development seeks to open up lines of attack; the player who's behind in development seeks to keep those lines closed. If you can combine a superior development with open lines of attack, you quickly find that whatever tactics you employ seem to always work out in your favor. On the other hand, if those lines remain closed, you soon find that your advantage in development isn't nearly so great an asset and that your work is really cut out for you in winning the game.

Perusing Some Possibilities for First Moves

In this section, you examine some alternative first moves. See whether you can understand why these moves are good or not so good from the twin perspectives of development and control of the center.

Taking note of two good first moves

Consider the most common first move in all of chessdom. By advancing the pawn in front of the white king two squares (1. e4; see Chapter 6 for info on chess notation), white occupies one central square and attacks another. The attacked square is indicated by an X in Figure 13-1. (The pawn could, of course, attack the other square to its right, but I'm talking about central squares here.)

From the perspective of control of the center, this move is obviously a useful one. Is the move also useful, however, in aiding the development of your pieces? Yes — absolutely. Here's why:

- ✔ Notice how the pawn's advance opens a line for the bishop's development. (The bishop's line of development is indicated by Xs in Figure 13-2a.)

- ✔ The bishop, however, isn't the only piece that now enjoys an open line. What about the queen? The queen also has a line open for her development (see Figure 13-2b).

So white's opening move proves useful not only for controlling the center but also for developing pieces. No wonder this particular opening move is so popular.

The next example looks at the second most popular opening move in chess: moving the queen's pawn forward two squares (1. d4); see Figure 13-3. By moving this pawn, white accomplishes pretty much the same thing as in the case of moving the king's pawn. Notice how the pawn occupies one central square and attacks another, which is marked with an X. In terms of controlling the center, the moves in these two examples are pretty interchangeable.

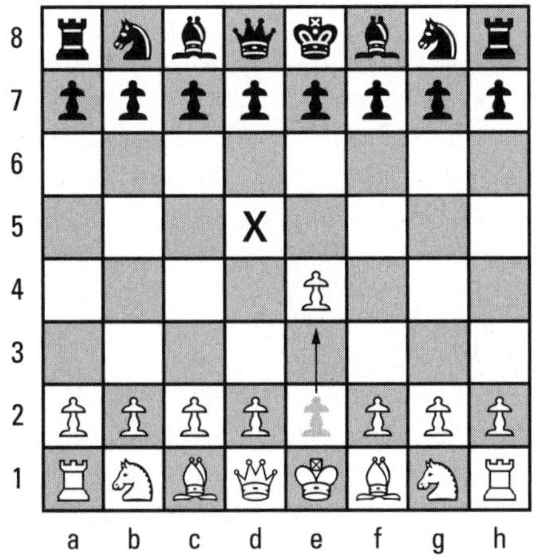

Figure 13-1: Advancing the pawn in front of the king.

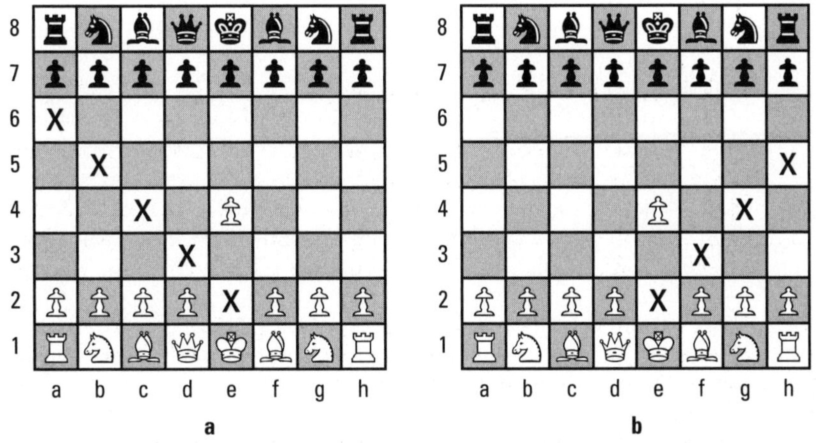

Figure 13-2: The king's pawn move opens two lines of development.

a

b

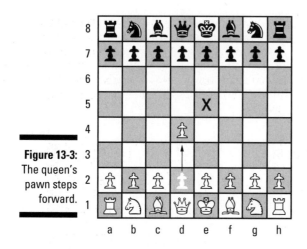

Figure 13-3:
The queen's
pawn steps
forward.

In terms of development, these moves are also very similar. With the move of the queen's pawn, a diagonal path opens up for a bishop, just as in the first example (see Figure 13-4a). But this time, the queen doesn't have an open diagonal — only a couple of squares along the file (see Figure 13-4b). The initial advance of the queen's pawn, therefore, doesn't do quite as much for development as does the initial advance of the king's pawn.

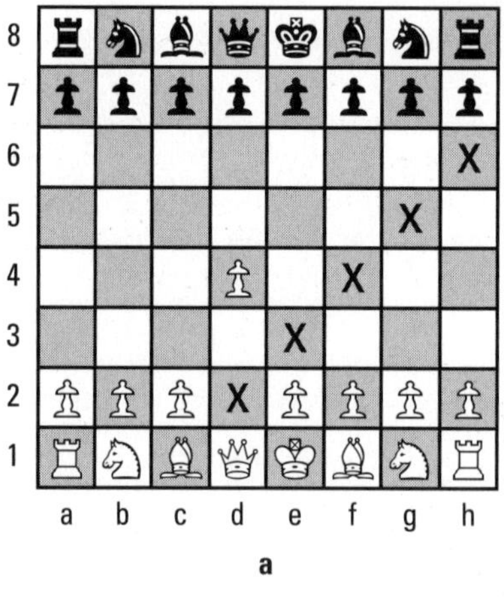

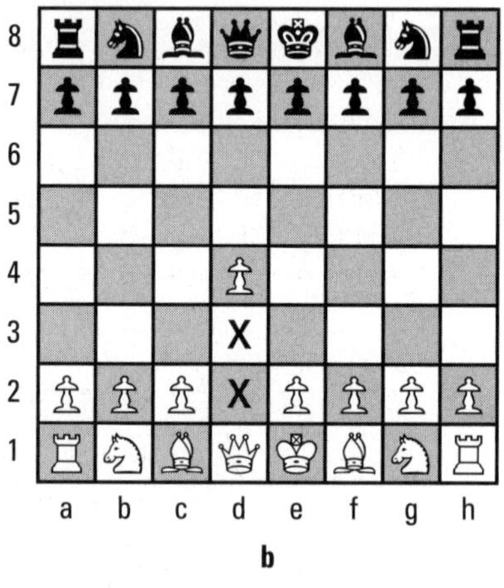

Figure 13-4:
The queen's
pawn clears
a path for
the bishop
but not for
the queen.

a

b

Surveying some not-as-good first moves

If you keep going with opening possibilities for white, you see that no other move accomplishes quite as much as the two choices in the preceding section.

The move shown in the next example — advancing the queen's bishop pawn forward two squares (1. c4) — is fairly popular at all levels of tournament play. The pawn attacks a central square (marked by X) without occupying one (see Figure 13-5a). Although this move opens up a diagonal for the queen (see Figure 13-5b), it doesn't help the bishops in any way; experienced chess players, therefore, don't consider the move quite as strong an opening as the two choices in the preceding section.

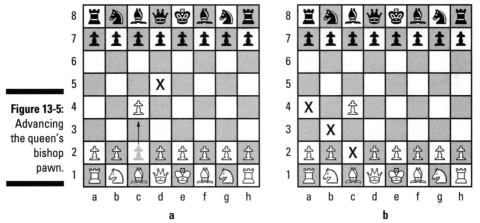

Figure 13-5: Advancing the queen's bishop pawn.

a

b

The following example — advancing the king's bishop pawn forward two squares — is even weaker when it comes to development. In the setup shown in Figure 13-6, the king's bishop pawn also attacks a central square (marked by X), but no other piece is helped by this advance. In fact, the king's safety is called into question because a diagonal is now open that black may use as a path to attack the king. There is now the possibility of an attack by either the black queen or dark-squared bishop along this diagonal.

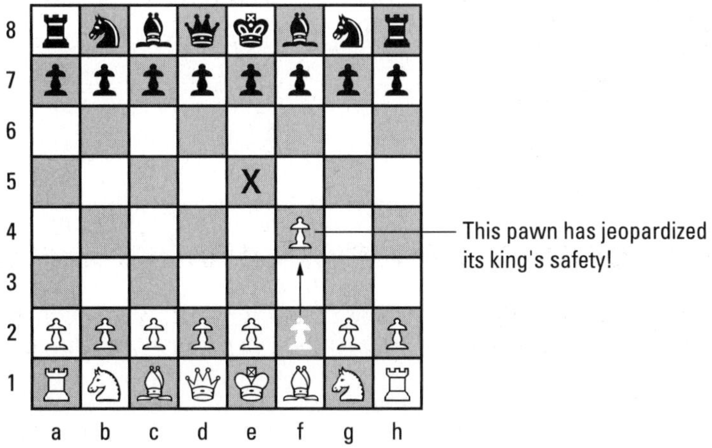

Figure 13-6: The king's bishop pawn steps into the limelight.

— This pawn has jeopardized its king's safety!

Figuring out the fianchetto as a first move

Pawn moves that are farther from the center of the board are generally very weak. However, one exception is the *fianchetto* (see Chapter 10), which occurs whenever you develop the bishop on either flank. This move may seem strange because, at first glance, the single-square advance by the knight pawn does little in terms of controlling the center (see Figure 13-7a). But this move is almost invariably followed by the development of the bishop to the square formerly occupied by the pawn (1. g3 and 2. Bg2, for example). The Xs in Figure 13-7b show that the bishop is now attacking the key central squares from a safe distance. This move can open a fairly effective attack but generally isn't as difficult to counter as the moves examined in the earlier section "Taking note of two good first moves."

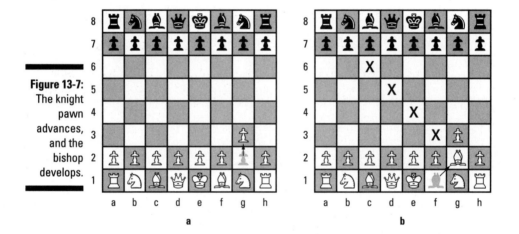

Figure 13-7: The knight pawn advances, and the bishop develops.

a

b

Exploring Common Chess Openings

Listing every chess opening ever used is impossible, but I can at least draw your attention to some of the more common ones. If you simply follow the basic opening principles described in this chapter, you're likely to play a decent game. But if you don't know the French Defense from the Spanish Game, people may question your chess heritage. If you hope to impress anyone with your lofty knowledge of the game, you should be able to identify the following openings by name. And if you go to a chess club, you'll find this vocabulary very useful in terms of speaking to others. For example, you can say to your fellow chess lover, "I saw that you played a Sicilian in your last game. Can you show me how it went?"

The hard part about many openings' names is that they're not always universally recognized. The Internet didn't exist 50 years ago, and local customs prevailed regarding naming conventions. Some became universally known based on a widely read publication or two, and some are still known by multiple names, depending on the part of the world you're in or from. For example, in the United States, chess players call the following opening sequence the *Ruy Lopez,* after the player who popularized it. But in other parts of the world, the same opening is known more commonly as the *Spanish Game,* after the country where it became popular.

It's impossible for me to give enough guidance to play the following openings even passably well in this amount of space. The point of this chapter, then, is to give you the basic principles of opening play. I don't recommend memorizing reams of variations, because that would do more harm than good. If you retain the basic principles, you'll do well. If you try to remember too many specific sequences from this book, your learning may suffer.

A popular double king pawn opening: The Ruy Lopez (the Spanish Game)

All double king pawn openings begin, naturally, with the advance of both kings' pawns two squares (1. e4 e5), as Figure 13-8 shows. Several popular openings begin in this manner, but by far the most popular is the Ruy Lopez.

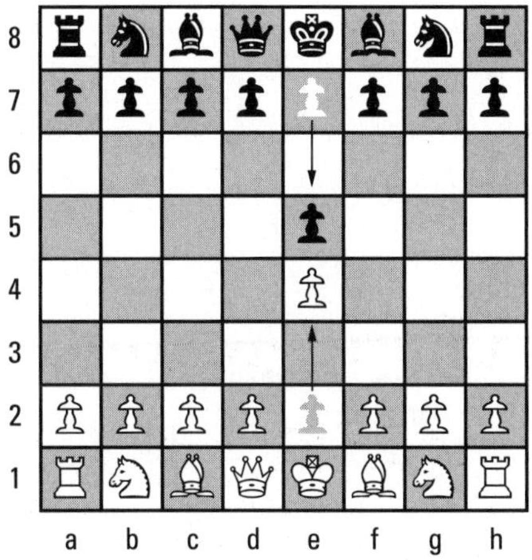

Figure 13-8: Double king pawn moves.

The Ruy Lopez begins with the mutual advance of the kings' pawns (refer to Figure 13-8). White's next move of a knight to f3 (2. Nf3) attacks black's e-pawn. Black's response, moving a knight to c6 (2. ... Nc6), defends the pawn (see Figure 13-9a). White's next move of the king's bishop to b5 (3. Bb5) defines the game as a Ruy Lopez (see Figure 13-9b).

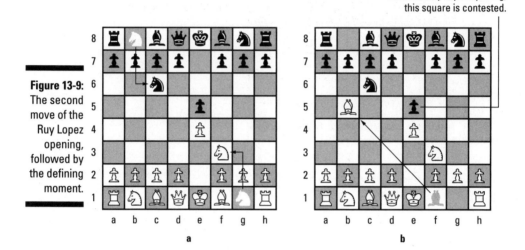

Figure 13-9: The second move of the Ruy Lopez opening, followed by the defining moment.

With the Ruy Lopez opening, this square is contested.

a

b

I've always liked the logic of this opening. After the pawns move, the white knight comes out to attack the black pawn. The black knight comes out to defend it. The white bishop comes out to attack the black knight that defends the black pawn. Further play is characterized by the struggle around the control over the black pawn (or more precisely, the *square* the black pawn occupies): White wants to capture it safely. Black wants to maintain it, and white's intent is to wrestle it away.

Different strokes: Other black replies to white's first move of the king's pawn

The following sections describe some other replies to white's first move of the king's pawn two squares (1. e4). These are replies other than the black king's pawn moving two squares (1. … e5), as I describe in the preceding section.

The French Defense

I describe the French Defense (1. e4 e6) in more detail in Chapter 9, but the basic idea is to fight for the light-colored center squares. The white king's pawn moves forward two squares; black replies by moving his king's pawn forward one square. The defense is very solid but has a drawback: The black light-squared bishop gets trapped behind the pawn chain (see Figure 13-10).

With the French Defense, this bishop is trapped.

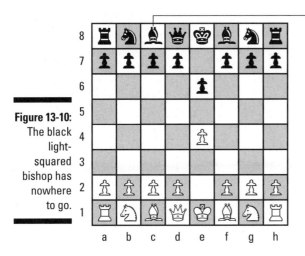

Figure 13-10: The black light-squared bishop has nowhere to go.

The Sicilian Defense

The Sicilian Defense (1. … c5) is very popular at all levels. After the white king's pawn moves forward two squares, a black bishop's pawn moves forward two squares. Usually, a white center pawn is traded for this black *wing* (side) pawn, as shown in Figure 13-11, which leads to an imbalance. Black then has two center pawns (the d and e-pawns) to white's one (the e-pawn) — but white has compensating advantages in space and time (see Chapter 3 for details on these elements). The imbalance produces tension because judging who has the greater advantage in this scenario is difficult.

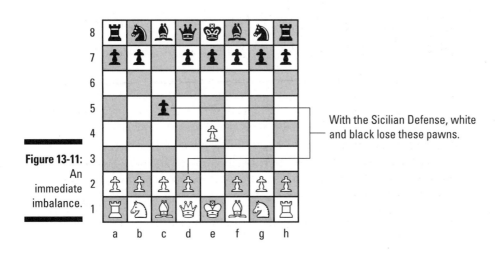

With the Sicilian Defense, white and black lose these pawns.

Figure 13-11: An immediate imbalance.

Ladies first: Double queen pawn openings

Besides moving the king's pawn forward two squares, the other most common first move for white is to advance the queen's pawn two squares (1. d4), as I explain in the earlier section "Taking note of two good first moves." If black responds the same way (1. ... d5), as shown in Figure 13-12, then you have a *double queen pawn game.* I describe two popular double queen pawn openings in the following sections.

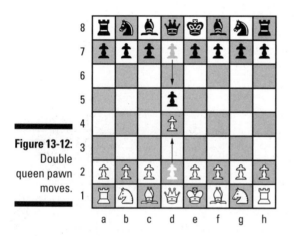

Figure 13-12: Double queen pawn moves.

The Queen's Gambit

The most usual opening that begins with double queen pawn moves is the Queen's Gambit (1. d4 d5 2. c4); see Figure 13-13. The *Queen's Gambit,* which is the offer of the c-pawn for capture, can be accepted or declined, and I cover both alternatives in Chapter 12.

With the Queen's Gambit opening in Figure 13-13, the center black pawn must decide whether to accept or decline the gambit:

- ✔ Figure 13-14a shows you the accepted version (2. ... dxc4). In other words, the center black pawn captures the white c-pawn.

- ✔ Figure 13-14b illustrates the declined version (2. ... e6) — that is, black refuses to take the white pawn on the c-file and instead defends the d-pawn with the e-pawn.

The Slav

The *Slav* (1. d4 d5 2. c4 c6) was popularized by the Russian grandmaster Mikhail Ivanovich Chigorin in the late 19th century. The opening is still a prime weapon today, even in the highest levels of competition. In it, after white moves her c-pawn two squares forward; black defends her d-pawn with her c-pawn without blocking her light-squared bishop (see Figure 13-15).

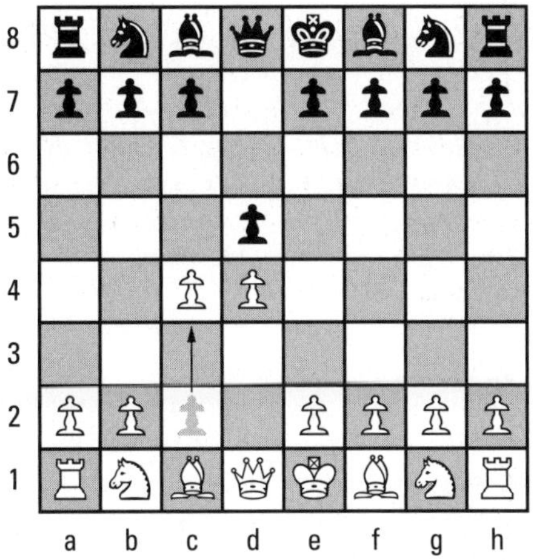

Figure 13-13:
The Queen's Gambit.

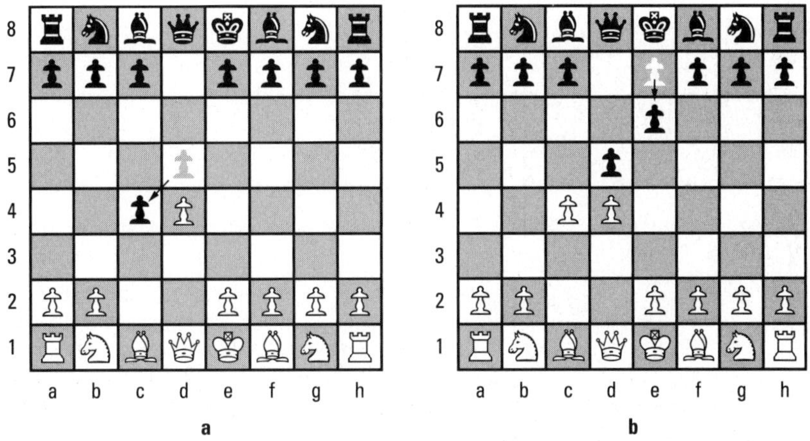

Figure 13-14:
The Queen's Gambit, accepted and rejected.

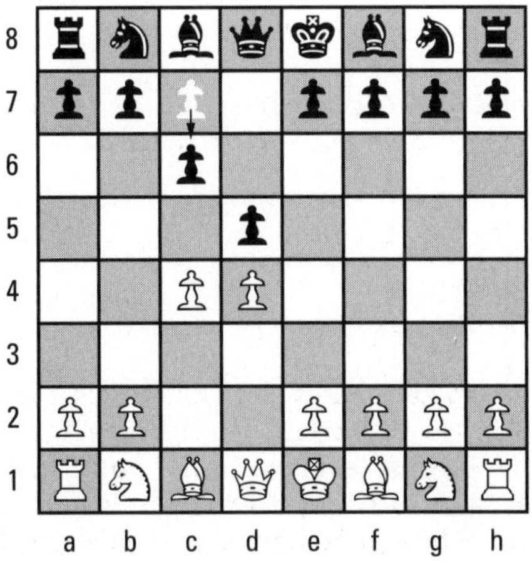

a

b

Figure 13-15:
The Slav opening.

Going back in time: Indian Defenses

Besides moving the black queen's pawn forward two squares, the other most common reply to white's first move of the queen's pawn is to move out the king's knight (1. ... Nf6), as shown in Figure 13-16. This move leads to what are usually referred to as the *Indian Defenses* — King's Indian or Queen's Indian — both of which are considered very reliable today.

This naming convention comes from the precursor to chess, *chaturanga,* which originated in India during or before the seventh century A.D. A game of chaturanga commonly opened with the development of a bishop on the wing. (In chess, this wing development is called a *fianchetto,* which I describe in Chapter 10.) Black makes the knight move first in order to prevent white from establishing a center pawn duo (see Chapter 3) by advancing the king's pawn two squares. This move is followed by a fianchetto on either wing.

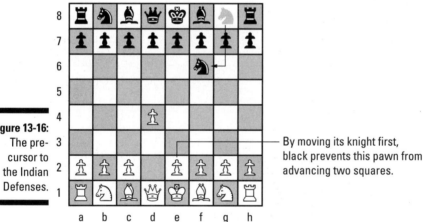

Figure 13-16: The precursor to the Indian Defenses.

By moving its knight first, black prevents this pawn from advancing two squares.

 You're better off playing openings that are a bit easier, such as the double queen pawn game that I describe earlier in this chapter, when you're starting out. You can graduate to the Indian Defenses after you gain more experience.

The King's Indian

In the *King's Indian,* the bishop is fianchettoed on the kingside (see Figure 13-17). Black usually castles quickly (see Chapter 5 for more on castling) and only then starts to attack white's center pawns with her own. This move is an extremely popular way to combat the queen's pawn opening, but it's also a very complicated one.

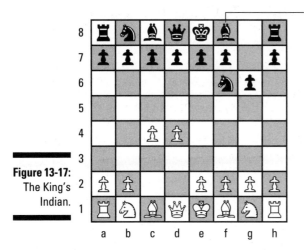

With the King's Indian, black develops this bishop and prepares to castle.

Figure 13-17:
The King's Indian.

The Queen's Indian

In the *Queen's Indian,* the bishop is fianchettoed on the queenside (see Figure 13-18). The strategy is fairly similar to that of the King's Indian. Black tries to attack the white center only after castling. The bishops attack the center from the safety of their fianchettoed positions, which helps black accomplish this counterattack.

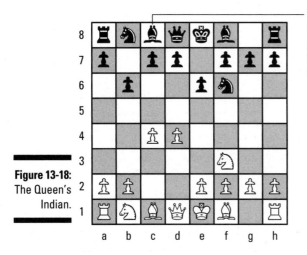

With the Queen's Indian, black develops this bishop first to prepare for an eventual castling to the queenside — all before attacking the center.

Figure 13-18:
The Queen's Indian.

Weird opening names

Although most of the names given to chess openings make a good deal of sense because they're named after a person or place, some opening names have far less mundane origins. Be warned that these names are far from universally recognized, but most players know what you mean if you refer to any of these three openings:

✔ The Dragon

✔ The Orangutan

✔ The Hedgehog

Less familiar but still generally understood are these openings:

✔ The Vulture

✔ The Rat

✔ The Kangaroo

One chess opening is even called the *Woozle,* but don't ask me why. In the United States, chess players call another opening the *Fried Liver Attack* — so you see, just about anything goes!

To get credit for a new opening system, you must play that opening in a major tournament or publish your analysis to back up your claim. Don't try too hard, however, because coming up with something no one has tried before is very, very difficult these days.

Chapter 14

Making Headway during the Middlegame

*T*he *middlegame* commences after the pieces are developed and the opening phase of the game ends. You don't have an arsenal of theory for use in the middlegame as you do in openings and endings. The absence of any vast repository of standardized middlegame theory means that you're usually on your own during this phase of play — but it also means that this part of the game is where your own personal creativity can shine through the most.

The middlegame is extremely difficult to play well. Quite often, players who are otherwise quite good at the game find themselves unable to navigate these murky waters adequately. They may know the opening principles and understand where to put their pieces initially, but after those moves, they're at a loss as to what to do next.

But be of good cheer — especially if you find yourself among the ranks of the middlegame-challenged — for the middlegame, too, has its own governing principles to guide your creative play. Openings and endings may involve some tactics, but middlegames are replete with tactics galore. (Need a quick refresher on tactics? Flip to Chapter 7.) Don't forget, however, that good tactics come from good plans. So in this chapter, I provide some details to help you in your tactical planning for the middlegame. If you bone up on your tactics and stick to these principles, you can play this phase of the game quite well indeed.

I could say many more things about the middlegame. The best teacher, however, is experience. You can gain a great deal of experience by playing over the games of the masters and studying their moves, but the best way to navigate a successful middlegame is simply to play several games yourself. My best advice is to read this chapter, where you discover how to formulate a plan for your game and gather some tips for the road on attacking your opponent in the most effective way possible through this aggressive phase of the chess battle. After you've tucked the fundamentals under your hat, scrounge up an opponent, play an opening of your choosing (refer to Chapter 13), and practice formulating and implementing your middlegame strategies.

Formulating a Middlegame Plan

Chess isn't a game that you can easily reduce to the simple sum of its parts. You may understand each element in isolation but still struggle to put the total package together or come to the correct understanding of any given position. Nevertheless, in the middlegame, you must be able to judge a *position* (the arrangement of the pieces on the board) correctly — or at least adequately — before you can hope to formulate the correct plan. If you can't plan well in chess, you end up aimlessly shuffling pieces about, hoping for a glaring error from your opponent. Players who fall into this category of non-planners are referred to in chess circles as *woodpushers.* The moral? Don't be a woodpusher. Instead, consider the governing principles for planning in the following sections.

Any time you don't know what to do in a chess game, just tell yourself to make a plan — you can achieve many fine victories if you simply evaluate a position and attempt to come up with the appropriate plan for that position. Think to yourself something like the following: "I'm going to advance my pawns and weaken my opponent's pawns and then attack them with my pieces." Decide which move helps you best carry out that plan, and make that move. After every move (your own and that of your opponent), reevaluate your plan in light of the changed situation. Perhaps your original plan is still appropriate, but maybe an even better idea occurs to you. Try not to switch aimlessly back and forth between plans; rather, have a specific reason to either stick with your plan or change to a new one. If the new idea seems about the same as the old one, stick with the old one.

Evaluating the position

To formulate a plan, you must first evaluate the position on the board, and to be successful, your plan must correspond to the demands of the position. If your pieces and pawns are poised to attack on the kingside, for example, then that is where you must attack.

Every position must be judged on its own merits. The rules of chess have so many exceptions that a blind adherence to any formula is doomed to failure. Some players wail that no justice is to be found in chess because they can be doing everything right according to the general guiding principles and still lose. The more mature among us refer to "the equalizing injustice of chess," by which we mean that the exception that spoils your plan today may be the exception that spoils your opponent's plan tomorrow.

In his book *Modern Chess Strategy* (published by Dover), Ludek Pachman puts forth the following factors to consider in evaluating any certain position:

- ✔ **The material relationship:** The material equality or the material superiority of either side (see Chapter 3).
- ✔ **The power of the individual pieces:** A factor that's tied to the pieces' mobility (see Chapter 2).
- ✔ **The quality of the individual pawns:** The pawn structure (see Chapter 3)
- ✔ **The position of the pawns:** The pawn formation (see Chapters 9 and 10).
- ✔ **The safety of the king:** See Chapter 3.
- ✔ **The cooperation among the pieces and pawns:** See Chapter 10.

The elements of piece mobility and king safety take priority in the middlegame. The rapid mobilization of your forces enables you to attack your opponent, and if you can induce a weakness in the enemy king's position, you may be able to win material or play directly for checkmate. Even if your opponent safeguards the king, you still may be able to force some other sort of concession, which is usually enough to pave the road to victory.

Pieces can move around quite quickly and change the nature of the game. Plans may need to be adopted or dropped if this type of change occurs. You can't stick to a plan that your opponent has thwarted but must readjust yourself to the new position instead. This sort of thing may occur many times in a single game.

Taking advantage of the pawn structure

The pawns are less mobile than the pieces, so you can more readily fix the placement of pawns. The conclusion, therefore, is that the essential characteristic of the pawn *formation* (mobile, locked, and so on — see Chapters 9 and 10 for more on pawn formations) and *structure* (doubled, isolated, and so on; see Chapter 3 for more on pawn structures) during the middlegame is your most trustworthy guide to the feasibility — and your adoption — of any particular plan.

I can think of no better illustration of the idea of the preeminence of pawn structure than the example shown in the following series of figures. This example comes from a composition written by W. E. Rudolph in 1912 and published in the French chess journal *La Stratégie*. (Positions that are constructed by an individual are called *compositions* to distinguish them from positions that happen to occur in actual play.) I first encountered the composition in the classic work *Pawn Power in Chess,* by Hans Kmoch (published by Dover).

In Figure 14-1, black is way ahead in material — but the position is inevitably a draw! Because they're scenarios created by an individual, compositions

begin with a declaration of whose turn it is to move and what the desired outcome is. In this case, white gets to move and can force a draw despite black's
material advantage. The pawn formation is the key to finding the proper plan.
White can lock it up tight.

White first moves the light-squared bishop up from the first rank to check
black's king (1. Ba4+; see Chapter 6 for the scoop on chess notation), as
shown in Figure 14-2a. Black has no choice except to capture the checking
bishop with the king (1. ... Kxb4); see Figure 14-2b. Otherwise, white has a
perpetual check on the black king (the bishop checks from the fourth rank,
then from the third, then from the fourth, and so on, because the black king
can only toggle back and forth between b5 and c4).

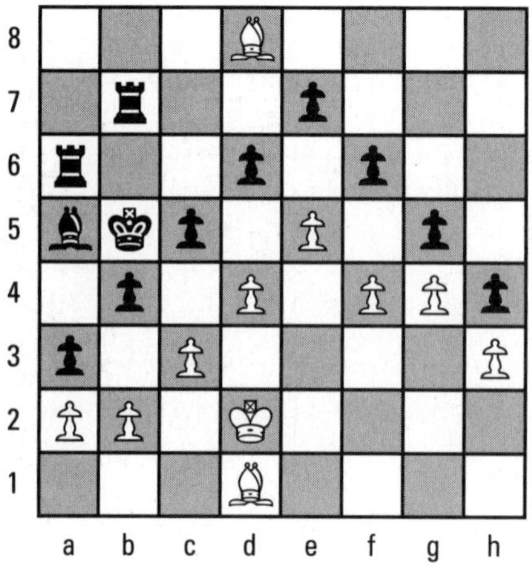

Figure 14-1:
Black is
ahead in
material, but
white
has the
right plan.

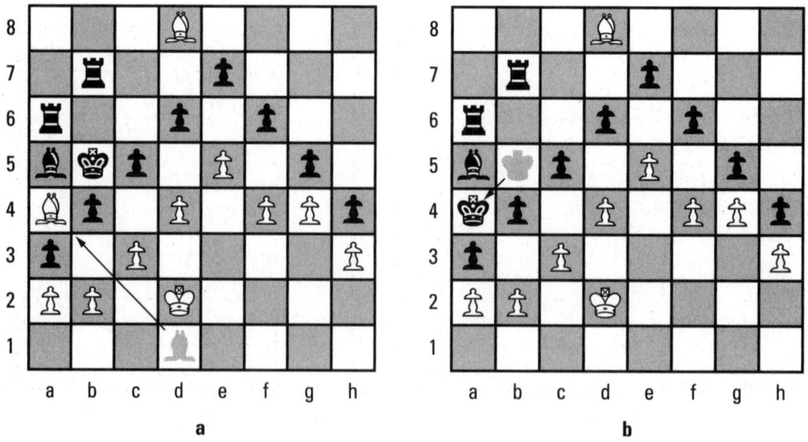

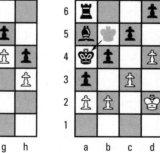

Figure 14-2:
The white
bishop
sacrifices
himself to
the black
king.

a

b

What follows next is as amusing as it is instructive. On each turn, white advances a pawn to check the king. White must carry out the plan in precisely the right order, or black will open an escape valve for his king. However, if white faithfully carries out the plan, black has no choice but to go along for the ride, because the black king has only one legal move on each turn.

White delivers check by moving the b2 pawn to b3 (2. b3+), as Figure 14-3a shows, and the black king must move to the only available square, b5 (2. ... Kb5); see Figure 14-3b.

White uses the exact same idea in Figure 14-4a. The pawn on c3 moves to c4 (3. c4+) and again checks the harassed black king, who has only one safe square to which he can move, c6 (3. ... Kc6); see Figure 14-4b.

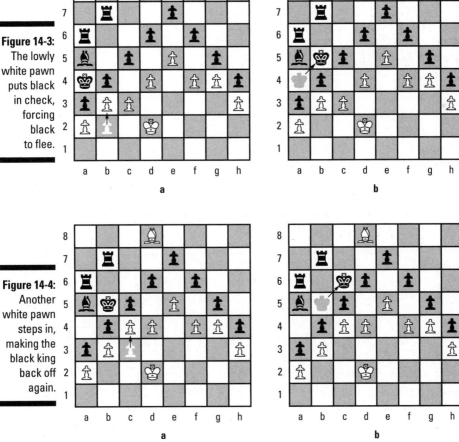

Figure 14-3: The lowly white pawn puts black in check, forcing black to flee.

Figure 14-4: Another white pawn steps in, making the black king back off again.

For a third time, white uses a pawn to check the black king (4. d5+), moving the d4 pawn to d5 (see Figure 14-5a), and the black king moves to the only square available to him, d7 (4. ... Kd7); see Figure 14-5b.

One last time, white gives check with a pawn (5. e6+) by moving the e5 pawn to e6 (see Figure 14-6a). Now, the black king finally has some choice as to where to move, but this new freedom doesn't matter anymore. Black can take the bishop (5. ... Kxd8), as shown in Figure 14-6b, or not — but black can never break through the fortress of pawns covering the board, despite being two rooks and a bishop ahead!

White seals the position with a final pawn move from f4 to f5 (6. f5); see Figure 14-7. Neither side can cross the neutral zone staked out by the reverse pawn wedges, so the game ends in a draw! As you can see, sometimes material advantage just doesn't matter.

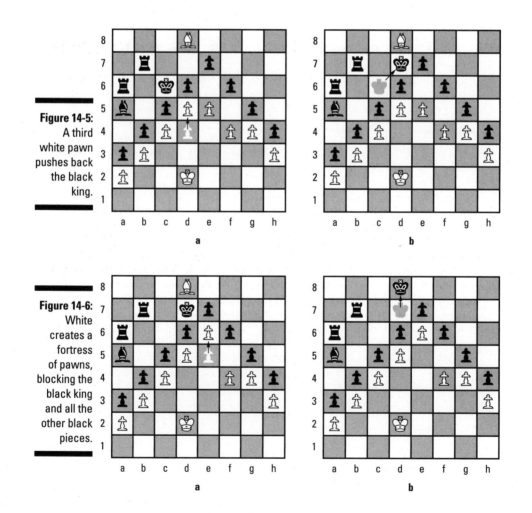

Figure 14-5: A third white pawn pushes back the black king.

Figure 14-6: White creates a fortress of pawns, blocking the black king and all the other black pieces.

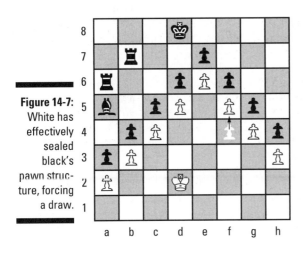

Figure 14-7: White has effectively sealed black's pawn structure, forcing a draw.

Looking for ways to use a minority attack

In a real game of chess, the pawns aren't quite as dominant as in the preceding section, but they do influence the placement of the pieces and the selection of plans. A more typical example of the pawn's influence on the middlegame is the *minority attack,* which is an advance of one or more pawns on a wing where the opponent holds the majority, in order to weaken the opponent's pawns and make them a target of attack. The following example shows this plan in practice.

The position shown in Figure 14-8a occurred in a game between Vasily Smyslov, who played white, and Yuri Averbakh, who played black, in the great Zurich tournament of 1953. In the game, Smyslov wanted to use the minority attack by advancing his queenside pawns and exchanging them for black's. For example, his plan may have been to eventually play b4, a4, and b5, forcing one of black's queenside pawns to be isolated and even threatening to make black's c5-pawn backward on the file white was most powerful on. But Averbakh, by moving his a-file pawn forward to a5 (1. ... a5), didn't allow it (see Figure 14-8b). By grabbing more space on the queenside before white could, black prevented white's original plan and forced him to come up with a different one. From this point on, in a game like this one, black must then respond to the new plan and to the next one, and the next one, if need be. If white makes a mistake, however, the initiative may pass to black, making it white's turn to try and thwart black's plans.

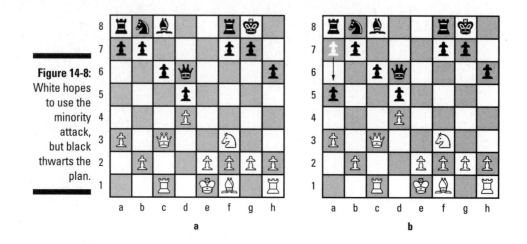

Figure 14-8:
White hopes
to use the
minority
attack,
but black
thwarts the
plan.

Attacking during the Middlegame

Old hands at chess have a saying: If you have a temporary advantage, you must attack. Otherwise, the advantage usually slips through your fingers. Attacking is a fundamental part of the game, but you must not attack too soon, or your effort will peter out ineffectually. You first must build up your position, by securing some advantage, to the point that launching an attack is warranted — you need to secure your position and weaken your opponent's.

You have no hard and fast rules to consider for deciding when to launch an attack. This ambiguity raises the level of decision-making involved in attacks to an art form. The great geniuses of the game seem to have an intuitive sense of when to commence an attack and how to punish a premature one launched by their opponents.

In the following sections, I provide some guidance on attacking during the middlegame — specifically, attack types to keep an eye out for and general attacking principles to employ.

Over time, you figure out when attacks work and when they don't — and why. Keep in mind that everyone fears a strong attacker. No one wants to end up on the wrong side of a brilliant win!

Watching out for and defending against certain types of attacks

Although most games of chess go their own individual route, they almost always have one thing in common. Attacks can feature different moves by different pieces, but you can generally sort them into similar categories.

Vladimir Vukovic (1898–1975) wrote a tremendous book on this subject called, quite naturally, *The Art of Attack in Chess* (Everyman Chess). In the book, he adopts the following classification system for attacks:

✔ The main action isn't in fact an attack on the king, but such an attack is possible in the position. (In other words, the primary objective is not a direct attack on the king, but the possibility is always in the air.)

✔ A player's action really does contain a direct threat to the opponent's king, but his opponent can stave off this threat at a certain price — for example, by giving up material or spoiling his position.

✔ The attacker carries out an uncompromising mating attack; a considerable amount of material may be invested in the attack as long as a mate is certain in the end.

A lengthy course in attack is beyond the scope of this book, but you still can make considerable progress in your attacking ability by reading the chapters on strategy (Chapter 12) and tactics (Chapter 7). By successfully implementing strategic concepts, you soon find that you can build a sound foundation for an attack against your opponent's king and then employ the specific tactics necessary to deliver checkmate.

Keeping some basic principles in mind

You can make a few generalizations about attacking during the middlegame as long as you understand that every position is unique and that exceptions are lurking like fleas just waiting to bite you in the ankle. The following are a few of these generalizations:

✔ **Attack if you control the center.** If you attack without controlling the center, you're exposed to a counterattack in the center, and your forces may be split. (Flip to Chapter 12 for more about controlling the center.)

✔ **Meet a flank attack with action in the center.** If your opponent attacks on either side of the board, your attack in the center divides and conquers your opponent's forces.

✔ **Be prepared to develop quickly to any area.** Your rapid deployment of pieces to one area of the board may be decisive if your opponent can't respond as rapidly. This is not a question of development.

✔ **Place queens in front of bishops and behind rooks during an attack.** The bishop isn't powerful enough to lead an attack, and the queen is too powerful to risk if the rook can do the dirty work in her place.

✔ **Don't place your knights on the sides of the board.** Knights control too few squares from the side of the board, and their attacking power is severely reduced there.

✔ **Attack in the case of opposite-colored bishops.** Because the bishops on opposite-colored squares (called "opposite-colored bishops" in the chess world) can't be exchanged for one another or control the same squares, the attacker has what sometimes amounts to an extra piece.

✔ **Exchange pieces to help your defense.** You have fewer pieces to trip over one another if you exchange some of them, and the attacker has fewer pieces with which to threaten you. (See Chapter 12 for more details on exchanging pieces.)

✔ **Put the rooks on open files (and the same file).** Putting the rooks on an open file and then on the same file (which is called *doubling*) whenever possible is helpful. Other pieces can zigzag their way into enemy territory. The rook requires an open file in order to invade successfully. Two rooks acting together can control more territory than one alone.

✔ **Put rooks on your seventh rank.** Rooks on a player's seventh rank can usually attack opponent's pawns that have remained on their original squares; sometimes the rooks can trap the opponent's king on the back rank.

✔ **Advance pawns to open lines.** The opening is the time to develop your pieces, not to waste time with excessive pawn moves. Conversely, in the middlegame the pieces are already developed; it may then be appropriate to make additional pawn moves in order to open lines or create weaknesses in your opponent's position.

✔ **Always guard against a counterattack.** Never leave your king exposed! Chess players very often spoil promising positions in their zeal to attack because they forget to first take a few small precautions. Sometimes taking a move or two to safeguard your own king's position before initiating or resuming your more aggressive pursuits is the proper thing to do.

✔ **Use knights in closed positions and bishops in open ones.** Bishops need open lines in order to profit from their long-range attacking abilities. Knights are more effective in skirmishes at close quarters, and closed positions are more apt to produce that sort of skirmish.

✔ **Attack where you control more space.** If you do so, you have more room to maneuver your pieces, and your opponent has less. You then have more squares to choose from when posting your pieces, and you may be able to swiftly shift your pieces from one point of attack to another while the defender struggles to meet your threats.

Chapter 15

Exiting with Style in the Endgame

· ·

In This Chapter

▶ Knowing why the endgame is so darn important

▶ Looking at all the angles and laying out a roadmap

▶ Ending with the mighty and the lowly: King and pawn endings

▶ Scrambling to avoid a draw: Rook endings

▶ Letting the minor guys duke it out: Knight and bishop endings

· ·

"**W**hy should I worry about the endgame?" a friend once asked me. "I never get to one." He meant that he either won or lost a game well before the endgame entered into the picture. My response: The reason he never got to an endgame was because he didn't know anything about one.

My point? Good endgame knowledge informs your opening and middlegame knowledge. In other words, you can't understand why certain opening moves are good or bad unless you understand the consequences they have in the endgame. You're also unable to formulate a good plan in the middlegame if you can't evaluate the plan's implication for the endgame.

In this chapter, I describe general endgame strategies and present some specific examples of winning techniques. (Flip to Chapters 13 and 14 for details on the opening and middle phases of a chess game.)

Putting the Endgame into Perspective

Just as middlegame planning flows logically from the opening, the endgame logically develops from the middlegame. The *endgame* arrives after the players lose a majority of pieces and clear much of the board. Attacks become more difficult to execute with this reduction in material (mating attacks are normally out of the question), and the emphasis of play shifts away from tactics to strategy (in terms of this book, from Chapter 7 to Chapter 12). The importance of individual pieces may undergo a marked change in value, and the roles of the pawns and the kings become more prominent. Whatever material remains is of paramount importance, and the only way to increase it is through one or more pawn promotions (see Chapter 5).

Endgames are deceptively complex. Because so few pieces remain on the board, the natural tendency is to conclude that endgames are easier than middlegames or openings. In fact, this phase is equally complicated; the difference is that it's easier to *study* than the earlier two phases. The openings and middlegames have too many possible variations to make heads or tails of them. The endings, however, are clearer in that an idea may be proved or disproved to win.

You can find a massive amount of documentation on the endgame in chess. Experienced players know of many positions — or types of positions — that lead to wins, losses, or draws. By studying the individual pieces in various endgame positions, you can then begin to understand them in combination with others. This strategy helps you to understand middlegame positions and even openings, so you can see that the road to chess mastery begins with the endgame.

In many cases, you can anticipate the endgame as early as in the opening, where one side plays for an advantage in pawn structure that the player can exploit only in the endgame.

Unfortunately, no shortcuts are available to help you master endgame positions; you must study them if you intend to become a chess master. If you'd rather just play than study, however, you'll quickly find that learning just a few basic positions and a few common themes is usually sufficient. In this way, you come to understand a good deal about many endgame positions and can figure out others as you play.

Getting a Handle on the General Winning Endgame Strategy

All endings are different, but the following methodologies can serve you well as a guide to devise the correct endgame plan:

- ✔ **Advance your king.** The king comes out of hiding in the endgame and becomes a critical factor. Advance the king toward passed pawns or toward pawns that are weak and vulnerable to attack. Otherwise, generally advance the king toward the center.

- ✔ **Try to create a passed pawn.** Promoting a passed pawn is relatively easier than promoting any other pawn. (See Chapter 3 for more on passed pawns.)

- ✔ **Push your passed pawns and try to promote them.** As the great grandmaster and writer Aaron Nimzowitsch once said, passed pawns have a lust to expand. Don't go overboard, however. Advance the passed pawn only if doing so is safe. Advancing a pawn into the enemy's teeth, where its capture is certain, is essentially pointless. (Flip to Chapter 5 for details on pawn promotion.)

✔ **Blockade your opponent's passed pawns.** You want to prevent them from advancing toward their *queening squares* (the squares directly in front of the pawns on the opposite end rank, where the pawns get promoted — see Chapter 5).

✔ **Offer to exchange pieces.** Generally speaking, the more material that's still on the board, the more complicated the ending. Don't exchange from a winning ending into a drawn ending, of course, but stay alert to the possibility of exchanging down into a simpler — yet still winning — endgame. (Check out Chapter 12 for an introduction to exchanging pieces.)

✔ **Know your pieces.** Steer the game into the type of ending where your pieces are more suited to winning than your opponent's. If your pawns are still sitting on the same-colored squares as your bishop, for example, try not to go into the ending in the first place! You probably have better chances of securing an advantage in the middlegame.

Further, if you have more pawns than your opponent, exchange pieces, not pawns. A pawn advantage increases as the number of pieces diminishes. But if you have fewer pawns than your opponent, exchange pawns, not pieces. A pawn disadvantage decreases as the number of pawns diminishes.

Also keep in mind that protected passed pawns are very strong, as are outside passed pawns. Passed pawns that are both outside and protected are usually decisive (see Chapter 3 for more on these types of passed pawns).

✔ **Understand the basics.** If you can study only a little bit of chess, study the endgame. Learn the basic winning and drawing techniques for the various endings, and you should find yourself playing the openings and middlegames much better, too!

The Geometry of the Chessboard

You were probably taught that a straight line is the shortest distance between two points. While this is a geometric fact (not counting wormholes) in everyday life, it's a geometric option on the chess board. Distance is counted on the chessboard not by inches, feet, or parsecs, but by squares. You may need to get from Point A on the chessboard to Point B, but your opponent may not want you there. She may block one or two of your pathways during the endgame, so checking out all the possible routes is wise. You have fewer alternatives in the endgame, by definition, so it can become possible to consider all of them.

Consider the case of the king, who's instrumental during the endgame. The king moves one square at a time in any direction. If you think that the shortest route from a1 to a8 in Figure 15-1 is to move the king in a straight line, you're correct. However, alternatives exist that are just as short.

The path a1-b2-a3-b4-a5-b6-a7-a8, shown in Figure 15-2, is just as short. Getting from a1 to a8 takes seven moves if you march in a straight line and seven moves if you skate from side to side! As long as you get where you're going in the same number of moves, it doesn't matter how you do it.

The least intuitive method may be the one shown in Figure 15-3. The king first marches toward the center (d4), and only then makes a dash to a8.

All of these methods are equivalent in that they take seven moves, but considering your alternatives before deciding on a course of action is important because only one of them may lead to victory.

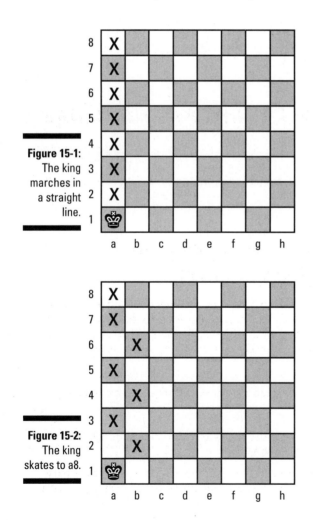

Figure 15-1:
The king marches in a straight line.

Figure 15-2:
The king skates to a8.

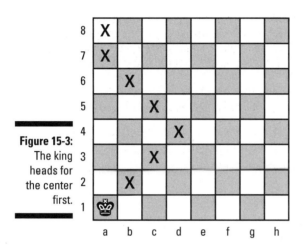

Figure 15-3:
The king heads for the center first.

Typical Stories: Pawn and King Endings

The most basic type of ending is the king-and-pawn versus king-only ending. However, you may also encounter endings that feature kings with multiple pawns. In the following sections, I describe several different endings involving pawns and kings.

When a pawn and the enemy king race to the queening square

Sometimes the game boils down to a race for the queening square between the pawn and the enemy king. In that case, if the lone king can't prevent the pawn from attaining its promotion to a queen, that king will end up checkmated. If the king can prevent the pawn's promotion, the game ends up a draw.

You have two easy ways to determine whether the king can prevent a pawn from promoting:

- ✔ **Count the squares between the pawn and the queening square and between the king and that square.**

- ✔ **Use the pawn square method.** This method, which chess players also call the *rule of the square* or the *pawn quadrant,* works best if you have a lot of squares to count.

The counting method

This first example details the counting method. Here's the question at hand: With white's turn to move in Figure 15-4, can the black king prevent the white pawn from reaching the queening square? (Don't worry about a missing white king — the important part is to concentrate on the race of the pawn and the black king to the queening square, h8.)

If you simply count the squares, you can see that the white pawn can queen before the black king can stop its advance to the last rank. The white pawn needs four moves to queen, which means that the black king has only three moves in which to control the queening square. But, the black king needs four, so black's king is one square short of controlling the queening square, and his doom is sealed.

The pawn square method

You can also determine black's inability to stop the white pawn from queening by applying the principle of the pawn square. The idea behind the *pawn square* is to create an imaginary square shape, which you start by extending a line from the pawn to the queening square. Because all sides of a square are of equal length, you can then create a mental picture of the other sides of the square, as shown in Figure 15-5, where the Xs mark the boundaries of the pawn square.

The rule goes as follows: If the enemy king is outside the pawn square, and the pawn is on the move, then the pawn can queen. If the enemy king is on or inside the square, however, he can stop the pawn from queening. So in this case, as the previous counting squares method shows, the white pawn is in the clear, and black is a goner.

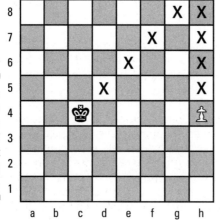

Figure 15-4: Counting the squares in the paths to the nearest queening square.

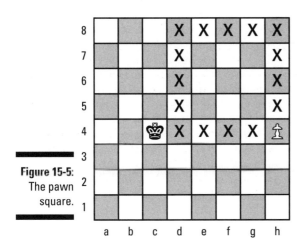

Figure 15-5:
The pawn
square.

When the kings face off: Opposition

Sometimes, simply stopping the straightforward march of the pawn (as described in the preceding section) isn't enough for the black king. In some positions, the pawn can queen with the assistance of its own king. Knowing exactly when a king and a pawn can defeat a lone king and when they can't is crucial to the understanding of endgames. That's where the opposition comes in.

If you think that "opposition" refers to your opponent, think again. This term refers to a fundamental and frequently occurring situation in king and pawn endings. If you want to study and become completely familiar with just one single concept in the endgame, make it the opposition. Many nuances to the opposition are beyond the scope of this chapter, but this tactic is described in more detail in many works on the endgame.

Opposition occurs when the two kings face one another, as shown in Figure 15-6, and one must make way for the other, because it's illegal for one king to attack the other. The king that moved last is said to "have the opposition," because the other king must give ground.

Quite often, the opposition determines whether a game is won, lost, or ends in a draw. Often, however, as in the example shown in Figure 15-7, you must know which side moves next to correctly evaluate the position. Here's the essence of the opposition: If the kings face one another and are separated by an odd number of squares, then the player who moved last has the opposition. (This situation is one of the few times in chess when you'd like to say, "I pass!") In the following sections, I show you what happens when black has the opposition and when white does.

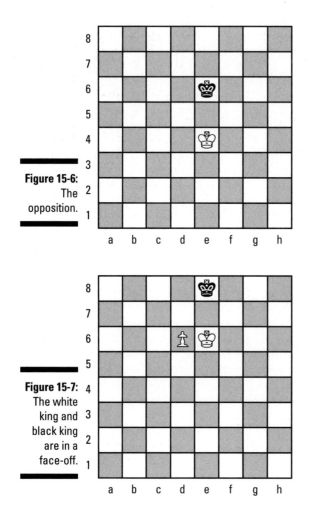

Figure 15-6:
The opposition.

Figure 15-7:
The white king and black king are in a face-off.

White's turn

Suppose that it's white's turn to move in Figure 15-7. A king move by white would be useless (the king can only retreat, not advance), so white has no better option than to advance the pawn (1. d7+), as shown in Figure 15-8a. Now black moves the king to occupy the queening square (1. ... Kd8); see Figure 15-8b.

White must now either let the black king capture her pawn or give stalemate by moving into a protective position behind the pawn (2. Kd6), as shown in Figure 15-9. Remember that stalemate is a draw (see Chapter 4 for more details).

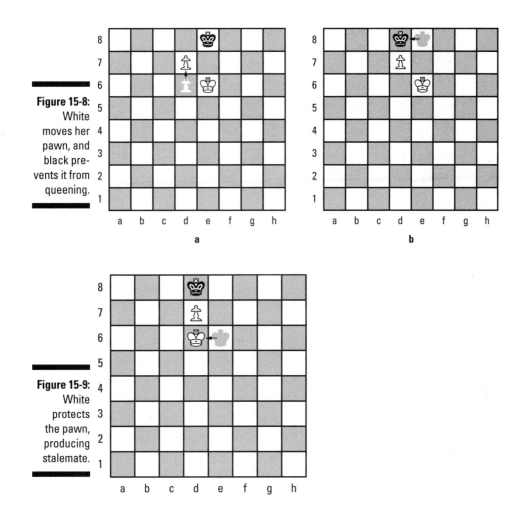

Figure 15-8:
White moves her pawn, and black prevents it from queening.

a

b

Figure 15-9:
White protects the pawn, producing stalemate.

Black's turn

If, on the other hand, black moves next in the original position shown in Figure 15-7, then white can eventually queen the pawn and win the game. Black can't advance her king toward the white king, and the best chance black has now is to cover the queening square (1. … Kd8), as shown in Figure 15-10. Otherwise, the advance of the pawn would cut off black from this key square, and white would then queen the pawn on the next turn.

White can now advance the pawn in safety (2. d7), because the king is protecting it, as shown in Figure 15-11a. Black must move away to the only square in which the king isn't in check (2. … Kc7); see Figure 15-11b.

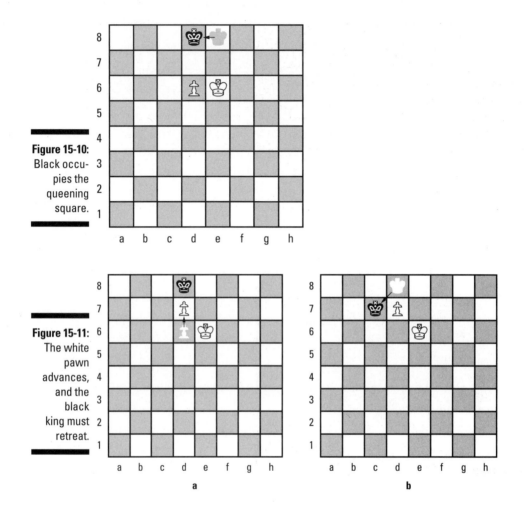

Figure 15-10: Black occupies the queening square.

Figure 15-11: The white pawn advances, and the black king must retreat.

a

b

This move enables white to advance the king (3. Ke7) and control the queening square, as Figure 15-12 shows. Black's only available moves are away from the queening square — which only prolongs black's agony. The white pawn can then advance to the last rank and get promoted to a queen; checkmate soon follows.

Endings with king and rook's pawn versus king always end in draws if the weaker side can get to the queening square. This outcome is inevitable because the stronger side can't approach the queening square with her king and can't advance her pawn without giving stalemate (the black king has no escape route off to the side in the case of the rook's pawn). The rook's pawn's inability to drive away a defending king can be magnified by adding what chess players call the *wrong bishop*. In Figure 15-13, white has an extra bishop as well as a rook's pawn, but it's the wrong-colored bishop because it can't control the pawn's queening square (a8), whereas a light-colored bishop could. Despite white's material advantage, this position is a draw.

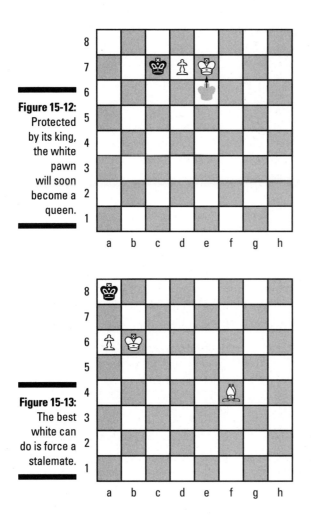

Figure 15-12:
Protected by its king, the white pawn will soon become a queen.

Figure 15-13:
The best white can do is force a stalemate.

When you can whittle down the material: Simplification

After you know that a certain ending is a sure win, you can sometimes use a process called simplification to reach it. *Simplification* maintains material equality but reduces the overall amount of it, which makes calculations less complicated. In Figure 15-14, white can capture first the black queen followed by the black rook, and reach a king and pawn ending that's known to be a winning one.

How does white go about forcing this ending by simplification? White first captures the black queen with her own queen (1. Qxd8+), as shown in Figure 15-15a. Black is then forced to capture the white queen with her rook (1... Rxd8), as shown in Figure 15-15b, because the king cannot otherwise escape check.

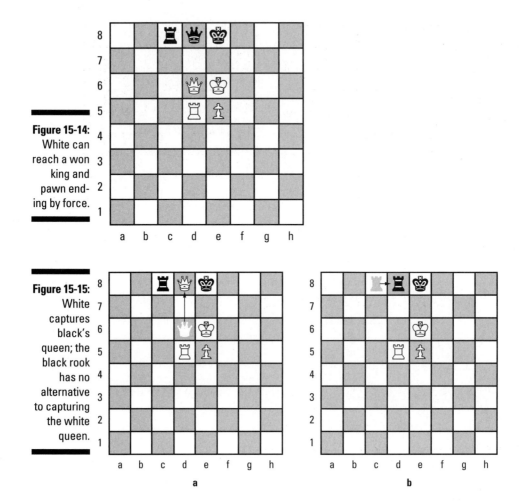

Figure 15-14: White can reach a won king and pawn ending by force.

Figure 15-15: White captures black's queen; the black rook has no alternative to capturing the white queen.

a

b

White then captures the black rook with her own rook (2. Rxd8+), as shown in Figure 15-16a. Black must then capture the white rook with her king (2. ... Kxd8), as shown in Figure 15-16b.

White can now gain control over the pawn's queening square (e8), as shown in Figure 15-17, which is known to be a winning position.

When each side has more than one pawn

Endings with a king and pawns versus a king and pawns can be deceptively complicated. You do have a few guidelines to follow, however.

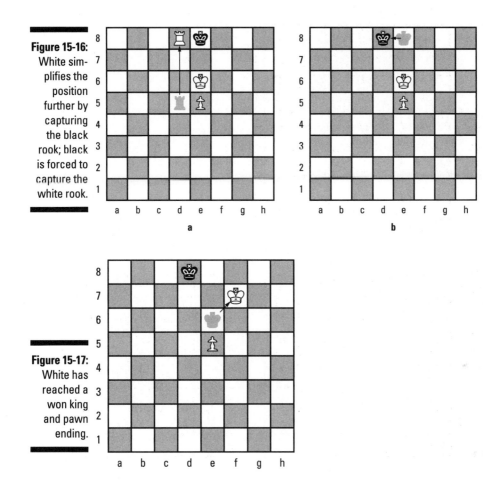

Figure 15-16: White simplifies the position further by capturing the black rook; black is forced to capture the white rook.

Figure 15-17: White has reached a won king and pawn ending.

Use one pawn to restrain two

Sometimes, trying to count the number of pawn moves necessary to determine whether a situation is a win or a draw (can a pawn queen?) can be confusing. When trying to limit the number of your opponent's strong pawns, see whether you can restrain two for the price of one. Consider, for example, the position shown in Figure 15-18.

Hitting on the correct first move for white — advancing the pawn on b2 two squares (1. b4) — is a simple matter (see Figure 15-19). White can restrain two black pawns by blocking the path of the pawn on b5 and by threatening to capture black's a-pawn should it move to a5.

Advance an unopposed pawn

If you're faced with a choice of which pawn to advance, advance the pawn that doesn't face an opponent. In Figure 15-20, white moves the unopposed pawn on g2 two squares forward to g4.

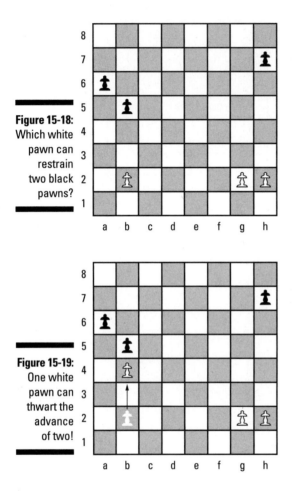

Figure 15-18:
Which white
pawn can
restrain
two black
pawns?

Figure 15-19:
One white
pawn can
thwart the
advance
of two!

In Figure 15-21, you can see the consequence of advancing a pawn on the same file as an opposing pawn. If white advances the h-pawn two squares instead of the g-pawn (1. h4), then black's response is to restrain both of those pawns by moving the h-pawn up two squares (1. ... h5)! (See the preceding section for this technique.)

Get a passed pawn

The next position is one that I show to all my students. This position vividly demonstrates that the power of a passed pawn is often worth all the knights in Columbus. (Chapter 3 provides details on passed pawns.)

A superficial glance at the position tells you that the two sides are even in material but that the white king is too far away from the action (see Figure 15-22). A deeper look, however, suggests that the important point isn't the position of the white king but the advanced position of the white pawns. How can white turn this setup into an advantage? By creating a passed pawn!

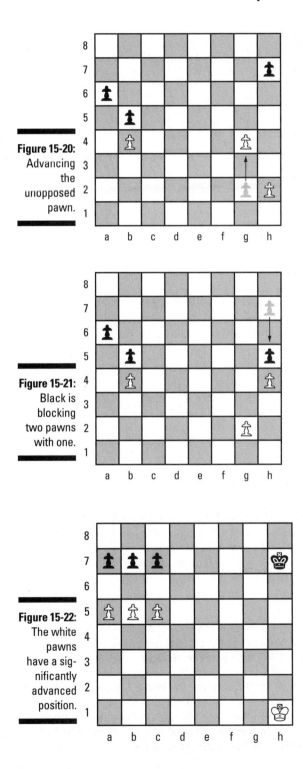

Figure 15-20: Advancing the unopposed pawn.

Figure 15-21: Black is blocking two pawns with one.

Figure 15-22: The white pawns have a significantly advanced position.

With its first move, advancing the middle pawn (1. b6), white threatens to capture one of the defending black pawns and then to queen with that pawn on the following move (see Figure 15-23a). This threat forces black to capture the forward white pawn (1. ... cxb6); see Figure 15-23b. Which pawn black uses to capture white's marauder really doesn't matter.

White advances another pawn (2. a6) with the same threat of capturing and queening on the next two moves (see Figure 15-24a). Black must again capture the attacking white pawn (2. ... bxa6), as shown in Figure 15-24b.

Following the two white pawn sacrifices, the nature of the overall position is radically altered. Upon moving forward one square to c6 (3. c6), white now has a passed pawn, which has a clear path to the queening square, as shown in Figure 15-25.

Regardless of what black does now, white can queen the pawn in two moves. After white queens the pawn, the win is straightforward.

Always be on the lookout for an opportunity to create a passed pawn that can continue marching unimpeded toward the queening square. In the preceding example, the two pawns who gave their lives so that the third could achieve promotion deserve burial with full military honors!

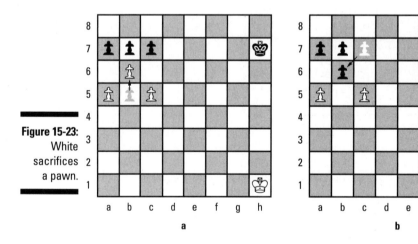

Figure 15-23: White sacrifices a pawn.

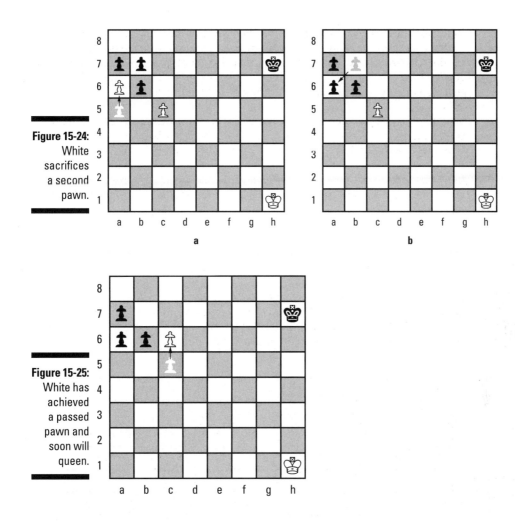

Figure 15-24: White sacrifices a second pawn.

a

b

Figure 15-25: White has achieved a passed pawn and soon will queen.

The Oh-So-Common Tricksters: Rook Endings

Rook endings are the most common endings in chess — mainly because rooks are usually the last pieces you develop and the last you and your opponent exchange. These endings, however, are awfully tricky — even masters commit elementary mistakes.

Akiba Rubinstein (1882–1961), a grandmaster from Poland, is generally considered to have been the finest rook and pawn expert of his time. His handling of these positions has instructed entire generations who followed him, and this legacy now belongs to chess heritage. Of course, few people can play like Rubinstein. One of his contemporaries, Dr. Siegbert Tarrasch, summed up my feeling about rook and pawn endings when he said, "All rook and pawn endings are drawn." That claim isn't true, of course, but it sure feels like it sometimes. My advice: Checkmate your opponent before you reach one of these endings!

Rooks are aggressive pieces and become despondent if relegated to passive defense. Keep this characteristic in mind, especially if you're defending an inferior position. Following are several guidelines for rook endings:

- ✔ **Activate your rook.** Sometimes you can even give up a pawn to turn a passive rook into an aggressive one. The sacrifice may well be worth it.

- ✔ **Put your rooks behind passed pawns.** You can best position your rook behind a passed pawn, whether it's yours or your opponent's, because the rook's mobility increases any time the pawn advances. The next best rook position is to the side of passed pawns, and the least desirable position is in front of passed pawns. (Flip to Chapter 3 for more on passed pawns.)

- ✔ **Advance connected passed pawns against rooks.** Connected passed pawns are most effective against rooks because it's difficult for the rook to stop them both. So, advance these pawns together.

- ✔ **Put your king on the queening square.** If you're defending your king with one rook against a rook and a pawn, occupy the queening square with your king, if possible. This strategy makes it harder for the pawn to promote.

- ✔ **Harass your opponent's king with your rook.** If defending, you may want to harass the enemy king with repeated checks by your rook. Harass from a safe distance, however, keeping your rook as far away from the enemy king as possible to avoid losing it.

- ✔ **Look out for the draw.** When both sides have pawns all on one side of the board, rook endings are often drawn.

Bishops and Knights: Minor Piece Endings

The endings that involve minor pieces are a little bit easier to understand than rook endings. Knights are better than bishops if the endgame commences with pawns in locked positions (immobile), but bishops become stronger than knights in open positions with pawns on both sides of the board. A knight can restrict a bishop's movement only with great difficulty, while a bishop can far more readily restrict a knight's movement — especially if the knight is positioned at the side of the board.

Consider the position shown in Figure 15-26. Here, the black bishop covers all the squares, marked by Xs, to which the white knight can potentially move. This example serves to illustrate one of the advantages of having a bishop instead of a knight in an ending. The bishop can often trade itself for the knight and potentially turn the game into a favorable king and pawn ending. The knight, however, rarely has this option.

In some cases, however, you'd rather have a knight than a bishop. Such a situation is demonstrated in Figure 15-27. In this example, because the white bishop is on a dark square and by definition can't attack anything on a light square, it can't attack any of the black pawns and must passively defend the white pawns. Only black has winning chances in this case, thanks to the knight's ability to move from a light square to a dark square and back. The black knight can theoretically occupy any of the squares, but the white bishop can't. By improving the position of the knight and king, black may be able to force white into further concessions and even win the game.

In the following sections, I describe three situations in which these advantages come into play: knight versus knight, knight versus bishop, and bishop versus bishop.

In all minor piece endings, neither bishop and king nor knight and king can deliver checkmate by themselves. This inability on the part of the knight and bishop to force checkmate in endings means that the weaker side needs to try to exchange as many pawns as possible. If the weaker side eliminates all the pawns, even by sacrificing a piece to do so, then the game is drawn.

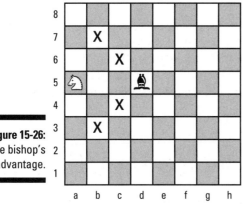

Figure 15-26:
The bishop's
advantage.

Medieval times, chess-style: Knight versus knight

When knights square off against knights, the action is defined by the piece's lack of long-range attacking ability. Hand-to-hand fighting is much more common, so keep these rules in mind:

✔ **Use your knight to blockade.** Anchor your knight to the square in front of a passed pawn. This strategy prevents the pawn from moving without diminishing the knight's attacking power. Knights are good soldiers and don't take offense at performing guard duty, as rooks and queens do.

✔ **Beware of outside passed pawns.** Outside passed pawns are especially effective against knights. Knights are good at short-range attack but weak at long range, because they can influence only one side of the board at a time.

✔ **Sacrifice the knight to get a passed pawn.** Consider sacrificing the knight to create an unstoppable passed pawn. (Need the scoop on passed pawns? Check out Chapter 3.)

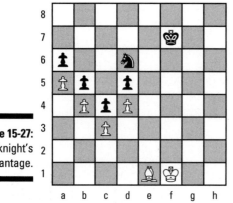

Figure 15-27: The knight's advantage.

In Figure 15-28, black has succeeded in blocking the white pawns on the kingside (they can't force their way to a queening square). Black's outside passed pawn on a6 is threatening to advance toward its queening square.

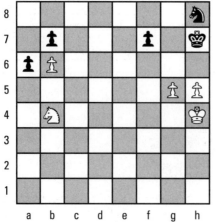

Figure 15-28: Black's pawn on a6 has the potential of queening.

White can prevent this potential queening by capturing the a6 pawn with her knight on b4 (1. Nxa6) and thereby sacrificing it, as shown in Figure 15-29.

If black captures the white knight with her pawn on b7 (1. ... bxa6), as shown in Figure 15-30a, then white has an unstoppable passed pawn on the b-file (see Figure 15-30b) and will win.

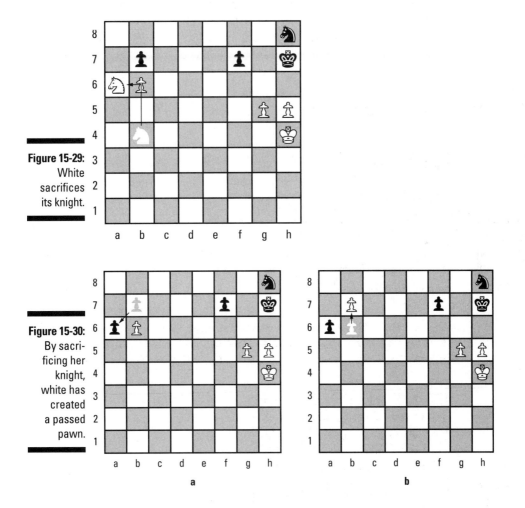

Figure 15-29: White sacrifices its knight.

Figure 15-30: By sacrificing her knight, white has created a passed pawn.

a

b

Survival of the fittest: Knight versus bishop

Here are some things to keep in mind for endings involving knights and bishops.

- ✔ **Use bishops in open positions.** Knights like closed positions (where piece movement is restricted), and bishops like open ones (where piece movement is relatively easy), because their mobility increases. The bishop's superiority to the knight lies in its ability to attack both sides of the board at once. The knight can't defend on one side and attack on the other simultaneously, but the bishop can. Endings are usually open, so bishops tend to be superior in the endgame.

- ✔ **Reduce the mobility of bishops with pawns.** By placing your pawns on the same-colored squares as the opponent's bishop, you can restrict the bishop's mobility. Ideally, you want your opponent to restrict her own bishop. Be careful not to place your pawns where the bishop can attack and win them. Follow this rule only if it restricts the bishop's mobility and the pawns are safe from capture.

- ✔ **Look for won king-and-pawn endings.** A king-and-pawn ending is easier to win than any other type of ending. If you can trade your piece for your opponent's and go into a won king-and-pawn ending, do it! (I describe these types of endings earlier in this chapter.)

- ✔ **Use bishops if the pawns are spread out.** The bishop's advantage increases when pawns are spread out on the board. The less symmetrical the position of the pawns, the better the bishop's situation.

A religious battle: Bishop versus bishop

Two completely different types of bishop-versus-bishop endings exist: when the bishops are on the same-colored squares and when they're on opposite-colored squares (commonly called "bishops of opposite color" or "opposite-colored bishops").

- ✔ **Look out for a draw with opposite-colored bishops.** Bishops of opposite color increase the chances of a draw: They can never capture one another! In addition, opposite-colored bishops can't get past each other's blockade.

- ✔ **Trade same-colored bishops if you're stronger.** In same-colored bishop endings, you can force the weaker side to give ground by offering to exchange the bishops. Put your bishop on the same diagonal as the one your opponent's bishop is on. Support your bishop with the king. If you have more pawns, your opponent won't want to trade and will be forced to cede the diagonal to you.

- ✔ **Use a long-range bishop to control a passed pawn.** The bishop can prevent the advance of a passed pawn by controlling the square in front of the pawn. Keep in mind that the bishop can control a square from a long distance.

  The farther apart passed pawns are, the better the stronger side's chances are of winning. If the pawns are close together, the enemy king can help establish a blockade. If they're farther apart, a blockade isn't possible. The king can be used on one side or the other, but not both.

Part IV
Getting into Advanced Action

The 5th Wave

By Rich Tennant

©RICHTENNANT

"Well, Mr. Humphrey, it appears that playing chess online for hours on end certainly <u>DOES</u> have some side effects."

In this part . . .

*I*f you want to play chess, you have to have someone (or something) to play with you. In this part, I give you the scoop on the various types of competition, from clubs and tournaments to computers and the World Wide Web.

Chapter 16

Playing in Competition

. . . .

In This Chapter

▶ Going to a club to prime your competitive skills

▶ Getting the skinny on tournaments

▶ Heading abroad with your game

▶ Being nice when you play face to face

▶ Refusing to forsake the PJs: Correspondence chess

. . . .

*I*f you're like me, you'll be nervous the first time you enter a tournament. Don't let that stop you! World champions had to play in their first tournament, too, and most chess aficionados remember what it feels like to not know the ropes. Just address your questions to the first quasi-official person you lay eyes on, and chances are you may make a new friend in the process. To give you firm ground to start on, I've included this chapter to bring you into the loop.

Here, I discuss chess clubs for those of you who want to boost your game while getting your social kicks. Then, for whenever you feel ready to exercise your competitive edge, I tell you where to find a tournament, how to act when you arrive at one, what to expect, and, of course, the good etiquette rules to remember while you're there. And if you want some competition but don't want to travel, I have a great option for you: correspondence chess.

Practice Makes Perfect: Joining a Club First

I usually advise my students to get involved in a club prior to playing in a tournament. A club is usually a friendlier environment and the best place to get your feet wet. You'll probably meet some tournament veterans who may be willing to take you under their wings. That's how most chess greats got started in tournament play.

Different clubs meet at different times, and some are larger than others. A club's membership may range from beginner to master, and the competitions may be informal or deadly serious. You have to visit one to find out what it's like. Each club usually has a director who can answer any questions you may have and help you find someone near your skill level.

To find a club near you, go to the online club directory page for the United States Chess Federation (USCF) at www.uschess.org. Click on "USCF" on the left side of the screen, then click on "Clubs and Tourneys" in the left-hand column, and then click on "Chess Clubs." There, you can find the name and contact information for any organization affiliated with the USCF.

Breaking Down U.S. Tournament Basics

After you've been in a chess club for a while, you may feel ready to jump into tournament play — but you need to know some basics first. In the following sections, I explain how to find tournaments, watch your time as you play, and establish a rating. I also describe the three main types of tournaments played in the United States.

In order to play a tournament game, you should know all the rules of competition (check out the fifth edition of the USCF rule book; see Appendix B) and be familiar with chess etiquette (which I discuss later in this chapter).

Finding tournaments

Normally, tournaments are run by a tournament director and require membership in the USCF and an entry fee. You can find all the information you need about the organization, as well as forms for becoming a member, on the USCF website at www.uschess.org.

U.S. tournaments are advertised in *Chess Life,* the monthly publication of the USCF, which is included with your membership dues and is available on the USCF website. *Chess Life* has a section that includes upcoming events and the names and phone numbers of the tournament directors. This listing will look like Greek to you the first time you see one, because it has all sorts of codes and shorthand. If you're a novice, call the director, tell him that you're an unrated player, and ask any questions you may have. Everyone was a beginner at some point, and tournament directors will take the time to show you the ropes.

Watching your time

You don't need a chess clock in order to play an informal game of chess, but you do need one in order to play a tournament game. (You bring your own clock, chessboard, and chess set to a tournament; see Appendix B to find some good sources for this equipment.) An analog chess clock has two faces (a digital one has two readouts) — one for each player. You depress a mechanism on your side of the clock to start your opponent's clock. Black starts white's clock at the beginning of the game, and after white moves, white stops his own while simultaneously starting black's.

Depending upon the tournament, the length of time allocated (called the *time control*) for the game varies. Each player may have 90 minutes to make 30 moves, for example, or he may have two hours to make 50. If any player exceeds the time limit while failing to make the minimum number of moves, he forfeits the game. Such a forfeit (called a *loss on time*) is treated just like any other loss for rating purposes and tournament standing. In other words, losing on time yields the same result as being checkmated.

Earning ratings

Tournament chess in the United States is certified and rated (meaning that everyone gets a numerical evaluation of his performance) by the USCF. *Ratings* in chess are a measure of expected performance versus known opposition, and they fluctuate based on your results: wins, losses, and draws. Beginners get their initial ratings by playing in tournaments against people with established ratings.

The ratings given by the international governing body in chess, called the *Fédération Internationale des Échecs* (FIDE, pronounced *fee*-day), are sometimes referred to as *Elo ratings* after one of the rating system's prime developers, Arpad Elo. The USCF uses a similar rating system, which is generally 50 to 70 points higher than the FIDE one. The FIDE system, however, doesn't rate players below a certain skill level, and treats them as unrated. The USCF system divides the rating population into classes, as shown in Table 16-1.

Table 16-1	The USCF Rating System
Points	*Class*
2400 and up	Senior Master
2200–2399	Master
2000–2199	Expert

(continued)

Table 16-1 *(continued)*

Points	Class
1800–1999	Class A
1600–1799	Class B
1400–1599	Class C
1200–1399	Class D
1199 and below	Class E

Note: Conventional wisdom used to hold that the average tournament player has a rating in the Class C range, but this is almost certainly not true. Achieving a rating in the C class is quite an accomplishment, because tournament players tend to be quite serious about their chess. Casual players may be very strong, of course, but usually active tournament players tend to be the strongest in the country.

The USCF class system has led to the development of class prizes. A typical Swiss system tournament (see the next section) offers cash prizes in each of the rating divisions, which allows the organizer to demand high entry fees. This setup can lead to a sort of ruthless competition, which is another reason to start out in clubs (which I describe earlier in this chapter) or smaller events, where the competition is still fierce — but friendlier.

Familiarizing yourself with the types of tournaments

Generally speaking, tournament competition comes in three varieties: the Swiss system, round robin, and match. The Swiss system, or Swiss for short, is the most popular in the United States. Matches and round robin competitions are usually more expensive to organize.

The Swiss system

Most weekend tournaments in the United States are run according to the rules of the Swiss system. The *Swiss system* orders all players by their rating (and ranks unrated players alphabetically) and splits the list in half. The top player of the top half is paired against the top player of the bottom half, and so on, until the bottom player of the top half is paired against the bottom player of the bottom half. In case of an uneven number of players, the bottom-most player is usually given a full-point bye (which means he is paired in the next round as if he had won — after all, it wasn't his fault that an opponent wasn't available).

Watching out for sandbaggers

When high-fee, high-class prize tournaments became popular, some chess players began trying to manipulate their own ratings. These players would intentionally lose rating points in low-cost events in order to play in a class below their true strength in the big-money tournaments — with the hope of defeating weaker competition and collecting relatively large cash prizes. This unethical practice is referred to as *sandbagging*. Calling a player a sandbagger is one of the worst chess-related insults!

Winners get one point, draws score one-half point, and losers get zero points. In the next round, winners play winners, losers play losers, and so forth, following the same procedure of dividing the lists in half and pairing the people in the two halves accordingly, within the various score-groups.

Gradually, you begin to play players of your approximate strength because — in theory, anyway — you should be scoring roughly the same amount of points against the same kind of competition. The strongest players, or the players having the best tournament, are increasingly likely to play one another as the tournament goes on. The winner is the player who scores the greatest number of points.

Usually, the first rounds of a tournament run under the Swiss system involve mismatches. Strong players play weaker players, especially early on in the tournament. Some players use a dubious strategy, called the *Swiss Gambit*, designed to avoid the toughest competition. This strategy involves allowing a draw with a weaker player, which gets the gambiteer easier pairings (the winners play other winners, but the gambiteer plays someone else who only drew) in the next few rounds. The hope is that in the later rounds, the strongest players will be playing each other — and the gambiteer will sneak into the prize money by playing inferior competition. This strategy, like any other designed to manipulate results, is just as likely to backfire as succeed. Who knows whether you'll really get weaker pairings? In all cases, you should play your best.

Round-robin tournaments

A *round-robin* tournament is one where everyone plays everyone else. These tournaments are regarded as a more accurate judge of a player's performance than Swiss system tournaments because they don't involve "lucky" pairings. Round-robin tournaments are used to determine most national championships and are the norm in international tournaments. A drawback to this type of tournament is that it normally takes a longer period of time to complete and is therefore more expensive to produce.

An offshoot of the round robin is the *Quad,* where the tournament is divided into groups of four players of roughly equal strength, who then play one another. This type of system is popular in the United States because it's inexpensive and avoids mismatches.

Match competition

Match competition isn't technically tournament competition because it involves only two players, but it's another popular form of competition and can be rated. In a match, one player plays another for a predetermined number of games. This head-to-head competition is the purest method for determining the stronger player and is usually adopted in order to determine the world champion — or the world champion's challenger.

Exploring Tournament Chess around the World

The main difference between U.S. and international tournaments is that they play by two different sets of rules. The basic rules of how to play are the same, of course, but the rules governing competition have some differences.

- ✔ In general, FIDE's rules rely more on the discretion of the officials, called *arbiters,* to resolve any disputes or enforce claims.

- ✔ USCF rules are more involved and dictate specific actions in specific situations to a much greater degree. That's why its rule book is so big and undergoes periodic revision.

Some international tournaments are by invitation only, but many Swiss events (see the preceding section) are open to anyone. You play by FIDE's rules and for a FIDE rating, but otherwise the experience is similar to a U.S. tournament.

FIDE comprises the member nations of the world who pay dues and elect FIDE officials (the USCF is the official representative of the United States). The organization also supervises the world championship and Chess Olympiads, where countries send teams to compete. As such, FIDE is responsible for awarding titles to an unlimited number of individual players, such as the following:

- ✔ **Grandmaster (GM):** The grandmaster title is the highest title awarded by FIDE and is earned by turning in excellent performances (called *norms*) in competition with players who already own the title.

- ✔ **International master (IM):** The international master title is secondary to the grandmaster and is also achieved by making norms in events that include a sufficient number of grandmasters or international masters.

The schism in world championship chess

In 1993, the FIDE world championship match was supposed to be between Russia's Garry Kasparov, the then-current champion, and England's Nigel Short, Kasparov's rightful challenger. However, Kasparov wasn't happy with the prize fund, so he ditched FIDE and helped found the Professional Chess Association (PCA).

The Kasparov-Short match was held under the sponsorship of the PCA, and FIDE was left with a sham match between two players whom Short had already defeated. Kasparov won the match convincingly and defended his title against Viswanathan Anand of India in 1995. The primary sponsor of the PCA was Intel — but after the 1995 match, Intel withdrew its support, and the PCA was history.

Negotiations for a reunification match between players with a claim to being champion continued to flounder. A non-FIDE-sanctioned match between Kasparov and Vladimir Kramnik of Russia (see Chapter 19 for more on these two) in 2000 ended in Kasparov's defeat. Although most people still considered Kasparov the world's best player, he was thwarted in his attempts for a rematch.

These goings-on call into question a fundamental historical division in chess: Does the title of world champion belong to the titleholder, or to the organization that grants it?

For a few years the chess world lived with the bizarre notion of two world champions. Most serious players considered Kramnik the actual champion during this time, but FIDE organized what it termed "official" championships won by different players. Finally, a reunification match was held in 2006 in which Kramnik defeated Bulgaria's Veselin Topalov to seemingly settle this issue.

FIDE further muddied the waters by introducing a world championship tournament, which supposedly replaced the more traditional match format. In 2007, Viswanathan Anand won the tournament to become the "official" champion. Thankfully, in 2008, Kramnik and Anand played a match won by Anand. Anand defended the title in 2010 against Topalov, and is considered the undisputed champion as of this writing. Order has finally been restored.

✔ **FIDE master (FM):** The FIDE master title is the third and last awarded by FIDE. The recipients are players who maintain a rating of 2300 or above, which is master class, in FIDE-sanctioned events.

Miss (or Mister) Manners: Tournament Etiquette

Chess is supposed to be fun, but quite often people take it very seriously. When you play Mr. or Ms. No Fun, you should know the do's and don'ts of chess etiquette.

Don't smoke 'em if you got 'em

A famous story in chess circles tells about one grandmaster complaining about another who kept an unlit cigar next to the chessboard. "It's a no-smoking tournament," the former complained to the tournament director. The director, quite rightly, pointed out that the cigar was unlit. The grandmaster persisted, however, claiming that his opponent was threatening to smoke! This absurdity has at least some basis in the chess world, because it has a saying that the threat is stronger than the execution!

Chess etiquette is especially important in tournament chess. In a serious encounter, both players are staring at the board for hours at a time. Your hypersensitive opponent will surely notice a raised eyebrow, and a sneeze may cause someone to go into shock. Heaven forbid that you'd have a nervous tic or a habit of drumming your fingers or humming (mostly) to yourself. Chess players have complained about all these things and more.

You may properly address your opponent during the game only to offer a draw. If you have a complaint, the safest course of action is to bring it up to the tournament director. If the game is only for fun, use common sense — but above all, avoid distracting an opponent who's thinking about a move.

Chess at these levels is an incredibly tense activity, and players get no physical release. Even otherwise placid individuals have been known to lose their cool over a real or imagined infraction. The best thing to do is just play for the fun of it, but even then it's important to know the basics that I describe in the following sections.

Calling your loss

Chess coaches regularly instruct beginners to never give up and always play out the game to checkmate. "No one ever wins by resigning," they say. Although this point may be true, sometimes a loss is inevitable, and wasting your opponent's time when you both know you're doomed is just plain rude. I explain when and how to resign in the following sections.

When to resign

If you're hopelessly behind in material or face imminent checkmate, you may as well start another game. Over the course of your lifetime, you may spend hours hoping to save one or two completely lost positions when instead you could be spending that time starting over from scratch. Moreover, you rarely — if ever — learn anything from these types of hopelessly lost positions. You're much better off spending your time figuring out where you went wrong and then trying not to get into that mess again.

Did Kasparov cheat?

During one tournament game against Judit Polgar, Garry Kasparov made his move and seemed to take his hand away from the piece for a split second. He then moved the piece to another square. The shocked Polgar didn't make a claim but later indicated that she thought the champion had indeed taken his hand off of the piece. Kasparov denied doing so.

However, the game was videotaped, and a careful review of the tape showed that Kasparov did in fact let go of the piece. Unfortunately, chess doesn't have instant replays, and no protest was possible after the game was over. If even world champions break the rules, what hope do the rest of us have?

Your opponents may possibly enjoy seeing you squirm, and not mind continuing on. More likely, however, they'll be annoyed that you don't know when to resign and may refuse to play with you anymore. In fact, I quit going to one club in particular because the players there kept playing on in hopeless positions. I found myself driving home well after midnight week after week. If the members had known when to resign, I might have continued to play there.

The bottom line, however, is that *resignation is a personal decision.* You should never resign just because your opponent wants you to, but you should resign when you objectively decide that you have no way to save the game. After the conclusion is inevitable, you may as well shake your opponent's hand and go your merry way.

How to resign

Just as important as knowing when to resign is knowing *how* to resign. The formal method is not to throw your hands in the air and start crying, but to tip your king over on its side. This action is a universally recognized surrender. Then it's important that you extend your hand to congratulate your opponent — this show of sportsmanship is a valued ritual in chess. It demonstrates that you have at least a touch of class.

Many players shake hands after the game but then undo the goodwill gesture by complaining that they should have, by all rights, won the game themselves. "If I'd just done this, instead of that, it would have been curtains for you," they sometimes say. This talk is just childishness. Far more effective is to ask, "What would you have done if I'd played this instead of that?" This approach accomplishes a couple of things:

> ✔ It acknowledges that your opponent's opinion, by virtue of the victory, may have some validity.

✔ It allows you to listen to your opponent's ideas. You're much better off picking your opponent's brain in this manner than trying to explain away why you lost the game.

Sometimes both you and your opponent will spend considerable time discussing the game. Chess players call these *post mortem* sessions. Try to be respectful during these sessions and concentrate on learning — not proving a point. You'll make many chess friends if you follow this advice.

Offering a draw

If you've determined that you can't checkmate your opponent, and if you don't think your opponent can checkmate you, you may want to verbally offer a *draw* (or a tie). Offering a draw under any other circumstances may be considered annoying, and your opponent may report you to the tournament director. What's worse is that the draw offer may be accepted or rejected, and you may still get scolded. In other words, if you make an improper draw offer, your opponent has the right to accept it *and* complain about it.

Under tournament conditions, you may make a draw offer only *after* you've made a move and *before* you've started your opponent's clock. Never offer a draw to your opponent on his time. That behavior is a breach of etiquette, and repeated offenses may cause you to lose the game by forfeit.

If you make a draw offer without making a move, your opponent has the right to ask to see your move and then decide whether to accept or reject your offer. Repeated draw offers may be considered annoying, so wait until the position has changed substantially before making another offer.

If the exact position on the board (with all the same conditions — for example, castling privileges and en passant opportunities) is about to be repeated for the third time with the same player to move, you can claim a draw without asking. Of course, to do this, you must have a complete written score of the game to prove your claim. However, you must do so *before* making the move that would repeat the position for the third time, because the claim must be made on your own time and a tournament director must witness the move.

Being careful what you touch

One of the touchiest subjects in chess is the *touch-move rule*. This rule simply means that if you touch a piece, you must move it — if doing so is legal. If you touch a piece that has no legal move, you're free to move any other piece. The move is considered complete when you take your hand off the piece.

Sometimes one player claims that the other touched a piece, and the second player denies doing so. If witnesses are nearby, the director may be able to make an informed decision. In the absence of witnesses, the claim generally isn't upheld on the first complaint. If you accidentally bump a piece or knock one over, you should say, "I adjust" and replace the dislodged piece.

Furthering the touch-move rule, a frequent cause of complaints is the hand hover. The *hand hover* occurs when a player positions his hand over a piece and leaves it there. The hand hover is a distraction, and you shouldn't do it — so goes the warning by José Capablanca (see Chapter 19 for more on that guy). You should never obscure your opponent's sight of the board unless you're in the act of moving, so don't reach for a piece until you've decided to move it.

Straightening your pieces

Sometimes a pawn or a piece may not be resting completely on one square or another. You're allowed to adjust that pawn or piece — or even a whole bunch of them — but only if you do it on your time and if you warn your opponent first. The French phrase *j'adoube* (juh-*doob*; "I adjust") is considered to be the proper warning, but it's also okay to use the English translation.

As long as you've issued the *j'adoube* warning, the touch-move rule is temporarily waived. Keep in mind, however, that you can't say "*j'adoube*" or "I adjust" *after* you've touched a piece!

Saving snacks for later

Generally, it's considered improper to eat or drink anything at the chessboard except for water or coffee. Of course, if you're playing in your own living room, all bets are off. The home team determines the ground rules in that case.

My worst experience with food at the chessboard came in my very first big tournament in New York. It was the last-round game, and whoever won would clinch a sizable prize. My opponent came to the board with a sloppy meatball sandwich and proceeded to get the sauce all over his hands. He then decided to adjust all my pieces, covering them with the sauce.

I was too inexperienced to complain and too young to shrug it off. Instead, I let my opponent's rudeness affect my play, which is what my opponent had hoped would happen, and managed to lose rather badly. Needless to say, this scenario was a severe breach of chess etiquette, and I should have complained to an official at once.

The worst losers in chess history

Mike Fox and Richard James, in their delightful book *The Even More Complete Chess Addict* (published by Faber and Faber), nominate the following three candidates for the title of "worst loser in chess history." In their own words:

✔ **Taking the bronze:** Former world champion Alexander Alekhine, a notoriously temperamental loser. At Vienna in 1922, Alekhine spectacularly resigned against Ernst Grünfeld by hurling his king across the room.

✔ **In the silver medal position:** Another famous loser, Aaron Nimzowitsch. At a lightning chess tournament in Berlin, he said out loud what everyone has at one time

felt. Instead of quietly turning over his king, Nimzo leapt onto his chair and bellowed across the tournament hall: "Why must I lose to this idiot?" Not nice, but everyone knows the feeling.

✔ **The gold medal, plus the John McEnroe Award for bad behavior at a tournament:** A lesser-known Danish player (reported in the *Chess Scene* and who was unnamed), who lost as a result of a finger slip involving his queen (refer to the earlier section "Being careful what you touch"). Unable to contain his despair, he snuck back into the tournament hall in the dead of night and cut the heads off all the queens.

Going the Distance: Correspondence Chess

Correspondence chess was originally played by sending postcards of chess moves through the mail (some people still call it "postal chess"). With the rise of the Internet, however, tournaments and competitions have also taken on a new form via e-mail and web servers (see more on cyberchess in Chapter 17). Clearly, you have to know chess notation in order to participate (and I explain it in Chapter 6), but after you get the hang of it, you'll find that correspondence chess is an excellent way to find opponents from outside your geographical area without leaving the comfort of your home.

To find opponents, you usually need to belong to an official correspondence chess organization; just enter "correspondence chess" into your favorite search engine.

Chapter 17

Hitting the Net with Computer Chess

. . . .

. . . .

*G*etting good at chess requires practice. Playing lots of what chess players call *off-hand* (just for fun) games gives you a chance to try out the skills you pick up in this book without putting a lot at stake.

When I got serious about chess, I was very lucky to live in a metropolitan area that was home to an active chess club where I could meet other players. But even so, I couldn't always find a playing partner at the times that were best for me. I was lucky to play once a week. Since then, computers, chess software, and the evolution of the Internet have revolutionized the way players study and play chess. You can now play, on your own PC, a program that can defeat even grandmasters. Even better, you can play chess at all hours of the day and night against opponents from around the world, and follow the top tournaments in real time from the comfort of your home.

In this chapter, I give you a bit of the interesting history of computer chess, and tell you how it differs from human-to-human chess (aside from the obvious fact that a computer doesn't breathe). I also give you a primer on general chess sites, electronic chess instruction, chess databases, chess computer programs, and online play.

Although I point you to the sites that have a solid history, the Internet is always changing and evolving. An online search can quickly put you on track to find whatever you want — just enter what you're looking for in your Internet browser.

Building a Better Player: A Brief History of Computer Chess

One of the very first challenges that computer programmers took on was the creation of chess programs, because they saw chess play as one of the ultimate challenges in computer applications. First, programmers had to decide on the best approach to simulate chess play. Then, as new technologies exploded on the scene, chess programs evolved accordingly. A couple of landmarks are particularly notable.

Developing a suitable approach

During the early days of computer development, chess was considered the ideal application for artificial intelligence (AI). The reasoning was that if someone could create an AI application to play chess like a human does, scientists' understanding of how the human mind works would dramatically increase. At that point, other simulations would be possible, or so the thinking went. However, computers really don't think the way humans do, and the emphasis in computer chess eventually shifted from playing a chess game as a human would to simply playing as well as possible.

The early AI approach was to use what were called *heuristics,* whereby computers would play by using certain rules of thumb — what chess players like to call general principles — to try to map out the game the way a human would. The downside of this method was that it turned out to be very difficult to write programs to make computers "think" like humans.

A different method programmed the computer simply to analyze as many moves and variations as possible, as far ahead as possible. This approach was the number-crunching method — what programmers call *brute force.* The disadvantage of this technique was that the computer wasted time looking at silly moves a human wouldn't even consider.

Early on, both approaches seemed equally valid because both led to equally bad play. Soon, however, with the development of integrated circuits (ICs), or *chips,* the speed of modern computers increased many times over, and brute force triumphed. Nowadays, little effort is made to have a computer play like a human would play. Instead, programmers simply try to calculate as many positions (or *ply* in computer-speak) as possible, with some heuristics to give a bit of guidance to the search. At the time of this writing, even commercially available chess programs on a home PC can analyze millions of moves per second! (I can handle perhaps two or three moves in that time — not exactly brute force, but I do have some highly developed heuristics!)

Looking at landmarks in development

One computer landmark for chess players took place back in 1977, before PCs were everywhere. People could buy a chess set with a built-in computer that was ready, without complaint, to play any time! Dubbed Chess Challenger I, this stand-alone chess computer was developed by business-man Sidney Samole, who was inspired by a game of 3D chess (don't try this at home!) between Captain Kirk and the Enterprise's on-board computer in the original *Star Trek* series. Samole loved playing chess but didn't have the time for a game when other people were available. Chess Challenger I was a big hit, even though it didn't really play very well.

Before long, competitors emerged and began developing chess computers that played much better. These computers looked very much like chess sets with extra-thick boards, and you could buy them in department stores. You could even adjust their playing strength, because playing someone — or, in this case, some chip — that's a lot weaker or a lot stronger than you doesn't provide as much training as playing someone whose ability is closer to your own.

Another computer chess milestone took place in the 1990s. Garry Kasparov, who, in my opinion, is the greatest chess player in history (see Chapter 19 for details), played two matches against IBM's Deep Blue, which, running on a mainframe supercomputer, was the best chess-playing program at the time. When Deep Blue won the second match, a great deal of hand-wringing ensued. This loss wasn't one for humanity, as many believed, but rather was a triumph of research and engineering.

Then came the widespread availability of PCs and the rapid development of the Internet, and buying a special machine to play chess against became a thing of the past. Inexpensive chess programs that can routinely defeat all but the very best players were developed to run on the average household PC, and websites that allow you to play chess online entered the scene. Today, you can play chess any time, day or night, on a moment's notice, with-out leaving your chair.

A (Down) Load of Information: General Chess Websites

Many great websites are available to give you general information on chess. For example, most member-nations of the World Chess Federation (also known as FIDE, its French acronym) offer websites. Because you're reading this book in English, here are three sites you may be interested in (for other national websites, go to www.fide.com):

- ✔ **U.S. Chess Federation (USCF):** www.uschess.org
- ✔ **Chess Federation of Canada:** www.chess.ca
- ✔ **English Chess Federation:** www.englishchess.org.uk

Some of the most important chess information you can get from your computer is about other humans. All three of the preceding sites give you the contact information for every official club in each nation. The USCF alone has hundreds of community and school clubs across America. These are the perfect places for you to go to get involved with chess in your area. Playing games and going over them afterward with other club members is a great learning experience. And the best part of chess is still social. Despite the wonderful resources online, playing other people face-to-face remains the most fun! (Check out Chapter 16 for more details about in-person chess competition.)

In addition to connecting you to other chess players, many sites give you a lot of information about chess. The following are three of my favorites. Like most developed chess websites, they offer you lots of good books and equipment to buy. But they give lots of information away for free — including essays on how to improve your game and reports on the latest chess events around the world.

- ✔ **The Week in Chess:** Go to the home page of the London Chess Centre at www.chess.co.uk and click on "TWIC" (The Week in Chess) for an amazing array of free information, such as the results and games from the most recent international tournaments.

- ✔ **Chess Life Online:** Head to the U.S. Chess Federation's website at www.uschess.org, click on "USCF" on the left, and then click on "Chess Life Online" in the vertical menu on the left side of the page. This online magazine, edited by former U.S. women's champ Jennifer Shahade, must be singled out. It covers the latest U.S. chess events in an entertaining fashion.

- ✔ **ChessCafe:** At www.chesscafe.com, top chess columnists from all over the world cover a potpourri of chess topics. The site's list of links to other chess websites (just click on "Links" in the horizontal menu at the top of the page) is an amazing resource in itself (and lets me save lots of space here!).

Schooling Yourself: Electronic Chess Instruction

Over the past several decades, tremendous progress has been made in the use of computers as chess-teaching tools. Some programs are specifically designed to teach chess to kids, such as Chesster. You can find it at www. chessbase.com. (Click on "Shop" and enter "Chesster" in the search bar that appears at the top of the resulting page.)

New DVDs seem to appear daily as well. Sites such as www.chesscafe. com, www.chessusa.com, and those of other major chess retailers are well stocked with new arrivals.

Plenty of online sites offer free instruction: Chessopolis offers extensive links to chess tutorials and lessons at www.chessopolis.com/tutorials.htm. Another information-rich site is chess.about.com.

All in One Spot: Chess Databases

A chess database is just like any other sortable database of information, but it contains chess games. If you want to see all the games that Garry Kasparov played in 1990, for example, you can sort the database to list only those games. You can even search databases containing millions of games for the exact position that occurred in one of your own games to see what others did! (You can actually do this type of search for free at the immense German online database at www.chesslive.de.)

Serious chess players care about chess data; they want as many games as possible in a format that makes the games easy to both sort and play through. Some chess data and programs that handle it for you are for sale. ChessBase has developed into the industry standard. (Go to www.chess base.com, click on "Shop," and then click on "ChessBase" in the vertical menu on the left.) Chess Assistant also has a loyal following; you can purchase it at any of the online chess retailers (see Appendix B).

Some chess databases are available free online. A nice, free web-based database is www.chessgames.com. You may also want to check out Scid, sophisticated freeware that works with Windows, Linux, Mac, and even Pocket PC. Go to www.scid.sourceforge.net. You can even install an engine, like the powerful but free Crafty (see the next section) into Scid so that it analyzes the games of your choice with you.

As you hunt for free chess games on the Internet, you'll run across a database format called *PGN,* which stands for *portable game notation.* The beauty of a PGN file is that games are stored in plain text in the standard notation I use in this book (and thus can be opened in Microsoft Word or Notepad), but they're also stored in a way that can be processed by chess computer programs. So, when you find a PGN file online that contains games you want, you don't need a special program to print it to play over the games on your own board. You can also install the game in your chess database, if you have one on your computer. Or, you can simply install a PGN reader to play through the games onscreen without the fuss of setting up a real board and set. One free PGN reader is Winboard, which can be downloaded at `www.gnu.org/software/xboard`. (But make sure to look over games on a real board and set from time to time — after all, your most important games will be in 3D!)

A PGN file can contain a single game or thousands of games in a database. Specialized PGN databases can give you a wonderful amount of valuable information. You can get databases of many games with your favorite openings. For example, if, after reading Chapters 9 and 13, you think you may want to specialize in the French Defense against 1. e4, you can download a database of games that start with the French Defenses.

Here's the great part: Lots of free PGN files are available online. Two websites that offers free PGN databases from well-organized, clear menus are `www.pgnmentor.com` and `www.chessopolis.com/chessfiles/`. But you can also just try searching online for whatever interests you, for example, "Caro Kann PGN."

Another terrific way to improve your game with the help of a chess database is to play over the games of a grandmaster — or even a world champion — whose games appeal to you. Maybe you like the openings the GM plays, the way she manages to whip up an attack, or her defense against the attacks of others. Chess is like other sports in this regard — if you study a hero you especially admire, you'll pick up a lot of tips for your own game. You can build or download databases (some in free PGNs) that pull together many games of top players.

The Little Engines that Could: Chess-Playing Computer Programs

Many commercial chess-playing computer programs (chess players call them *engines*) are available. Most of them can beat just about anyone. You can find the following popular programs for sale online at major online chess retailers: Rybka, Fritz, Hiarcs, and Shredder. In addition, `www.chessbase.com` offers some of the most sophisticated chess software on the planet. Although expensive, this advanced software is a must for professionals. The chess world is mostly Windows based, but Mac users can have their fun, too. (The powerful Shredder program offers a Mac version.)

Don't be discouraged. These programs beat nearly everyone most of the time. Nevertheless, having a program that's stronger than you are has its advantages. These programs share their evaluations with you so you can see where they think you made a mistake. They also suggest improvements in your play, which can be a very useful tool. By studying where you went wrong and considering a program's suggestions, you may learn some valuable lessons that can elevate your future play.

What a Site: Playing Chess Online

You can find two types of sites for playing chess online: free and pay-to-play. The pay-to-play sites are for serious chess players, so unless you count yourself among them, stick to the free sites. Whether you're paying to play or playing for free, you need to register and create an online ID. (Some pay-to-play sites allow you to play as a guest in order to get you to try their software, but you won't have full functionality until you register.)

- ✔ **Free sites:** Pogo (www.pogo.com; just enter "Chess" in the search bar at the top of the home page where it says "Find A Game") and the Free Internet Chess Server (www.freechess.org) are the most common.

- ✔ **Pay-to-play sites:** The Internet Chess Club (www.chessclub.com) and Playchess (www.playchess.com) are the most popular ones, although others are available. On these sites, you can choose from a wide range of human and computer opponents. Opponents are always available, because the sites' audiences are worldwide. You can even configure these sites to save your played games automatically on your hard drive so that you can analyze them later — a crucial move if you want to improve.

A variety of time controls — determining how fast you must play — are offered on these sites. Many players play blitz chess, with each game taking only a few minutes, but all sorts of time controls have their adherents.

If you aren't ready to play online, you can still watch and learn. Most of these sites allow you to click on a game in progress, so you can then follow the action in real time. The highest-level tournaments are broadcast over the Internet nowadays, and millions of eyeballs are tuned in. However, you normally have to be a registered user at one of the pay-to-play sites in order to join in the fun.

You may want to consider a trial membership on the pay-to-play sites, which is usually available, just to see whether a particular site is for you. Commentary by strong players accompanies many live broadcasts, and some means are usually provided for players of all abilities to ask questions or make their own observations.

Live lessons are also regularly scheduled, and old ones are archived. So you have other reasons to join rather than simply to play. But the play is the best part. Finding regular sparring partners who are roughly your equal in strength is one of the real joys of chess on the Internet. You can make enduring friendships with people whom you would otherwise never meet. Go ahead — log on!

Part V
The Part of Tens

ALTHOUGH A STRONG PLAYER, URI KAPROV WAS ALWAY SUSPECTED OF USING PERFORMANCE-ENHANCING DRUGS

In this part . . .

Every *For Dummies* book has a part that features lists of ten good-to-know facts, tips, or whatever, so of course I was eager to jump on the bandwagon. In this part, I give you the rundown on the most famous chess games ever played. I provide the complete notation so you can follow along with your own board and chess set and recap the games in your own living room. I also present the best players of all time, which is always a good way to begin an argument. Most chess players have their favorites, and I'm no different.

Chapter 18

The Ten Most Famous Chess Games of All Time

Some games are a part of chess players' common chess heritage, including the ten I detail for you in this chapter. Every game here will be familiar to some extent to just about every tournament player (in fact, some of these games are so well-known that they even have names!), and being able to speak intelligently about them is important. This knowledge establishes your reputation as a good talker — if not a good player!

Most of these games are from a long time ago; older games appear so often in lists such as this for several reasons:

✔ Older games have been included in many more references than the newer ones, and more people are likely to have studied them.

✔ Everyone today can understand these games — but some of the best games of recent years are more difficult to follow.

✔ Players of long ago didn't understand defense as well as players do today, and their lack of defense led to amazing games that are simply unlikely to occur in modern competition.

Of course, many people will have different lists of the top-ten most famous games (maybe even David Letterman!), but the ones in this chapter are the most important to me.

Before You Begin: Understanding the Games

In order to enjoy the games in this chapter, you must understand chess notation, which details the moves, and *annotation,* or commentary on those moves. See Chapter 6 for my explanation of this notation (and get out your board so that you can follow along better).

When chess players write about chess games, we tend to follow a few simple conventions:

- ✔ The player who played white is listed first.
- ✔ The place and year of the game are included if known.
- ✔ The name of the chess opening is included.
- ✔ The comments refer to the moves that precede them.

For you grammatical types, please note that chess players don't always spell out complete sentences. The notated moves themselves are often a part of the comment that follows them.

Interestingly enough, for a class of people who claim to be logical, the names of the chess openings are often a subject of debate. This situation is sort of similar to a bunch of scientists fighting for credit for inventing or discovering the same thing. Quite often, the decision of what to call the opening comes down to a matter of personal preference. In this book, I use the names that are commonly accepted by chess players in the United States.

Conventions such as these make it easier to know which game in particular you're reading about. After all, Garry Kasparov and Anatoly Karpov have played more than 160 games of chess against each other. We have to have some way of differentiating among them!

Annotating a famous game is always dangerous. Not only can you be wrong, but you may break the spell these games cast over people the first time they see them. However, I've found it worth taking the risk in most cases, because, for many people, some explanation is better than none.

Adolf Anderssen versus Lionel Kieseritzky: The Immortal Game

London, 1851 (King's Gambit)

Nowhere is it more evident than in the Immortal Game that the players of the mid-1800s loved attack first and material last!

1. e4   e5

2. f4   exf4

3. Bc4   Qh4+

Anderssen wants to develop rapidly, even if it means losing the right to castle.

4. Kf1   b5

Kieseritzky shows an equal disdain for anything other than rapid development.

5. Bxb5   Nf6

6. Nf3   Qh6

Most analysts have roundly criticized this move by Kieseritzky, but the German grandmaster Robert Hübner has demonstrated that it's better than the suggested 6. ... Qh5.

7. d3

Hübner suggests that 7. Nc3 would have been better.

7. ... Nh5

The move 7. ... Bc5 has been suggested as superior. However, don't take these suggestions as evidence that these players weren't very good. Anderssen and Kieseritzky were simply playing by the principles that were understood at the time. Rapid development and attack were all that really mattered to them.

8. Nh4

This move is sometimes praised as an example of Anderssen's great feel for the attack, but other analysts have decided that 8. Rg1 would have been even better.

8. ... Qg5

9. Nf5   c6

This last move attacks the bishop and unpins the queen pawn, but perhaps 9. ... g6 — immediately attacking the overly aggressive knight — would have been better.

10. g4

Hübner suggests that 10. Ba4 would have been more circumspect.

10. ... Nf6

Again, Kieseritzky should have played g6, attacking the knight.

11. Rg1   cxb5

Black violates the principle of development over material! This error by Kieseritzky is interesting and, according to Hübner, the decisive mistake. He suggests 11. ... h5.

12. h4   Qg6

13. h5   Qg5

14. Qf3   Ng8

15. Bxf4   Qf6

16. Nc3   Bc5

17. Nd5

The move 17. d4 would have gained a tempo, but then the game wouldn't have had this brilliant finish.

17. ... Qxb2 (See Figure 18-1.)

18. Bd6

Almost every text gives this move two exclamation points in honor of its brilliance. Hübner, however, gives no fewer than three better moves and gives the move a question mark. Nevertheless, it leads to the following immortal conclusion:

18. ... Bxg1

19. e5   Qxa1+

20. Ke2   Na6

21. Nxg7+ Kd8

22. **Qf6+** Nxf6

23. **Be7#**

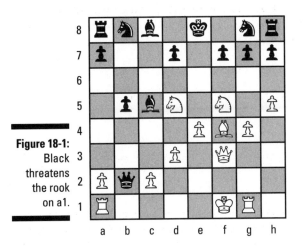

Figure 18-1:
Black
threatens
the rook
on a1.

The way that Anderssen combined his few remaining pieces in such a way as to overcome Kieseritzky's huge remaining army is most remarkable. Even if Anderssen and Kieseritzky didn't play the absolutely best moves, they certainly played the most entertaining ones!

Adolf Anderssen versus J. Dufresne: The Evergreen Game

Berlin, 1852 (Evans Gambit)

This game was given its name by Steinitz. It was a friendly (non-tournament or match) game, which makes its preservation all the more remarkable.

1. **e4** e5

2. **Nf3** Nc6

3. **Bc4** Bc5

4. **b4** Bxb4

5. **c3** Ba5

6. **d4** exd4

7. **0-0**

The Evans Gambit was an old favorite of the Romantic-age players and is still dangerous today. White sacrifices material for an advantage in development and for open lines for the pieces.

7. ... d3

Dufresne's response is weak. Either 7. ... dxc or 7. ... d6 would have been better.

8. Qb3   Qf6

9. e5   Qg6

The pawn is immune to capture. If 9. ... Nxe5 10. Re1 d6 11.Qb5+, white would have won the black bishop on a5.

10. Re1   Nge7

11. Ba3   b5

In those days, development was considered to be more important than puny amounts of material.

12. Bxb5   Rb8

13. Qa4   Bb6

14. Nbd2   Bb7

15. Ne4   Qf5

This position is difficult to play correctly, but this last move is simply a waste of time.

16. Bxd3   Qh5

Now Anderssen begins one of the most famous combinations in all of chess history.

17. Nf6+!   gxf6

18. exf6   Rg8

19. Rad1!

Obviously, Anderssen has already conceived of the brilliant finish.

19. ... Qxf3 (See Figure 18-2.)

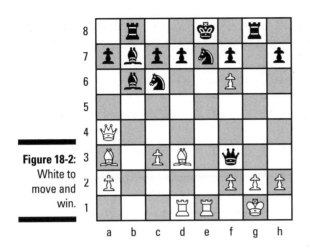

Figure 18-2:
White to move and win.

One can only speculate whether Dufresne ever saw Anderssen's combination coming!

20. Rxe7+   Nxe7
21. Qxd7+!   Kxd7
22. Bf5+! Ke8
23. Bd7+ Kf8
24. Bxe7#

Paul Morphy versus Duke Karl of Braunschweig and Count Isouard

Paris (at the Opera), 1858 (Philidor Defense)

This offhand game is one of the most instructive examples of how to develop rapidly and attack. It was what chess players refer to as a *consultation game*, where one player (in this case, Morphy) plays against two opponents, who are allowed to help one another select black's moves. Legend has it that the duke was roundly criticized in the next day's papers for playing a game of chess at the opera!

1. e4   e5
2. Nf3   d6
3. d4   Bg4

A weak move, but one that has a certain logic to it. The white knight and pawn are attacking black's pawn on e5. Black's pawn is defended by only the d6 pawn. Instead of bringing up another defender (say, with 3. ... Nd7), black chooses to pin the knight. The drawback to this idea is that white has a tactic at his disposal that forces black to trade the bishop for the knight.

4. dxe5 Bxf3

Not 4. ... dxe5 5. Qxd8+ Kxd8 6. Nxe5, which would have won a pawn.

5. Qxf3 dxe5

Material balance has been restored, but Morphy already has one piece developed (the queen) and can now develop another. Morphy has a lead in development and the advantage of the two bishops.

6. Bc4 Nf6

Black must guard against the threatened capture on f7.

7. Qb3 Qe7

Morphy, with his move, renews the threat to capture on f7, and his opponents are forced to guard against it (by moving the queen) on their turn. This move guards f7 but blocks the king's bishop. Morphy's edge in development continues to grow.

8. Nc3 c6

Morphy could have won a pawn by 8. Qxb7, but after 8. ... Qb4+, he would have been forced to trade queens. Morphy correctly decides that continuing his development (because his advantage lies in that element) is more important than winning a pawn. Black takes a moment to guard the b7 square with 8. ... c6, which is a necessary precaution, but this move doesn't help his development.

9. Bg5 b5?

Another pawn move! This time Morphy decides that the time is ripe for sacrifice.

10. Nxb5! cxb5

11. Bxb5+   Nbd7

12. 0-0-0 Rd8

Both knights are pinned, and black can barely move, but how is white to capitalize?

13. Rxd7! Rxd7

Now Morphy has sacrificed a rook for two pawns, but his lead in development is so overwhelming that the material deficit is immaterial! Notice that the black king's rook and bishop have yet to move.

14. Rd1   Qe6

Duke Karl and Count Isouard reason that if they can trade queens, they'll survive the attack and win with their extra material. Morphy never gives them the chance.

15. Bxd7+   Nxd7 (See Figure 18-3.)

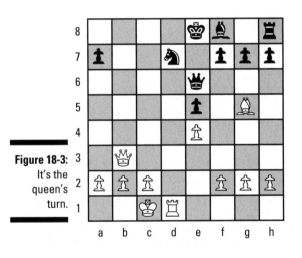

Figure 18-3:
It's the queen's turn.

16. Qb8+   Nxb8

The final sacrifice is of the queen, but Morphy willingly parts with her for checkmate!

17. Rd8#

Wilhelm Steinitz versus Kurt Von Bardeleben

Hastings (England), 1895 (Italian Game)

This game is famous for the concluding combination and for the report that Von Bardeleben didn't bother to resign but simply got up and walked away without a word.

1.	e4	e5
2.	Nf3	Nc6
3.	Bc4	Bc5
4.	c3	Nf6
5.	d4	exd4
6.	cxd4	Bb4+
7.	Nc3	d5

Steinitz (white) is willing to sacrifice a pawn (or more!) in return for a lead in development. Von Bardeleben declines the offer to win material (by 7. ... Nxe4) and immediately strikes back in the center. The struggle then shifts to a fight for control of d5.

8.	exd5	Nxd5
9.	0-0	Be6

Steinitz is again willing to sacrifice a pawn (9. ... Nxc3 10. bxc3 Bxc3) in return for speedy development, and again Von Bardeleben prefers to concentrate on reinforcing his control over what he perceives to be the key square, d5.

10.	Bg5	Be7

Steinitz develops with a threat (by attacking the black queen), which is usually very strong. Von Bardeleben must take a moment to defend against the threat. Now both white and black have four pieces developed, but white has also castled and is on the move.

11.	Bxd5	Bxd5
12.	Nxd5	Qxd5
13.	Bxe7	Nxe7
14.	Re1	f6

Steinitz initiated the preceding series of exchanges for a very subtle reason. Now Von Bardeleben can't castle, because he needs his king to guard the knight. He now hopes to escape his predicament by playing his king to f7 and then a rook to e8, but does he have time to do so?

15. Qe2   Qd7

16. Rac1   c6

If 16. ... Kf7 at once, 17. Qc4+ followed by 18. Qxc7 would have won a pawn for white.

17. d5!   cxd5

Steinitz sacrifices the d-pawn in order to clear the d4 square for his knight. The time gained to bring the knight into the attack is worth more than the pawn. Notice how Von Bardeleben's rooks still stand on their original squares.

18. Nd4   Kf7

19. Ne6   Rhc8

Steinitz is threatening to invade with 20. Rc7.

20. Qg4   g6

Von Bardeleben must guard against 21. Qxg7+ Ke8 22. Qf8#.

21. Ng5+   Ke8 (See Figure 18-4.)

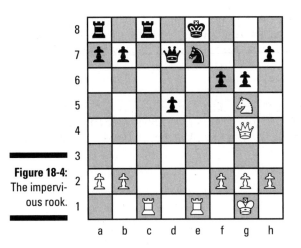

Figure 18-4:
The impervious rook.

22. Rxe7+   Kf8

An extraordinary situation. Black can't capture the white rook, but white can't capture the black queen! If 22. ... Qxe7 23. Rxc8+ (or 22. ... Kxe7 23. Re1+ Kd8, 24. Ne6+), white would have won, but 23. Rxd7 (or Qxd7) Rxc1# would have resulted in a win for black! Now a comical series of moves takes place where Steinitz's impudent rook essentially thumbs its nose at Von Bardeleben's king.

23. Rf7+   Kg8

Not 23. ... Kd8 24. Qxd7#.

24. Rg7+   Kh8
25. Rxh7+   Kg8
26. Rg7+   Kh8

Steinitz's checks haven't been without purpose. Now that Von Bardeleben's h-pawn has been eliminated, Steinitz can bring the queen into the attack with check. White must not allow black to play Rxc1+, which mates quickly, so keeping the black king in check is critical. By replacing the harassing rook with a marauding queen, white increases his attacking force by a decisive amount.

27. Qh4+ Kxg7
28. Qh7+ Kf8
29. Qh8+ Ke7
30. Qg7+ Ke8

If 30. ... Kd6 31. Ne4+ dxe4, 32. Rd1+ would have removed the mate threat and won the black queen.

31. Qg8+ Ke7
32. Qf7+ Kd8
33. Qf8+ Qe8
34. Nf7+ Kd7
35. Qd6#

Von Bardeleben walked away from the board without playing out the final sequence, which is bad manners but understandable in this case. He must have been completely frustrated by his inability to move anything other than his king for so long.

Georg Rotlewi versus Akiba Rubinstein: Rubinstein's Immortal Game

Lodz (Poland), Russia, 1907 (Tarrasch Defense)

This game is another one where the few remaining black pieces combined to overwhelm the vastly superior white pieces. Rubinstein's combination was remarkable in that he continued to offer material right up until the end; as such, the game is known as Rubinstein's Immortal Game.

1.	d4	d5
2.	Nf3	e6
3.	e3	c5
4.	c4	Nc6
5.	Nc3	Nf6
6.	dxc5	Bxc5
7.	a3	a6
8.	b4	Bd6
9.	Bb2	0-0
10.	Qd2	Qe7
11.	Bd3	dxc4

Rotlewi (white) and Rubinstein have adopted very similar setups. The setups have two subtle differences, however, both of which favor black. The first is that black waited to play 11. ... dxc4 until after white's king bishop moved, and this strategic delay gained a tempo for black. The second difference is that the black queen is better placed on e7 than white's queen is on d2. Black's queen is safe, whereas the white queen is exposed on the open d-file. Are these small advantages enough to allow black to win? Maybe — and maybe only if your name is Rubinstein.

12.	Bxc4	b5
13.	Bd3	Rd8
14.	Qe2	Bb7

As you can see, the positions are almost mirror images of one another. The difference is that Rubinstein has already castled and played his rook to d8. Clearly, black got an advantage in development out of the opening.

15. 0-0   Ne5

16. Nxe5 Bxe5

17. f4   Bc7

Is Rotlewi gaining an edge in the center, or is Rubinstein provoking weaknesses in the white king's position?

18. e4   Rac8

19. e5   Bb6+

20. Kh1   Ng4

The safety of white's king is clearly the most critical element at the moment — 21. Qxg4 Rxd3 clearly would have been better for black.

21. Be4   Qh4

22. g3 (See Figure 18-5.)

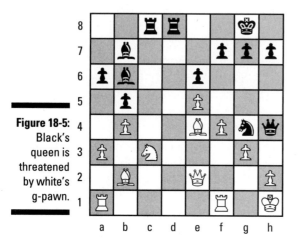

Figure 18-5: Black's queen is threatened by white's g-pawn.

22. ... Rxc3!

A remarkable sacrifice of a queen that white can't refuse. If 23. Bxc3 Bxe4+, 24. Qxe4 Qxh2#.

23. gxh4 Rd2!

Sacrificing a queen isn't enough for Rubinstein. He now throws a rook into the mixture.

24. Qxd2   Bxe4+

25. Qg2   Rh3!

And checkmate by ... Rxh2 is unavoidable. Notice that the white queen on g2 is pinned. Rubinstein wins!

Stepan Levitsky versus Frank Marshall

Breslau (Poland), 1912 (French Defense)

After Marshall's 23. ... Qg3!! move, the spectators were said to have showered the board with gold pieces! Although legends are more fun to believe, it should be noted that the chess journalist and international master I. A. Horowitz reported that Marshall's wife, Caroline, "disclaims even a shower of pennies."

1. d4   e6

2. e4   d5

3. Nc3   c5

4. Nf3   Nc6

5. exd5   exd5

6. Be2   Nf6

7. 0-0   Be7

8. Bg5   0-0

9. dxc5   Be6

10. Nd4   Bxc5

11. Nxe6   fxe6

12. Bg4   Qd6

13. Bh3   Rae8

14. Qd2   Bb4

Marshall now threatens 15. ... Ne4, which prompts Levitsky to exchange his bishop for black's knight. As a result, Marshall's pieces are more aggressively posted, and he's ahead in development. How can he translate this advantage into victory?

    15. Bxf6   Rxf6

    16. Rad1   Qc5

    17. Qe2   Bxc3

    18. bxc3   Qxc3

    19. Rxd5   Nd4

By exploiting the pin on the e-file, Levitsky retains material balance, but Marshall again gains time by centralizing the knight along with an attack on white's queen.

    20. Qh5   Ref8

    21. Re5   Rh6

Marshall again repositions a piece with a gain of time by the attack on the queen. The black pieces are now optimally posted for tactics.

    22. Qg5   Rxh3

Levitsky can't play 23. gxh3 because of 23. ... Nf3. Instead, he wants to play 23. Rc5 and 24. Rc7 with an attack of his own.

    23. Rc5 (See Figure 18-6.)

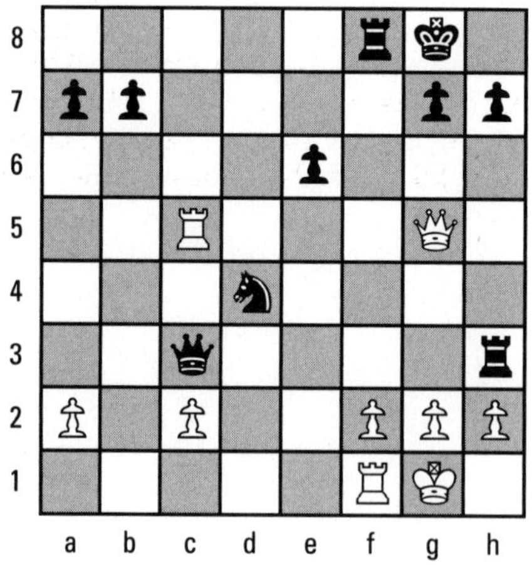

Figure 18-6: Black to move and win.

23. ... Qg3!!

Levitsky resigns! Levitsky had no fewer than three different ways (shown here with asterisks) to capture Marshall's queen — but all of them would have lost:

*24. hxg3 Ne2#

*24. fxg3 Ne2+

25. Kh1 Rxf1#

*24. Qxg3 Ne2+

25. Kh1 Nxg3+

And Levitsky couldn't have recaptured with 26. fxg3 because Marshall's certain response would have been 26. ... Rxf1#.

Emanuel Lasker versus José Raúl Capablanca

St. Petersburg (Russia), 1914 (Ruy Lopez, Exchange Variation)

This historical encounter pitted the world champion Emanuel Lasker against the sensational young José Raúl Capablanca. Lasker proved that he wasn't yet ready to roll over and die before the next generation. Besides the historical significance of the game, this match is noteworthy for Lasker's simple winning strategy, seemingly flowing right from the opening. Simple for him, that is! What this game lacks in brilliant combinations is made up for by the sheer elegance of Lasker's play.

1. e4 e5

2. Nf3 Nc6

3. Bb5 a6

4. Bxc6 dxc6

5. d4 exd4

6. Qxd4 Qxd4

7. Nxd4   Bd6

8. Nc3   Ne7

9. 0-0   0-0

Both sides have developed pieces and castled. Lasker has an edge in the center and consequently an advantage in space. He exploits this advantage by seizing even more space on the kingside. He isn't opening himself up to attack, as white did in the previous game. The players have already exchanged so much material that the chances of a decisive attack are slim.

10. f4   Re8

11. Nb3   f6

The threat was 12. e5, trapping the black bishop.

12. f5   b6

13. Bf4   Bb7

14. Bxd6   cxd

Lasker doesn't mind repairing Capablanca's damaged pawn structure because he has his sights set on the e6 square for his knight.

15. Nd4   Rad8

16. Ne6   Rd7

17. Rad1   Nc8

Notice how Capablanca's pieces are struggling to defend the d6 pawn without getting in each other's way. This dilemma is often the consequence of having a spatial disadvantage.

18. Rf2   b5

19. Rfd2   Rde7

20. b4   Kf7

21. a3   Ba8

Lasker has control over the center and has slowed Capablanca's advance on the queenside. He now improves the position of his king and seizes more space on the kingside.

22. Kf2   Ra7

23. g4   h6

24. Rd3   a5

25. h4   axb4

26. axb4 Rae7

27. Kf3   Rg8

28. Kf4   g6

29. Rg3   g5+

30. Kf3   Nb6

31. hxg5 hxg5

Lasker has now opened the h-file and takes control of it with a rook.

32. Rh3   Rd7

33. Kg3   Ke8

34. Rdh1 Bb7

Capablanca hopes that his position is defensible and merely marks time, but Lasker now takes the opportunity to bring his queenside knight into the game, even at the cost of a pawn.

35. e5!   dxe5

36. Ne4   Nd5

37. N6c5 Bc8

Capablanca can't guard everything and decides to give up a rook for one of the pesky knights. Lasker retains his trumps — the h-file and the spatial advantage — and now adds a slight material edge to the equation.

38. Nxd7 Bxd7

39. Rh7   Rf8

40. Ra1   Kd8

41. Ra8+ Bc8

42. Nc5

Capablanca resigns, because the threat of 43. Ne6+ is devastating.

Donald Byrne versus Robert J. Fischer: The Game of the Century

New York, 1956 (Grünfeld Defense)

Here, the young Bobby Fischer played one of the greatest games of all time. This game was quickly dubbed the game of the century, but it was certainly played in the spirit of the last century.

1.	Nf3	Nf6
2.	c4	g6
3.	Nc3	Bg7
4.	d4	0-0
5.	Bf4	d5
6.	Qb3	dxc4
7.	Qxc4	c6
8.	e4	Nbd7
9.	Rd1	Nb6
10.	Qc5	Bg4

This position is an interesting one. Byrne seems to have complete control over the center, which normally leads to an advantage, but notice that Fischer has completed the development of his minor pieces and castled. Byrne's king's bishop and rook are still on their original squares; he should have attended to his development and not bothered with his next move, which meets with a tactical response.

11.	Bg5?	Na4!

If Byrne had then played 12. Nxa4 Nxe4, 13. Qc1 Qa5+ would have won a pawn for black.

12.	Qa3	Nxc3
13.	bxc3	Nxe4
14.	Bxe7	Qb6

Fischer is willing to sacrifice his rook for white's bishop in return for an attack against white's king. Byrne decides to forgo the win of material in order to try to castle, but Fischer keeps the pressure on and gives him no time to bring his king to safety.

15. Bc4   Nxc3!

16. Bc5   Rfe8+

17. Kf1 (See Figure 18-7.)

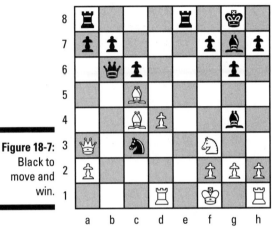

Figure 18-7:
Black to
move and
win.

17. ... Be6

An amazing queen sacrifice, justified by the white king's precarious position and black's lead in development! *18. Bxe6* would have been met by *18. ...* *Qb5+*.

18. Bxb6   Bxc4+

19. Kg1   Ne2+

20. Kf1   Nxd4+

21. Kg1   Ne2+

22. Kf1   Nc3+

23. Kg1   axb6

Black takes time out to capture the bishop because doing so doesn't lose any time. The capture includes a threat to take the white queen on black's next move.

24. Qb4   Ra4

25. Qxb6   Nxd1

26. h3   Rxa2

Fischer continues to gobble up material while improving the position of his pieces.

27. Kh2   Nxf2
28. Re1   Rxe1
29. Qd8+   Bf8
30. Nxe1   Bd5
31. Nf3   Ne4
32. Qb8   b5
33. h4   h5
34. Ne5   Kg7

By breaking the pin, Fischer allows the king's bishop to join in on the final assault.

35. Kg1   Bc5+
36. Kf1   Ng3+
37. Ke1   Bb4+
38. Kd1   Bb3+
39. Kc1   Ne2+
40. Kb1   Nc3+
41. Kc1   Rc2#

Deep Blue versus Garry Kasparov

Philadelphia, 1996 (Sicilian Defense)

No danger is inherent in picking this game for the list of the ten best chess games. Never has a chess game seen as much publicity as this initial match between IBM's computer and Garry Kasparov. In the first game of their six-game match, which I detail in this section, the computer caused a sensation by defeating the world champion. It was the first time a computer beat a world champion at regular tournament time controls, and the media all over the world picked up this story.

1. e4   c5
2. c3   d5
3. exd5   Qxd5

  4. d4   Nf6

  5. Nf3   Bg4

  6. Be2   e6

  7. h3   Bh5

  8. 0-0   Nc6

  9. Be3   cxd4

10. cxd4 Bb4?

This move gets the world champion into trouble. The normal course of action would have been to develop the bishop to e7. Kasparov is undoubtedly trying to get the computer into unknown territory because the computer's memory contains all these moves up to this point from previous games. It isn't "thinking" yet, just "remembering." Now it starts its own calculations.

11. a3   Ba5

12. Nc3   Qd6

13. Nb5   Qe7

14. Ne5   Bxe2

15. Qxe2 0-0

The computer's advantage is a subtle one. The knights have been allowed to make two moves each for the black knight's one.

16. Rac1 Rac8

17. Bg5   Bb6

18. Bxf6 gxf6

Black's move is forced because 18. ...Qxf6 19. Nd7 would have won material for white.

19. Nc4   Rfd8

Not 19. ... Nxd4 20. Nxd4 Bxd4, because of 21. Qg4+ and 22. Qxd4. The computer would never miss this kind of tactical trick. Now the computer ruins Kasparov's queenside pawn structure — a thing it "knows" is good to do.

20. Nxb6 axb6

21. Rfd1 f5

22. Qe3   Qf6

Kasparov is pressuring the pawn at d4. The computer now makes an excellent decision. Instead of becoming passive by defending the pawn, it chooses to advance it and attack. Well done!

23. d5   Rxd5

24. Rxd5 exd5

25. b3   Kh8

Kasparov tries to swing his rook to the g-file and attack. The computer correctly assesses that this attack isn't dangerous and simply begins to "eat" material on the queenside.

26. Qxb6 Rg8

27. Qc5   d4

28. Nd6   f4

29. Nxb7 Ne5

The computer wouldn't have fallen for 30. Qxd4 Nf3+, which would have won the white queen.

30. Qd5   f3

31. g3   Nd3

32. Rc7   Re8

Kasparov's attack looks very dangerous, but the computer isn't rattled by appearances.

33. Nd6   Re1+

34. Kh2   Nxf2

35. Nxf7+ Kg7

36. Ng5+ Kh6

37. Rxh7+

Kasparov resigns in the face of 37. ... Kg6 38. Qg8+ Kf5 39. Nxf3, where he would have had no threats and Deep Blue too many. Score: Silicon 1, Carbon 0. Of course, this setback just made Kasparov mad, and he proceeded to soundly defeat the computer in the rest of the match.

Kasparov didn't fare so well in his 1997 rematch with the computer, however: Deep Blue defeated its human opponent 3.5 to 2.5 in this six-game match. But don't jump to the conclusion that Deep Blue's victory automatically signals the superiority of computers in such matters. Visit the website www.chess.ibm.com to find out more about this match.

Garry Kasparov versus the World

MSN, 1999 (Sicilian Defense)

Using the Internet to watch live broadcasts of chess games became a popular pastime in the 1990s. Kasparov in particular generated huge numbers of hits to sites covering his games. The next step was to use the Internet to let everyone actually play a game against the master. The audience, which included grandmaster analysts and commentators, got to vote on which moves to play, and the most popular choices were the ones adopted. This game, which lasted several months, generated enormous publicity and had a tremendous amount of participation by both voters and viewers.

1. e4   c5
2. Nf3   d6
3. Bb5+ Bd7
4. Bxd7+   Qxd7
5. c4   Nc6
6. Nc3   Nf6
7. 0-0   g6
8. d4   cxd4
9. Nxd4 Bg7
10. Nde2 Qe6 (See Figure 18-8.)

This move was new at the time. However, the move gives Kasparov an opportunity to invade with his knight.

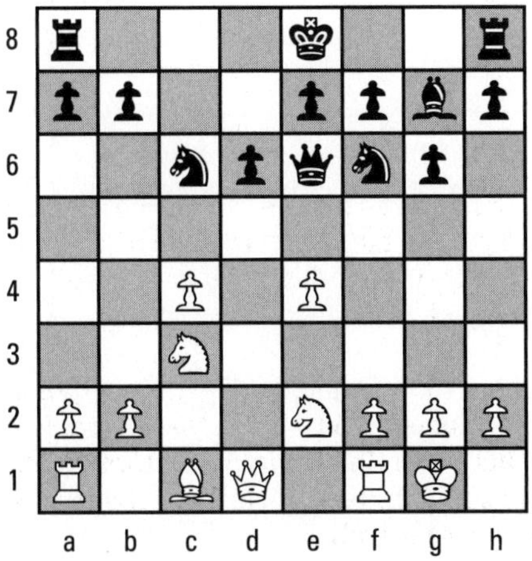

Figure 18-8: Black seeks to destroy white's d-pawn.

11. Nd5   Qxe4

12. Nc7+   Kd7

13. Nxa8   Qxc4

14. Nxb6+

Kasparov despairs of saving the knight and seeks to cripple black's queen-side pawns before losing it.

14. ...axb6

15. Nc3   Ra8

16. a4   Ne4

17. Nxe4   Qxe4

18. Qb3   f5

19. Bg5   Qb4

20. Qf7   Be5

21. h3   Rxa4

22. Rxa4   Qxa4

23. Qxh7   Bxb2

24. Qxg6   Qe4

25. Qf7   Bd4

26. Qb3   f4

27. Qf7   Be5

28. h4   b5

29. h5   Qc4

30. Qf5+   Qe6

31. Qxe6+

Kasparov must trade queens in this position if he wants to keep his winning chances alive. The move 31. Qd3 would have been answered by 31. ... Qg4.

31. ... Kxe6

32. g3   fxg3

33. fxg3   b4

34. Bf4   Bd4+

Kasparov later claimed that 34. ... Bh8 would have been sufficient to equalize the position.

35. **Kh1** b3
36. **g4** Kd5
37. **g5** e6
38. **h6** Ne7
39. **Rd1** e5
40. **Be3** Kc4
41. **Bxd4** exd4
42. **Kg2** b2
43. **Kf3** Kc3
44. **h7** Ng6
45. **Ke4** Kc2
46. **Rh1** d3
47. **Kf5** b1=Q
48. **Rxb1** Kxb1
49. **Kxg6** d2
50. **h8=Q** d1=Q
51. **Qh7**

Although the world is a pawn ahead, Kasparov has the better chances due to the advanced nature of his passed pawn on g5 (see Figure 18-9).

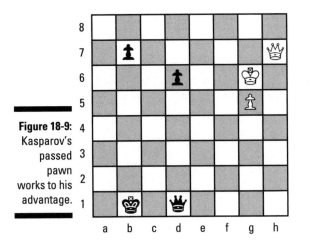

Figure 18-9: Kasparov's passed pawn works to his advantage.

51. ... b5

This move is a mistake. Analysis demonstrated that black could have drawn by playing 51. ... Ka1.

52. Kf6+ Kb2

Again, the king should have moved to a1. These apparently simple positions can be devilishly difficult to play correctly.

53. Qh2+ Ka1
54. Qf4 b4
55. Qxb4 Qf3+
56. Kg7 d5
57. Qd4+ Kb1
58. g6 Qe4
59. Qg1+ Kb2
60. Qf2+ Kc1
61. Kf6 d4
62. g7 1-0

The world resigns, because white's g-pawn is going to queen and inevitably win the game.

Chapter 19

The Ten Best Players of All Time (and a Few Others)

*I*f you want to start an argument, picking the ten best chess players of all time is a good way to do it. Many people feel very strongly about this particular issue, and several have written books about it. Elaborate cases have been made to try to prove who was the best ever by mathematically quantifying their performances and assigning them ratings.

I do no such thing, of course. (That would be too much work!) The way I've decided to judge the best players is by asking a simple question: How much did they stand above their contemporaries? I think this is the only valid way to compare players from different generations. Here they are in this chapter, along with their life span and country, in the order in which I think they most dominated their respective eras. I've also included a short fragment from one of each player's games in order to help you appreciate their brilliance. All of them have produced novel ideas which have advanced the state of the art in chess. (Want more names? At the end of this chapter, I provide a few honorable mentions and list a few players who never won the world championship but were amazing nonetheless.)

To understand the games I discuss in this chapter, you should be familiar with chess notation and annotation; see Chapter 6 for the scoop, and get out your board and chess set so that you can follow along better.

Garry Kasparov (1963–), Russia

Born in Baku, Azerbaizhan, Garry Kasparov won the world championship in 1985 in one of five titanic struggles with Anatoly Karpov (see the section on that guy later in this chapter). Not until he was finally defeated by Vladimir Kramnik in a 2000 match did I fully appreciate how dominant he'd been. Kasparov's tournament results during his peak, from the mid-1980s into the 21st century, were equally impressive. What moves him to the head of this list is the fact that he was so much more active than the majority of his predecessors. No one else demonstrated his or her superiority so convincingly so often.

Kasparov entered only the very strongest tournaments and routinely won them. Only Karpov could challenge him — and because Karpov is also one of the ten best players of all time, this restriction only adds to Kasparov's résumé. The two players were fierce combatants in what must be considered the greatest chess rivalry of all time.

The game position in Figure 19-1 shows Kasparov in action in 1994 against his younger rival and eventual conqueror, Russian grandmaster Kramnik.

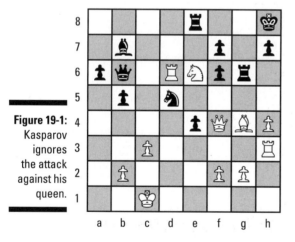

Figure 19-1: Kasparov ignores the attack against his queen.

A wild position! Kramnik's black knight on d5 attacks Kasparov's white queen on f4. Kasparov's knight on e6 is also threatened by black's pawn on f7. It's true that Kasparov could have captured black's queen with 27. Rxb6. But this would have started wholesale trading that would have led to a level game: 27. Rxb6 Nxf4 28. Nxf4 Rxg4 29. Rxf6. Here's what Kasparov did instead:

27. h5!!

Kasparov ignores the attacks on his major pieces and pushes a lowly pawn! In his mind's eye, Kasparov has seen that he can force a winning position by disregarding threats that would dominate the attention of lesser players.

> 27. ... Nxf4
>
> 28. hxg6 Qxd6
>
> 29. Rxh7+ Kg8

Black is a full queen ahead. At this point, Kasparov could have drawn by perpetual check with 30. Rg7+ Kh8 31. Rh7+, and so on. But he foresees much more!

> 30. gxf7+! Kxh7

The only legal move.

Black actually resigns before white can play 31.fxe8Q (see Figure 19-2), because black has no adequate defense to the threat of 32. Qf7+, with check-mate soon to follow.

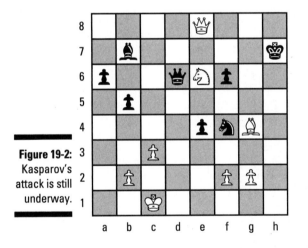

Figure 19-2: Kasparov's attack is still underway.

Anatoly Karpov (1951–), Russia

Although Garry Kasparov (see the preceding section) eventually eclipsed Anatoly Karpov, no one would dream of leaving Karpov off this list. Karpov won the championship by default when Bobby Fischer (whom I discuss later in this chapter) refused to defend his title. Many people considered this a black mark on Karpov's record because Karpov never actually won the title by playing a championship match, but I think that's silly. Perhaps this event is what spurred him on to incredible achievements in tournament chess in the 1970s and '80s.

Only the great Viktor Korchnoi was able to test him in match play, but even he couldn't beat Karpov, and Karpov dominated the tournament scene. (You can read more about Korchnoi in the later section "The Strongest Players Never to Be World Champion.") From 1978 to 1981, Karpov played in ten major tournaments and finished clear first or in a tie for first in nine of them. Karpov was clearly the dominant player after Fischer and before Kasparov.

I've moved Karpov up on this list since the second edition of this book because he battled so long and hard against Kasparov and competed on an almost equal level when they were both at their best. Elevating my estimation of Kasparov's greatness forced me to reconsider Karpov's.

Karpov was renowned for his positional genius. His pieces and pawns nearly always seemed to sit confidently on exactly the right squares. His "quiet" moves seemed to suck the life out of his opponent's game. Playing him has been compared to being slowly suffocated by a boa constrictor. But Karpov could produce a flashy combination as well — if it was really the best move! In the position from 1977 in Figure 19-3, Karpov is black against the Italian champion Stefano Tatai, whose white pieces have been restricted to the back three rows of the board. Importantly, Tatai's king is not yet castled. Cover the moves following Figure 19-3 with your hand and, before going on, try to find Karpov's next move.

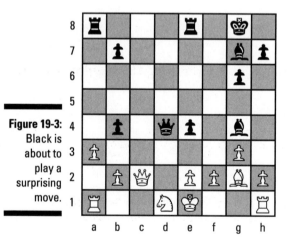

Figure 19-3: Black is about to play a surprising move.

23. ... Qd3!

An unpleasant surprise! Queen sacrifices are often completely unanticipated.

24. exd3

Had Tatai recovered from the shock in time, he might have tried 24. Qd2, but then Karpov would have been able to show off just how deeply he saw into this position (24. ... Qxd2+ 25. Kxd2 Rac8 26. axb4 Red8+, 27. Ke1 Rc2 28. f3 Rdd2 29. fxg4 Rxe2+) when white's position was hopeless. Alternatively, 24. Qxd3 exd3 would also have left white's king in the bullseye: 25. e4 d2+! 26. Kxd2 Red8+.

24. ... exd3+

Discovered check!

25. Kd2   Re2+

26. Kxd3

What now? Obviously, 26. ... Rxc2 27. Kxc2 would have left white ahead a whole rook. Ah, but wait, black can throw his other rook into the game with a check!

26. ... Rd8+

27. Kc4   Rxc2+

28. Kxb4   Rcd2

Black attacks the white knight on d1 three times, and it's guarded only twice. So . . .

29. f3   Bf8+

This move is much stronger than capturing the pawn on b7.

30. Ka5

30. Kb3 would have capitulated even more quickly after 30. ... Be6+, and it would have been checkmate in no more than three more moves.

30. ... Bd7

White resigns (see Figure 19-4). If Tatai had saved his bishop, he would have been mated in four moves: 31. Bf1 Bc5 32.Bc4+ Kh8, after which 33. ... Ra8+ and checkmate could no longer be prevented. 0–1

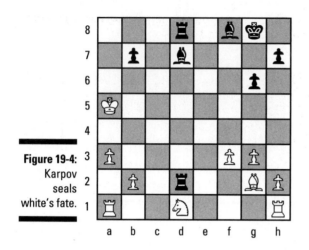

Figure 19-4:
Karpov
seals
white's fate.

José Raúl Capablanca (1888–1942), Cuba

José Raúl Capablanca was world champion from 1921 to 1927. Many people considered him the strongest player in the world prior to 1921, but he was unable to arrange a match with the then-champion, Emanuel Lasker (see the section on him later in this chapter).

When public sentiment became overwhelming in demand of a match, Lasker simply tried to resign his title to Capablanca. This behavior seems to add credence to the view that Capablanca was the better player years before the match finally took place. In fact, beginning in 1914, Capablanca lost only a single game over the next eight years.

Capablanca's dominance was so great that he was nicknamed "the chess machine." Even great players felt that he was unbeatable. Capablanca eventually became somewhat bored with chess because it was too easy. For him, it may have been.

In the game Capablanca-Benito Villegas from Buenos Aires in 1914, black has just played the move 17... cxd4 to arrive at the position shown in Figure 19-5.

Most players would play the seemingly routine move 18. Bxd4, but Capablanca has a better idea. He plays the following move:

18. Nxd7

If Villegas had played 18... dxe3, capturing white's queen, Capablanca would have continued with 19. Nxf6+ — see Figure 19-6.

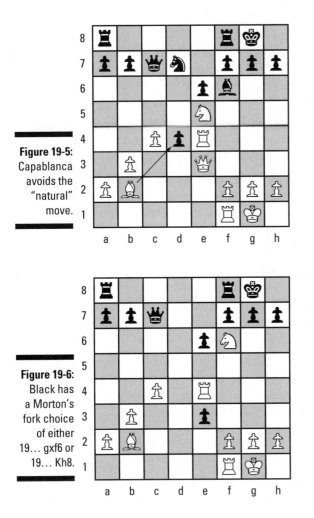

Figure 19-5: Capablanca avoids the "natural" move.

Figure 19-6: Black has a Morton's fork choice of either 19... gxf6 or 19... Kh8.

White would have delivered checkmate after 19... gxf6 20. Rg4+ Kh8 21. Bxf6#, but 19... Kh8 would also have lost to 20. Rh4, with the threat of 21. Rh7#. If black had avoided this threat by playing 20... h6, white would have gained the upper hand by playing 21. Rxh6+ gxh6 22. Nd5+, winning black's queen.

The truly great players could all see obvious moves, but they knew to look beyond them.

Robert James Fischer (1943–2008), United States

In 1971, Robert James Fischer (nicknamed Bobby) shocked the chess world by winning 19 consecutive games against an extremely high level of competition. This feat has been compared to throwing back-to-back no-hitters in major league baseball. During his peak playing period, from the mid 1960s into the early '70s, players spoke of "Fischer Fever," where they felt ill just having to play against him. Just as with José Raúl Capablanca (see the preceding section), Fischer had an aura of invincibility — which wasn't far from the truth. Fischer was head and shoulders above the best players of his day.

His abrupt withdrawal from chess was tragic. Rumors of Fischer sightings were rampant, and the public was often tantalized by stories of his impending reemergence. Unfortunately, Fischer waited more than 20 years before playing in public again. His behavior, always intense, became increasingly odd over the years and prevented him from ever again competing at the highest levels.

The position in Figure 19-7a occurred in the game Fischer-Bent Larsen from Potoroz in 1958. It's white's turn to move. How does white crack black's defense? White plays 22. Rxh5. See Figure 19-7b.

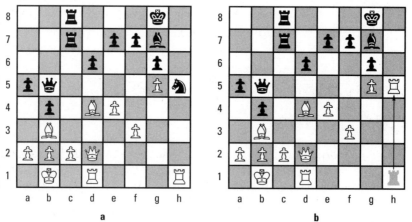

Figure 19-7: Fischer sacrifices his rook to open lines for his coming attack.

The white rook captures the black knight on h5, which was unusual because of the material sacrifice involved. In the old pre-Internet days, good study material from the games of the masters was hard to come by. This game, however, became famous, and to claim that by the 1970s all serious U.S. students of the game were familiar with this type of sacrifice is no exaggeration.

The game continues:

22. ... gxh5

23. g6   e5

24. gxf7+ Kf8

25. Be3   d5

This is the best try, but it fails to save the game.

26. exd5

White avoids 26. Bxd5 to steer clear of the response 26... Rxc2.

26. ... Rxf7

27. d6   Rf6

28. Bg5   Qb7

29. Bxf6   Bxf6

30. d7   Rd8

31. Qd6+ 1-0

If 31. ... Be7, 32. Qh6#. If 31. ... Kg7, then 32. Rg1+ wins the bishop and will mate. Sacrificing the exchange, as Fischer did in this game, in order to open lines of attack against the enemy king, is now part of every serious player's arsenal of weapons.

Paul Morphy (1837–1884), United States

Paul Morphy's career was meteoric. He burned brightly for a short period of time, in the mid-19th century, and then never played again. Moving him up or down this list depending upon how much or how little you value longevity is quite sensible.

Morphy defeated all the best players of his day with the exception of Howard Staunton — who managed to avoid playing Morphy. Most historians give Staunton no real chance of ever being able to defeat Morphy in a match. What set Morphy so far above his contemporaries wasn't that he won but *how* he did it. Morphy played scintillating chess. His games still serve as classic examples of how powerful rapid development can be.

After defeating the best and the brightest, Morphy retired from chess to set up his law practice in New Orleans. Unfortunately, what many believe to have been serious mental health problems surfaced and haunted him for the remainder of his days.

The position in Figure 19-8a occurred in a game between Louis Paulsen and Morphy in 1857. Notice how Paulsen's white bishop on c1 is in its original position and is blocked by white's own pawns. Paulsen is trying to drive Morphy's black queen off of the d3 square, so he can move his d-pawn and get that bishop into the game. Morphy, however, has something else up his sleeve.

Morphy plays 17... Qxf3. (See Figure 19-8b.) This sacrifice of the black queen rips white's kingside open and exposes the king to a relentless attack.

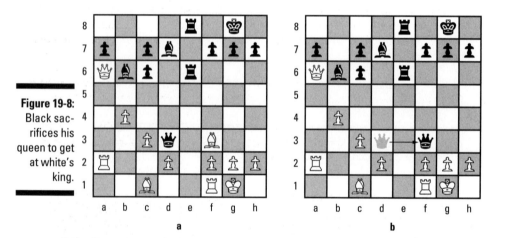

Figure 19-8:
Black sac-
rifices his
queen to get
at white's
king.

The game continues:

18. **gxf3** **Rg6+**

19. **Kh1** **Bh3**

Black attacks the rook and tightens the noose around the king's neck in the process.

20. **Rd1** **Bg2+**

21. **Kg1** **Bxf3+**

22. **Kf1**

Although 22... Rg2 would have led to the quickest checkmate, white was compelled to resign in any case after another handful of moves.

Emanuel Lasker (1868–1941), Germany

Emanuel Lasker is an interesting case. Some people put him first on the list, and others put him toward the bottom. The major criticism is that he played infrequently. The major argument in his favor is that he was world champion from 1894 until 1921 — longer than any other player in history. Many people believe that Lasker ducked the toughest opposition, but his tournament and match results clearly show that he was the world's best player for a considerable period of time.

Lasker established his credentials by winning four consecutive major tournaments (these tournaments were infrequent in those days): St. Petersburg 1895–96, Nuremberg 1896, London 1899, and Paris 1900. From 1895 to 1924, Lasker played in ten major tournaments, finished first eight times, second once, and third once. This achievement was clearly the best record of anyone during his time.

The following position occurs after the 14th move of the game Lasker versus Johann Bauer, which took place in 1889 in Amsterdam. (See Figure 19-9a.)

Bauer almost certainly expected 15. Qxh5, when 15. … f5 would have made black's position quite solid. We can only imagine what a surprise Lasker's 15. Bxh7+ must have been. (See Figure 19-9b.)

Figure 19-9: The beginning of what was to become known as the classic two bishop sacrifice.

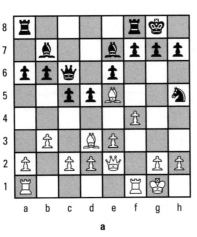

a

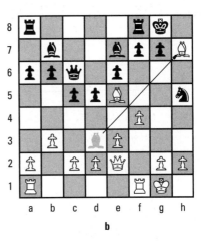

b

The game continues with the following moves:

15. ... Kxh7

16. Qxh5+   Kg8

17. Bxg7+!

The second bishop sacrifice destroys black's king cover. Garry Kasparov (whom I discuss earlier in this chapter) once wrote that today Lasker might try and copyright this idea!

17. ... Kxg7

18. Qg4+ Kh7

19. Rf3

This maneuver is known as a "rook lift" because the rook is "lifted" in front of the g- and h-pawns. The threat is 20. Rh3#.

19. ... e5

20. Rh3+ Qh6

21. Rxh6+ Kxh6

22. Qd7

This move is the sting at the end of the scorpion's tail. See Figure 19-10.

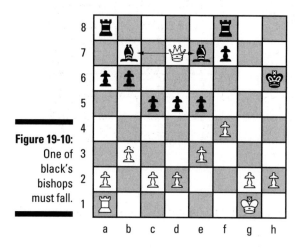

Figure 19-10:
One of black's bishops must fall.

The double attack on the black bishops means that one of them must fall. Black plays on, but the issue of who will win is no longer in doubt: 1-0 in 38 moves. Sacrifices such as the one in this game became part of the repertoire of every serious student of the game.

Wilhelm Steinitz (1836–1900), Austria

The first world champion, Wilhelm Steinitz was considered the best player in the world for a period of about 20 years. By virtue of his match and tournament record, Steinitz was probably the best player in the world during the late 1860s and certainly was by the early 1870s. From 1862 to 1894, Steinitz had an unbroken string of 24 match victories.

It wasn't until 1886, in a match versus Johann Zukertort, that a winner was officially given the title of world champion. Steinitz won with a score of ten wins, five losses, and five draws. He then successfully defended his title several times before losing, at the age of 58, to the young Emanuel Lasker (see the preceding section).

In a world championship match game against the great Russian player Mikhail Chigorin played in 1892 in Havana, the position in Figure 19-11a is reached after the 23rd move of the game. (Flip to the later section "The Strongest Players Never to Be World Champion" for more about Chigorin.)

The obvious move for Steinitz, as white, would have been to play 24. Bxd4+, but that would have allowed black to fight on with 24. ... Rf6. Instead, Steinitz administered the coup de grace with 24. Rxh7+. (See Figure 19-11b.)

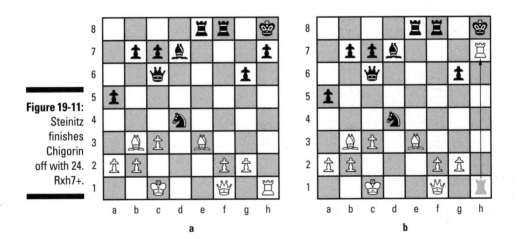

Figure 19-11: Steinitz finishes Chigorin off with 24. Rxh7+.

Sacrificing such a large amount of material is counterintuitive to most players.

The game concludes with the following moves:

24. ... Kxh7

25. Qh1+ Kg7

> **26. Bh6+ Kf6**
>
> **27. Qh4+ Ke5**
>
> **28. Qxd4+ 1-0**

Black resigns, because 28... Kf5 would have been met by 29. g4#.

Alexander Alekhine (1892–1946), Russia

Alexander Alekhine was single-minded in his pursuit of the world championship, and his drive eventually overcame José Raúl Capablanca's skill (I talk about Capablanca earlier in this chapter). Alekhine's results were never as dominating as those of the players higher on this list, but he still managed an impressive run. From 1921 through 1927, he competed in 15 major tournaments and won 8 of them. From 1930 to 1934, he won five strong tournaments but let his weakness for drink get the best of him. He lost the title to Max Euwe in 1935, primarily because of his poor physical condition.

Alekhine cleaned up his act and won the return match to regain the title, which he kept until his death. However, his last years were sad ones. His play was unrecognizable, and his physical condition continued to deteriorate. Nevertheless, Alekhine belongs on this list by virtue of his many tournament and match victories.

In one of the great tournaments of his youth (he wasn't yet 20), at Carlsbad, Germany, in 1911, Alekhine flashed the kind of inspired combinational play with which he would continue to shock and disorient his opponents. After 14 moves against the Polish-American master Oscar Chajes, Alekhine is white in the position shown in Figure 19-12.

Alekhine's white bishop on c4 is under attack by Chajes's black pawn on b5, a position that would cause most players to look for a retreat square. But most players aren't Alekine! He knows that black's uncastled king can be vulnerable, especially because much of his army is undeveloped.

> **15. Bxb5 Rxb5**

Black must capture, or the game is simply lost. So Chajes grabs the bishop and holds on for the ride.

> **16. Nxb5 Qxb5**
>
> **17. Rb1**

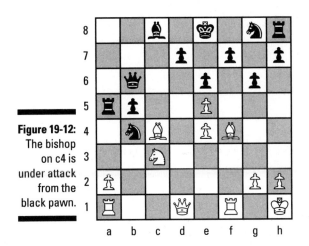

Figure 19-12:
The bishop
on c4 is
under attack
from the
black pawn.

White pins black's knight to his queen.

17. ... Ba6

Now black threatens 18. ... Qxf1+!, after which he would come out on top.

18. Qd6   f6

Black could have tried 18. ... Ne7, with the idea of castling to get the king out of the center. But after 19. Rfd1 Nc8 20.Qxb4 Qxb4 21. Rxb4, Alekhine would have been an exchange up with a remote passed pawn, winning easily. After Chajes's 18. ... f6, 19. Qxb4 would not have been a threat because black would simply have played 19. ... Qxb4, and after 20. Rxb4 Bxf1, Chajes would have had the better game. That's not what the fierce Alekhine has in mind!

19. Rfc1   Qd3

Black is trying to trade queens, which would ease his defensive burden, but Alekhine is not about to oblige him (see Figure 19-13).

20. Rxb4

White has a better move than capturing black's queen. If white had played 20. Qxd3 and black had responded with ... Nxd3, black would have had a tough but defensible game.

20. ... g5

21. Rd4   Qb5

Black's queen is defending the pawn on d7, but Alekhine has something up his sleeve (see Figure 19-14).

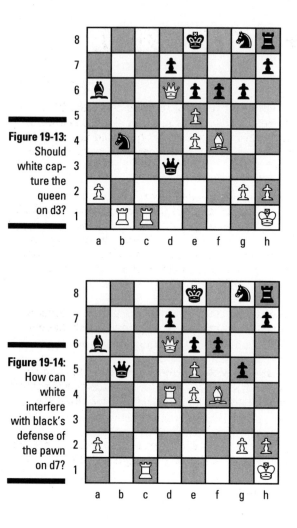

Figure 19-13: Should white capture the queen on d3?

Figure 19-14: How can white interfere with black's defense of the pawn on d7?

22. a4!

Watch how Alekhine chases the black queen away from its protection of d7.

22. ... Qb7

23. Rc7   Qb1+

24. Rd1

Black calls it quits. If he had saved his queen, he would have been mated quickly after 25. Qxd7+. 1–0

Mikhail Botvinnik (1911–1995), Russia

Mikhail Botvinnik won seven consecutive major tournaments from 1941 to 1948, including the tournament held to determine the champion upon Alexander Alekhine's death. There's little doubt that he would have defeated Alekhine (see the preceding section), and it seems certain that he was the best player of the 1940s.

Remarkably, Botvinnik was an engineer by profession and didn't dedicate himself to chess the way most of the champions did. He lost his title to Vasily Smyslov in 1957 but won it back in the return match the next year. He then lost to Mikhail Tal in 1960 but again recaptured the title in the return match. The *return match clause,* stating that the champion has a right to a rematch if defeated, was stricken in 1963 when he lost to Tigran Petrosian, and no one will ever know whether he would have managed to score the hat trick.

Despite a fairly tarnished record in championship match play, Botvinnik was clearly the best player in the world for many years. None of his challengers could make that claim.

In 1945 a famous radio match took place between the United States and the former Soviet Union. Botvinnik, as black, was paired on the top board against Arnold Denker. The position in Figure 19-15a is reached after white's 22nd move.

White is hoping to exchange queens and steer the game into an endgame, but Botvinnik has other plans. He plays 22... Rxh2+. (See Figure 19-15b.)

The game concludes with these moves:

23. Kxh2 Rh8+

24. Qh4

The alternatives were also grim. 24. Bh6 would have lost the queen to 24... Qxf4. Notice that the bishop would have been pinned and unable to capture black's queen. Also, the attempted move 24. Nh5 would have failed to 24. ... Rxh5+ 25. Kg3 Rxg5+, when it would have been the white queen's turn to be pinned.

24. ... Rxh4+

25. Bxh4 Qf4   0-1

The queen is now attacking both of white's bishops. Because white can only save one of them, Denker resigns.

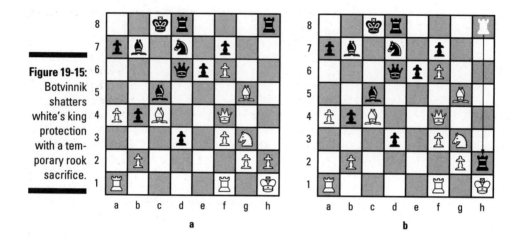

Figure 19-15: Botvinnik shatters white's king protection with a temporary rook sacrifice.

Mikhail Tal (1936–1992), Latvia

Mikhail Tal barely makes the top ten because health troubles kept him from performing at peak efficiency. Otherwise, he may have been much higher on the list. Mikhail Botvinnik (see the preceding section) once said, "If Tal would learn to program himself properly, he would be impossible to play."

Tal won the world championship title from Botvinnik in 1960 but lost the return match. Before this return match, Tal became unwell with kidney trouble but refused to postpone play. He eventually lost one of his kidneys and was never really well afterward.

Nevertheless, from 1949 to 1990, Tal played in 55 strong tournaments, winning or sharing 19 first and 7 second prizes. He won six Soviet championships, which were some of the strongest tournaments of that time. He also compiled a record of 59 wins, 31 draws, and only 2 losses in seven Olympiads. Famous for his intimidating stare, Tal joins José Raúl Capablanca and Bobby Fischer (both discussed earlier in this chapter) as the most feared opponents in history. When playing Tal, players were always afraid of winding up on the losing side of a soon-to-be-famous game.

In the position in Figure 19-16, Tal is white against Hungarian Lajos Portisch in 1965, at the time one of the world's elite grandmasters and a frequent candidate for the world championship.

Sitting in Tal's chair, most masters would have rescued the attacked light-squared bishop by counterattacking with 16. c5 and then playing 17. Bc4. But the Wizard of Riga has some magic in mind!

    16. Rxe6+   **fxe6**

The best of the 18th century?

François-André Danican Philidor (1726–95) of France was reported to be the best player of his time, and the surviving games show a striking superiority to that of most of his contemporaries in his knowledge of the game. Unfortunately, not enough information on this time period is available to truly document his dominance, and this lack of data keeps him from making the top ten.

However, he did author the most influential chess book of his age, *L'analyse des échecs*

(An Analysis of Chess), published in London in 1749. Philidor entered an important choir at the age of 6 and must be considered something of a musical prodigy. He learned chess when the court musicians had spells of inactivity and passed the time playing the game. When his voice broke around the age of 14, he began playing chess in earnest. Even so, his musical compositions were numerous, and some of them are even performed today.

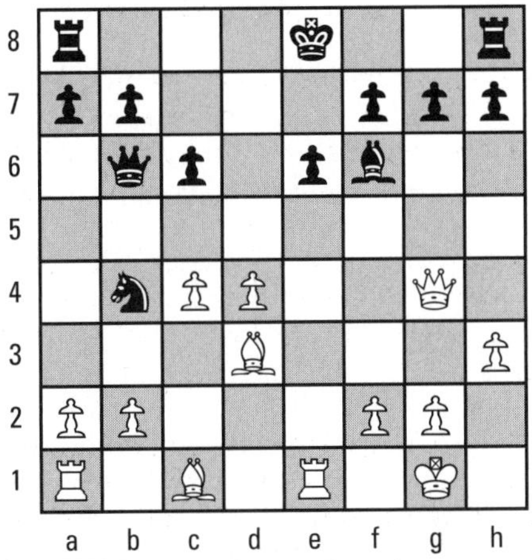

Figure 19-16:
White's bishop on d3 is attacked by black's knight on b4.

Of course, every other possible move would have been catastrophic.

17. Qxe6+   Kf8

We can't blame Portisch for not being fond of his position after 17. ... Be7 18. Bg6+ Kd8 (if 18. ... hxg6?, 19. Bg5 Qc7 20. Re1) 19. Bf5 Qxd4 20. Bf4 Re8, but it would have kept him in the game.

18. Bf4

Tal threatens 19. Bd6, checkmate.

18. ... Rd8

19. c5!   Nxd3

If black had saved his queen with 19. ... Qa5, then 20. Re1! would have sealed his fate; for example, 20. ... Nxd3 21. Bd6+ Rxd6 22. Qe8 mate.

20. cxb6 Nxf4

Although black has, in terms of the material point-count, more than enough pieces for the queen, Tal proves that Portisch is lost!

21. Qg4 Nd5

22. bxa7 Ke7

Although this move looks anti-intuitive, it is one of black's best in a bad position. He connects his rooks and heads for the queenside with his king.

23. b4! Ra8

After 23. ... Nxb4 24. Rb1 Rxd4 25. Qg3, Portisch's position would have been pitiful.

24. Re1+ Kd6

25. b5! Rxa7

Black is understandably eager to eliminate white's potential queen, but this permits Tal to deliver the *coup de grace!*

26. Re6+! Kc7

White has one final sacrifice to make in order destroy Black's position (see Figure 19-17).

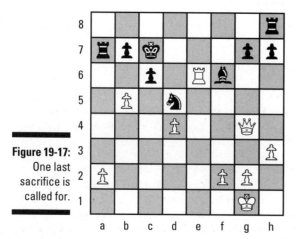

Figure 19-17:
One last
sacrifice is
called for.

27. Rxf6! gxf6

The moves 27. ... Nxf6 28. Qxg7+ would also have cost black a rook and the game.

28. Qg7+ 1–0

Honorable Mentions

Other world champions must be included in any such list, because they all were dominant to some extent. Although these players may not appear on every best-ever list, they deserve consideration:

- ✔ **Adolf Anderssen (1818–1879), Germany:** Although the title of world champion wasn't established during his day, Anderssen was arguably the best player of his time and deserves consideration as an honorable mention.
- ✔ **Max Euwe (1901–1981), Netherlands:** World Champion in 1935.
- ✔ **Vasily Smyslov (1921–), Russia:** World Champion in 1956.
- ✔ **Tigran Petrosian (1929–1984), Russia:** World Champion from 1963–1969.
- ✔ **Boris Spassky (1937–), Russia:** World Champion from 1969–1972.
- ✔ **Vishwanathan Anand (1969–), India:** Undisputed World Champion since 2007.
- ✔ **Vladimir Kramnik (1975–), Russia:** World Champion from 2000–2007.

The Strongest Players Never to Be World Champion

If you don't get enough controversy from trying to establish the best players of all time, ask who the strongest player to never win the world champion title was. That question usually does the trick. The prime candidates, in chronological order, are as follows.

- ✔ **Mikhail Chigorin (1850–1908), Russia:** Mikhail Chigorin played two championship matches with Wilhelm Steinitz and lost both of them, but these matches were considered to be closely contested, and the second match in particular could have gone either way. In 1893, Chigorin drew a tremendous fighting match with Siegbert Tarrasch, who also makes this list.

✔ **Siegbert Tarrasch (1862–1934), Germany:** From 1888 to 1892, Siegbert Tarrasch won five consecutive major tournaments. He never challenged Wilhelm Steinitz for the title — although he was certainly qualified to — reportedly due to his obligations as a medical doctor. When he finally got his chance against Emanuel Lasker in 1908, he was past his prime and soundly beaten.

✔ **Harry Nelson Pillsbury (1872–1906), United States:** Harry Nelson Pillsbury's first international tournament was Hastings 1895, one of the strongest and most famous tournaments in history. Unbelievably, he won the event ahead of Wilhelm Steinitz, Emanuel Lasker, Mikhail Chigorin, and Siegbert Tarrasch. No one had ever done anything like it before. His career tournament record against Lasker was four wins, four losses, and four draws — the best result among any of his contemporaries. His untimely death, due to illness, may have been the only obstacle between him and the title.

✔ **Akiba Rubinstein (1882–1961), Poland:** In 1912, Akiba Rubinstein won four major tournaments and was clearly at the top of his game. He then began negotiations with Emanuel Lasker for a title match. Sadly, he fared badly in the great tournament in St. Petersburg 1914 and lost his potential backing. Then World War I broke out; his best opportunity was gone.

✔ **Samuel Reshevsky (1911–1992), United States:** During the years 1935 to 1950, Samuel Reshevsky played in 14 major tournaments and won half of them. He finished lower than third only once. This record is all the more remarkable because he was only a part-time player and held a full-time, nonchess job. Born in Poland, he was perhaps the greatest child prodigy in chess history. He also continued to play at an extremely high level well into his 70s and once drew a match with Bobby Fischer in 1961.

✔ **Paul Keres (1916–1975), Estonia:** Paul Keres won some of the strongest tournaments in the late 1930s, but the advent of World War II dashed his title hopes. After the war, he was a candidate for the title no less than seven times but never made it to the finals. His near misses took on almost tragic proportions.

✔ **Viktor Korchnoi (1931–), Russia:** Viktor Korchnoi won four Soviet championships and competed as a candidate many times over the course of his career. He came within a hair's breadth of winning the title from Anatoly Karpov in 1978. Korchnoi was a defector from the Soviet Union, and all of that country's resources were used against him. Of all the players on this list, Korchnoi may have the strongest claim.

Part VI
Appendixes

The 5th Wave   By Rich Tennant

"'Yankees vs. Confederates', 'Navy vs. Army'...
there it is — 'Dogs vs. Vacuum Cleaners.'"

In this part . . .

In this part, I provide a handy glossary of terms that you can turn to anytime you need to know what a chess word means. I also provide a reference to other chess resources that you can use to find all the latest in chess-related gear as well as helpful information and cool websites to visit.

Appendix A

A Glossary of Chess

*O*ver the years, chess players have developed their own language — well, terminology — for communicating about the various moves, pieces, and so on. Bone up on the terms in this glossary, and you'll be sure to fit in at the nearest chess club — not to mention you'll have a much easier time wading through all the chess books on the market. Of course, you don't have to take a test when you reach the end of this book, so you don't need to commit these terms to memory. Just keep this glossary handy so you can find the information you need at any given moment. ***Note:*** If you encounter chess notation (square c6, 1. e3 Nc7, and so on), you may want to turn to Chapters 1 and 6, respectively, for a quick lesson on how to read it.

action chess: See ***rapid chess***.

active: The description of a move that increases your mobility; also the description of a piece that is mobile. See also ***passive***.

adjust: To touch a piece or pawn (generally to move it to the center of its square) without the intention of making an official move. A player should announce "I adjust" or "*J'adoube*" (juh-*doob*) before touching the piece. See Chapter 16 for more on chess etiquette. See also ***J'adoube*** and ***touch-move***.

algebraic notation: A system of recording the moves of a chess game (first devised in the 19th century) in which each square on the board has a unique identifier. From white's side of the board, the files are lettered from *a* to *h* moving from left to right, and the ranks are numbered 1 to 8, moving from bottom to top. Piece moves are designated by a one-letter abbreviation for the piece followed by its destination square. Pawn moves are designated by the destination square alone. Chapter 6 has the details on understanding algebraic chess notation. See also ***notation***, ***long algebraic notation***, and ***descriptive notation***.

annotation: Commentary on a chess game that attempts to explain the game in general terms or by examining alternatives to the moves played. Chapter 6 shows you the annotation symbols and their meanings.

arbiter: A person who ensures that the rules are observed, supervises the game(s), enforces the rules and his own decisions regarding them, and imposes penalties on players infringing on the rules. See also ***international arbiter***.

attacking move: An aggressive move that (often) elicits a defensive response.

back rank: A player's own first rank.

back-rank mate: Checkmate delivered by playing a queen or rook to an opponent's back rank when the king is kept from moving out of check by its own pawns.

backward pawn: A pawn that has pawns of its own color on adjacent files only in front of it, so it has no pawn protection of its own.

bad bishop: A bishop whose effectiveness is hampered by its own pawns.

bishop pair: Two bishops, usually compared to an opponent's two knights or bishop and knight. In many positions, the bishop pair has a slight advantage over these other two configurations of minor pieces due to greater mobility.

bishops of opposite color: A situation where one player has a bishop on the light squares and the other player has a bishop on the dark squares. Endings with bishops of opposite color are often drawn.

blindfold chess: Chess played without seeing the board or pieces. Originally a player was, in fact, blindfolded; now in blindfold chess a player usually sits with her back to the board. Famous players who have played simultaneous blindfold chess include François-André Philidor, Paul Morphy, Alexander Alekhine, and George Koltanowski.

blitz: Chess played very quickly. Each player is given a small amount of time, commonly five minutes apiece, in which to play the entire game.

blockade: A situation where one side is prevented from advancing. Originally, Aaron Nimzowitsch used the term to describe the blocking of a pawn by a piece.

blunder: A bad move that results in checkmate, the loss of material, or a seriously weakened position.

book move: The term for a standard move, one generally recommended in books cataloging openings or books concerned with the opening in question.

brilliancy: A game containing original, innovative, and sometimes surprising moves.

brilliancy prize: An award given for the best brilliancy at a tournament. The first brilliancy prize was awarded to Henry Bird in 1876 for his win over James Mason.

castling: A single move involving both the king and a rook. Castling kingside moves the king from e1 (e8 for black) to g1 (g8 for black) and the rook from h1 (h8 for black) to f1 (f8 for black). Castling queenside moves the king from e1 (e8 for black) to c1 (c8 for black) and the rook from a1 (a8 for black) to d1 (d8 for black). Castling is permitted only if the following conditions are met: The king isn't in check, neither the king nor the relevant rook has previously moved in the game, no pieces are between the king and the rook, and none of the squares the king must move across are attacked by an enemy piece or pawn. Chapter 5 has an illustrated explanation of castling.

center: The squares c4, c5, d4, and d5. Sometimes the term is also used to encompass the squares adjacent to these four.

centralization: The act of bringing pieces to the center where they can control the largest amount of the board.

cheapo: A slang expression for a swindle or a cheap trick that doesn't withstand serious scrutiny. See also *swindle*.

check: An attack on the opponent's king by either a piece or a pawn. When in check, a player must do one of the following: move the king out of check, interpose a piece or pawn, or capture the checking piece. Although it used to be common to utter the word "check" when making such a move, this practice is not only unnecessary but also is often frowned upon. Chapter 4 covers check possibilities. See also *checkmate*.

checkmate: When a king is in check and can't make any move to get out of check, the king is said to be checkmated (or simply "mated"), and the game is over. See Chapter 4 for checkmate information. See also *check*.

chess clock: A device made up of two clocks that records the amount of time each player uses while on the move. Only the clock of the player to move is running; after making his move, the player pushes a button that stops his clock and starts the clock of his opponent. See also *Fischer clock* and *flag*.

chess problem: A composed chess position that identifies that checkmate (or another conclusion, such as helpmate, where the solver is required to checkmate himself) is to be given in a specified number of moves.

chessic: An adjective noting that something is related to chess.

chessman: A term that refers to both pieces and pawns. Sometimes the term is shortened to *man*. The term *unit* is sometimes used interchangeably with chessman. See also *piece*.

classical: A style of chess play that developed in the late 19th century, emphasizing rapid development and control of the center with pawns. See also *center* and *development*.

closed file: A file that has at least one pawn of each color on it.

closed game: A game where piece movement is restricted by interlocked pawn chains and play centers on positioning pieces outside of the center, in anticipation of the opening of the position. Most of the pieces are usually still on the board and are behind the pawns, which may impede their movement. See also *open game*.

combination: A series of forced moves (usually involving a sacrifice) that leads to an advantage for the initiating player.

compensation: An advantage that compensates for a disadvantage elsewhere. For example, a gain of tempo may compensate for the loss of a pawn.

connect: To move rooks of the same color onto the same rank, unseparated by pieces or pawns.

consolidate: To maintain an established advantage.

consultation chess: A game in which at least one side consists of two or more players who consult with each other in the play of the game. One of Paul Morphy's most spectacular games was against the Duke of Brunswick (Braunschweig) and Count Isouard. This pair played Morphy in consultation and suffered a stunning loss. (Chapter 18 has the story on that famous game.)

cook: A defect in a chess problem.

correspondence chess: Chess played by mail. The earliest correspondence game whose moves have been preserved was played in 1804. Chess played via e-mail has also become popular. Unlike over-the-board play, the consultation of books and other materials is permitted in correspondence chess. Also known as *postal chess*. (See Chapter 16 for more details.)

cramped position: A position in which the pieces have little room to move. See also *closed game*.

crippled majority: A group of pawns on one side of the board that outnumber the opponent's pawns on this side, but that, because of structural weaknesses (for example, doubled pawns), can't result in the creation of a passed pawn. See also *majority*.

critical position: The point in a game where the decisive series of moves begins.

cross-check: A reply to a check that is itself a check. See also *check*.

crosstable: A chart in grid form that lists the complete results of a tournament.

decoy sacrifice: A sacrifice that entices the movement of an opponent's piece to a disadvantageous square. The move may place the hostile piece on a disadvantageous square or simply remove it from a part of the board where it was more effective. See also *sacrifice*.

descriptive notation: A system of recording the moves of a chess game based on the names of the pieces and places they occupy before the game begins. A move is given by the name of the piece moving, followed by the square to which it moves. This notation is now almost completely replaced by algebraic notation. See also *algebraic notation*, *long algebraic notation*, and *notation*.

desperado: A piece that is trapped or must inevitably be captured and that a player moves to inflict the greatest possible damage to the opposing side.

development: The movement of pieces from their initial squares. See Chapter 3 for the full scoop on development.

diagonal: Any contiguous line of squares along which a bishop may move. If a bishop isn't on one of the four corner squares of the board, it's on a square that represents the intersection of two diagonals, which are referred to as the *short diagonal* and the *long diagonal*.

diagram: An illustration depicting a chess position where white is at the bottom of the picture and black is at the top.

discovered attack: The movement of a piece or pawn that results in an attack by an unmoved piece. The stationary piece is now able to attack because the piece that was moved previously blocked the attack. See also *discovered check*.

discovered check: The movement of a piece or pawn that results in a check by an unmoved piece. See also *discovered attack*.

double attack: A simultaneous attack by a single piece or pawn on two pieces of the opponent. Any pawn or piece can theoretically make a double attack, except pawns on the a- or h-files.

double bishop sacrifice: The sacrifice of both bishops to open up the enemy king. The Lasker-Bauer game of 1889 at Amsterdam is the first documented, successful example of this maneuver. See also *sacrifice*.

double check: A discovered check in which the moved piece also gives check. Only the movement of the king can meet a double check. See also *discovered check*.

double round robin: A tournament where each contestant plays two games (one as white and one as black) with every other contestant. See also *match*, *round robin*, and *tournament*.

doubled pawns: Two pawns of the same color on the same file, which are nearly always a positional weakness.

draw: A completed chess game that has no winner. A draw can come about in several ways: by agreement of both players; by stalemate; by the declaration and proof of one player that the same position has appeared three times (with the same player to move and all other possibilities the same); by the declaration and proof of one player that there have been 50 moves during which no chessman has been taken and no pawn has been moved; by adjudication; or by the falling of one player's flag (on the chess clock) when her opponent has insufficient material to perform checkmate. See also *50-move rule,* and *stalemate.*

duffer: A disparaging term to describe a very poor player. See also *patzer*.

dynamism: A type of play where positional weaknesses are permitted in favor of aggressive counterplay. Dynamism developed out of the hypermodern school of chess play. See also *hypermodern*.

edge: The outside squares of the chessboard, namely the first and eighth ranks and the a- and h-files.

Elo scale: A system for ranking chess players in order of relative strength based on results in rated games. The important factor in comparing two players is the difference in their Elo ratings, not the absolute level of either rating. The Elo system was adopted by the United States Chess Federation (USCF) in 1960 and by FIDE in 1970. The system was devised by physicist Arpad Elo as an improvement to the system developed in 1950 by Kenneth Harkness.

en passant: French for "in passing," this term refers to the capture of a pawn that has moved two squares forward by an opponent's pawn on the fifth rank. You can capture en passant only immediately following the move of the enemy pawn two squares forward. The capturing pawn moves diagonally forward one square and captures the pawn as if it had moved only one square forward. An en passant capture is sometimes recorded with "e.p.": for example, exd5 e.p. (See Chapter 6 for more on chess notation and Chapter 5 for illustrated information on en passant.)

en prise: French for "within grasp." A chessman is en prise if it is left or moved to a square where it can be captured without loss to the capturing player. See also *hanging*.

endgame: Also called the *ending,* the endgame is the final state of the chess game, characterized by the relatively few pieces on the board. Players typically use the king more aggressively in the endgame than in the opening or middlegame. One of the most common concerns in this phase is the promotion of pawns. Check out Chapter 15 for detailed endgame information. See also *middlegame, opening,* and *promotion.*

endgame study: A composed chess position in which white must locate the unique win (sometimes a draw) according to the requirements set out by the composer. Studies tend to be more realistic than problems. Enthusiasts of studies value those of great originality and beauty. See also *problem* and *endgame*.

equalize: To achieve a position where the opponent's initiative is negated. For example, white usually has the initiative in the opening, and black works to equalize, or overcome, this initiative.

escape square: A square to which a king in check can move. Also called *flight square*.

Exchange: The capture of a piece or a pawn while giving up material of equal strength. When capturing a rook while giving up only a bishop or a knight, one is said to "win the Exchange." See also *minor exchange*.

fianchetto: The placement of a bishop on b2 or g2 for white and b7 or g7 for black. The term is derived from the Italian *fiancata*, meaning "moves played on the flank."

FIDE: Fédération Internationale des Échecs, the international chess federation founded on July 20, 1924, in Paris. FIDE (pronounced *fee*-day) has more than 150 member countries and concerns itself with all aspects of the game of chess.

FIDE master: The title below that of international master. A player with a FIDE master title usually has an Elo rating of at least 2350. See also *Elo scale*.

50-move rule: The chess rule that declares a game drawn when a player demonstrates that 50 moves have been played without the move of a pawn or without any captures. See also *draw*.

file: Any of the eight columns on a chessboard, denoted by an algebraic notation letter, for example the *a-file*. See also *algebraic notation*.

Fingerfehler: German for finger-slip, a description of an obvious but bad move made without thinking.

first board: Also called *top board,* a term to describe the board in a team match that usually has each team's strongest player.

Fischer clock: A clock that, in addition to serving the usual functions of a chess clock, adds a certain amount of time to each player's clock after each move, in order to avoid desperate time scrambles at the end of a game, which often result in poor moves. See also *chess clock*.

fish: A derogatory term for a chess player of little skill or experience.

five-minute chess: See *blitz*.

flag: Part of an analog chess clock. As the minute hand on the clock nears the 12, the flag is pushed upward. When the minute hand reaches 12, the flag falls. The falling of the flag indicates that the player's time has expired; if the requisite number of moves hasn't been played, the player is said to "lose the game on time." (In other words, the game is lost because time ran out, not because of the position on the board, although many games are lost on time when the position is poor and the losing player uses large amounts of time in an effort to try to find a way to save the game.) See also *chess clock*.

flank: Sometimes called a *wing*, the flank is one side of the chessboard, such as the a-, b-, and c-files or the f-, g-, and h-files.

flank development: Developing pieces on either flank (for example, in order to fianchetto a bishop). See also *development, fianchetto,* and *flank*.

flank openings: Openings where white doesn't make early advances of the d- or e-pawns but instead develops on the a-, b-, and c-files or the f-, g-, and h-files. The fianchetto is a common motif in flank openings. See also *fianchetto* and *flank*.

flight square: See *escape square*.

fluid pawn center: Any position where the center pawns can be advanced or exchanged.

fool's mate: The shortest possible chess game ending in checkmate: 1.g4 e5 (or e6) 2.f4 (or f3) Qh4 mate. See also *scholar's mate*.

forced move: A move for which only one reply is possible (or if more than one reply, all but one are undesirable).

fork: An attack on two enemy chessmen at the same time. See also *skewer*.

Forsyth notation: A compact and simple means of recording a chess position, devised by Scottish player David Forsyth. Beginning at the top left-hand corner of the board (a8), you record the position of the chessmen as well as the unoccupied squares, rank by rank. White's men are recorded with capital letters, and black's men with lowercase letters.

French bishop: Black's light-squared bishop in the French Defense, which tends to be very weak because of the black pawn on e6.

frontier line: Grandmaster Aaron Nimzowitsch's term for an imaginary line running between the fourth and fifth ranks.

gambit: Any opening that contains a planned sacrifice of material, usually to promote rapid development or control of the center.

Gens una sumus: Latin for "we are one family," this saying is the official motto of FIDE. See also *FIDE*.

GM: An abbreviation for international grandmaster. See also *international grandmaster*.

good bishop: A bishop unhindered by its own pawns and thus very mobile. See also *bad bishop*.

grandmaster: A shortened form of international grandmaster. See also *international grandmaster*.

grandmaster draw: A deprecating term for a short, drawn game between grandmasters where it's obvious that neither player has made any attempt at playing for a win.

Grandmaster of Chess: A title bestowed by Czar Nicholas II upon the finalists of the 1914 St. Petersburg tournament: Alexander Alekhine, José Raúl Capablanca, Emanuel Lasker, Frank Marshall, and Siegbert Tarrasch.

half-open file: A file on which only one of the players has a pawn or pawns.

half-pin: A pin in which the chessman subject to the pin may move along the same line (file, rank, or diagonal) that it shares with the attacker. See also *pin*.

handicap: A means of trying to equalize chances in a game played between opponents of greatly different strengths. Numerous methods of implementing a handicap exist. The stronger player may (among other things) treat a draw as a loss; play several opponents at the same time; give her opponent more time on the clock; give her opponent two moves in a row at the opening of the game; or remove one or more of her pieces from the board before play begins.

hanging: A slang term to describe an undefended piece left exposed to capture. See also *en prise*.

hanging pawns: Wilhelm Steinitz's term for two adjacent pawns that are on the fourth rank, can't be supported by other pawns, aren't passed pawns, and are on half-open files.

hole: Wilhelm Steinitz's term for the square directly in front of a backward pawn where an opponent's piece can't be attacked by a pawn.

hypermodern: A school of thought developed after World War I in reaction to the views of Wilhelm Steinitz and Siegbert Tarrasch. The most important idea of the hypermodern school is that occupation of the center isn't vital — one can put pressure on the center or even just carefully monitor it and still win. The leaders of the hypermodern movement — Aaron Nimzowitsch, Richard Réti, Gyula Breyer, Ernst Grünfeld, and Saviely Tartakower — were strong players and witty writers. Many hypermodern ideas are still considered valid today, but so are many of the ideas of Steinitz and Tarrasch.

illegal move: A move that is in violation of the laws of chess. If an illegal move is discovered during the course of a game, the game will be returned to the point it was at before the illegal move was made. The player who made the illegal move must move the piece he had previously moved illegally, if he can make a legal move with that piece. Otherwise, that player is permitted to make any legal move.

illegal position: A position that isn't the result of a series of legal moves. Thus, an illegal move necessarily leads to an illegal position. Other sources of illegal positions include incorrect positioning of the chessboard and incorrect arrangement of the chessmen, either at the beginning of the game or at the time an adjourned game is resumed. If possible, the position must be corrected; otherwise, a new game must be played.

Indian defenses: Hypermodern defenses to 1. d4 beginning with 1. ... Nf6. Indian defenses commonly employ a bishop fianchetto and slow development. The name comes from this slow development, common in India, which permitted pawn moves of only a single square, long after Europe had adopted the option of a two-square advance on the first move of a pawn. Chapter 13 has more details on these and other common openings.

initiative: The term used to describe the advantage held by the player who has the ability to control the action and flow of the game, thus forcing the opponent to play defensively.

international arbiter: A title first awarded by FIDE in 1951. A candidate is nominated by her federation and may be selected by the qualification committee if she has a complete knowledge of the rules of chess and FIDE regulations; is objective; has knowledge of at least two FIDE languages (English, French, German, Spanish, and Russian); and has experience in controlling at least four important tournaments, two of which must be international. See also *arbiter*.

International Computer Chess Association (ICCA): The association that organizes the annual World Computer Chess Championship and the World Microcomputer Chess Championship held every year.

international grandmaster: A title established in 1950 and awarded by FIDE. FIDE has detailed requirements for the title, which is awarded to only the best players in the world. A player with a FIDE grandmaster title, often abbreviated GM, usually has an Elo rating of at least 2500. See also *Elo scale* and *FIDE*.

international master: A title established and awarded by FIDE, often abbreviated IM. An IM is a stronger player than a FIDE master but not as strong as an international grandmaster and usually has an Elo rating of at least 2400. See also *Elo scale* and *FIDE*.

International Rating List: A list of the world's strongest players, compiled by FIDE by using the Elo rating scale. It was first published in July 1971. See also *Elo scale* and *FIDE*.

international woman grandmaster: A title established in 1976 and awarded by FIDE to the world's strongest female players. See also *FIDE*.

interposition: The blocking movement of a piece in between an attacked piece and the attacker.

isolated pawn: A pawn whose adjacent files contain no pawns of the same color. An isolated pawn is weak because other pawns can't defend that pawn or the square in front of it.

J'adoube: French for "I adjust," this expression (pronounced juh-*doob*) is used by a player on the move before touching a piece, generally to move it to the center of its square. A piece or pawn so adjusted doesn't have to be the man that will be the subject of the player's official move. See also *adjust* and *touch-move*.

key: The unique, first move in the solution to a chess problem. See also *problem*.

kibitz: To comment during a game, or during analysis following a game, within the hearing of the players. The term is often used in a pejorative sense and is in many occasions applied to the comments of a spectator for whom the players have little respect. See also *kibitzer*.

kibitzer: One who kibitzes.

king hunt: A prolonged attack on the opponent's king that usually dislodges it from a shielded, defensive position with a series of checks and sacrifices. A successful king hunt ends in checkmate.

king pawn opening: Any opening beginning with 1. e4.

kingside: The e-, f-, g-, and h-files.

knight fork: Any double attack by a knight. See also *double attack*.

knight's tour: A chess puzzle whereby the knight is moved 64 times, landing on each square only once. A solution is called *re-entrant* if the knight finishes on a square that is a knight's move away from the square where it began.

ladder: A fluid method of ranking chess players within a club or other group. The ladder is usually established by listing players according to their chess rating. Any player may challenge someone one step above him on the ladder (sometimes two or more places). If the challenger wins, that person moves up the ladder, and the opponent moves down.

laws of chess: The rules that govern the play of the game. During the 1850s, Howard Staunton was one of many players who first sought to establish a unified set of chess laws. FIDE established its own laws of chess in 1929. See also *FIDE*.

legal move: A move permitted by the laws of chess.

Legall's mate: A mating sequence appearing in the game between M. de Kermar Legall and Saint Brie in about 1750: 1. e4 e5, 2. Bc4 d6, 3. Nf3 Bg4, 4. Nc3 g6, 5. Nxe5 Bxd1, 6. Bxf7+ Ke7, 7. Nd5 mate.

lever: Hans Kmoch's term for two pawns, one white and one black, that are diagonally adjacent so that either can capture the other.

light piece: Another expression for a minor piece: a bishop or a knight.

light-squared bishop: A bishop that moves on light-colored squares.

lightning chess: Another term for speed or blitz chess. See *blitz*.

liquidation: The exchange of chessmen to stunt an opponent's attack, to solidify one's own advantages, or to improve one's own position.

long algebraic notation: A form of algebraic notation in which a move is designated by a letter indicating the piece moved, the square the piece moves from, and the square the piece moves to (for example, Bc1-g5). Pawn moves are designated by the starting square and the destination square (for example, e2-e4). See also *notation, algebraic notation,* and *descriptive notation*.

long castling: An expression sometimes used to describe castling queenside. See also *castling*.

Long Whip: The line in the King's Gambit: 1. e4 e5, 2. f4 exf4, 3. Nf3 g5, 4. h4 g4, 5. Ne5 h5.

losing the exchange: To exchange a rook for either a bishop or a knight.

Lucena's position: A well-known and well-analyzed rook and pawn ending first analyzed in the oldest surviving book on chess, written by Luis Lucena and published in 1497.

Luft: German for *air,* a flight square for the king.

major piece: A queen or a rook. See also *minor piece*.

majority: A player's numerical superiority of pawns on one flank. Such a majority is important because it may lead to the creation of a passed pawn. See also *passed pawn*.

Marshall swindle: Another expression for swindle, so named because Frank Marshall was well known for finding ways to play on in what seemed like lost positions. He named a collection of his games "Chess Swindles." See also *swindle*.

master: A title offered by many national chess federations to strong players. See also *national master*.

master tournament: A tournament held simultaneously with another tournament of greater strength, the latter usually containing many grandmasters as participants. The winner of the master tournament is often granted an invitation to the following year's higher-level tournament.

match: (a) A contest between two players only, as distinguished from a tournament. The term often refers to a contest of many games but is sometimes used to describe a single game. The first major chess match was between Louis Charles de la Bourdonnais and Alexander McDonnel in 1834. (b) A contest between two teams that is played on several boards.

mate: Short for checkmate.

material: The combined force of the chess pieces (see Chapter 3 for details).

mating attack: An attack that aims at checkmate.

mating net: A position where one player has mating threats.

mating sacrifice: A material sacrifice made to achieve checkmate.

mechanical move: A move made with little thought because it seems to be obvious.

middlegame: The part of a chess game that follows the opening and comes before the endgame. Consult Chapter 14 for details on the middlegame. See also *opening* and *endgame*.

miniature: (a) Also called *brevity*, a miniature is a short game — usually containing 20 moves or less. Many writers use the term only for entertaining games and, therefore, don't generally include draws in this category. (b) Any chess problem featuring seven or fewer pieces. See also **problem**.

minor exchange: Siegbert Tarrasch's term for the exchange of a knight for a bishop. Because he preferred bishops, he described the player who gave up the knight as winning the minor exchange. See also **Exchange**.

minor piece: A bishop or a knight. See also **major piece**.

minority attack: The advance of one or more pawns on a flank where the opponent has a pawn majority.

mobility: The ability to move one's pieces to important parts of the board quickly and easily.

My System: Aaron Nimzowitsch's immensely influential work describing his theory of chess, first published in English in 1929.

national master: A title granted by national federations to strong players, usually those with a sustained Elo rating of 2200 or above. See also **Elo scale**.

neoromantic: A style of play developed in the 20th century. This style incorporates the romantic tradition of aggressive attack and couples this aspect of play with a strong defense.

norm: The number of points a player in an international tournament must score to gain one qualification for a FIDE title. The weaker the tournament, the more points a player must score for any given norm. See also **FIDE**.

notation: Any means of recording a chess game. See also **algebraic notation**, **descriptive notation**, and **long algebraic notation**.

obstructive sacrifice: A material sacrifice to hinder an opponent's development. See also **sacrifice**.

odds: See **handicap**.

Olympiad: Tournaments organized by FIDE, now held every two years, in which teams from FIDE member countries compete for gold, silver, and bronze medals. The first Chess Olympiad was held in London in 1927. The first Olympiad for women chess players was held in 1957.

open file: A file that has no pawns. Sometimes called an *open line*. See also **file**.

open game: A term usually used to denote games that begin 1. e4 e5 and are characterized by piece mobility. See also **closed game**.

open tournament: A tournament that is open to any player.

opening: The beginning part of a chess game, during which the players develop all or most of their pieces. Head to Chapter 13 for info on the opening. See also *middlegame* and *endgame*.

opposite-colored bishops: See *bishops of opposite color*.

opposition: A position where the two kings are on the same rank, file, or diagonal. When only one square separates the kings, they're said to be in direct opposition. When three to five squares separate them, they're said to be in distant opposition. A player is said to "have the opposition" if the kings are in direct opposition and her opponent must move, thus allowing the player with the opposition to advance her king.

Orangutan: 1. b4. Also known as *Sokolsky's Opening, Polish Opening,* and *Polish Attack.*

organic weakness: Any permanent imperfection in a pawn structure.

outpost: A square on the fifth, sixth, or seventh rank that a pawn is guarding and that an enemy pawn can't attack.

outside passed pawn: A passed pawn away from most of the other pawns on the board.

over the board: A description of games played face to face, as opposed to correspondence chess.

overload: A situation where a pawn or piece must perform too many defensive functions and a weakness is created.

overprotection: Aaron Nimzowitsch's concept of concentrating many pieces and/or pawns — even more than may seem necessary — on an important square. This technique creates a strong square that interacts beneficially with the overprotecting pieces.

pairings: A listing of who plays whom at a tournament.

passed pawn: A pawn that has no enemy pawn opposing it on its own file or on any immediately adjacent file.

passive: (a) A description of a move that contains no threats; (b) A description of a piece with limited mobility — in other words, a piece that isn't active. See also *active*.

patzer: A weak player (taken from German). Sometimes used more specifically to describe a weak player who either doesn't recognize his deficiencies or who may boast of his ability.

pawn chain: A diagonal set of pawns that protect each other.

pawn formation: A pawn configuration associated with a particular opening. See Chapters 9 and 10 for more on pawn formations.

pawn grabbing: An insulting term to describe the act of winning pawns at the expense of development or countering an opponent's attack. Also known as *pawn snatching.*

pawn storm: The general advance of two or more connected pawns. A pawn storm may be employed to attack the king, to promote one of the pawns, or to keep some of the opponents' pieces away from another part of the board, among other things. Also known as a *pawn push,* a *pawn roller,* or a *steam-roller.*

pawn structure: A description of the overall position of one player's pawns on the board. Consult Chapter 3 for information on pawn structures.

perpetual check: A position where one player can continue to place his opponent's king in check without threatening checkmate. Such a game is drawn because either the player with perpetual check will eventually be able to make a threefold repetition of the position, or both players will agree to a draw. See also ***check, checkmate***, and ***draw***.

phalanx: A pawn structure where two or more pawns of the same color are side by side — in other words, on the same rank and on adjacent files. See also ***pawn structure***.

piece: A king, queen, rook, bishop, or knight. See Chapter 2 for an introduction to all the pieces and their powers.

pin: A piece or pawn that is immobilized because it stands between its king (or other piece) and an opponent's piece that would otherwise be attacking the king (or the other piece).

poisoned pawn: A pawn (often white's pawn on b2) that is undefended during the opening but that, if taken, often permits the player who gave it up to engage in a strong attack or to later win the piece taking the pawn.

positional sacrifice: A sacrifice of material that improves the position of the sacrificing player. See also ***sacrifice***.

postmortem: The discussion of a game after it's over.

prepared variation: An opening line that a player discovers in study before a tournament and that the player only makes public over the board. See also ***over the board***.

preventive sacrifice: A sacrifice made to prevent the opponent from castling. Also known as an *anticastling sacrifice*. See also *castling* and *sacrifice*.

problem: A composed chess position that identifies that checkmate (or another conclusion, such as helpmate, where you checkmate yourself) is to be given in a specified number of moves.

promotion: When a pawn reaches the eighth rank, it must immediately become a piece of its own color (except a king) at the player's choice — regardless of what pieces she may still have on the board. Generally, a player will promote a pawn to a queen. Flip to Chapter 5 for more about promotion. See also *under-promotion*.

prophylaxis: Aaron Nimzowitsch's expression for positional play in which your opponent's best moves and plans are prevented before they can take place.

protected passed pawn: A passed pawn that is protected by another pawn. See also *passed pawn*.

queen pawn opening: An opening begun by the advance of the d-pawn to the d4 square.

queening square: The eighth rank square to which a pawn is moved and then must be promoted. This promotion square is called the queening square because the promotion choice is nearly always a queen. See also *promotion*.

queenside: The a-, b-, c-, and d-files.

quick play: See *rapid chess*.

quiet move: A move that contains no immediate threat, doesn't make a capture, and isn't a check, but is often a strong move.

rank: Any horizontal row on a chessboard.

rapid chess: A chess game where each player has 30 minutes (or less, but not as fast as blitz chess) in which to complete the game; previously called *action chess* by FIDE. In the United States, the preferred term is *action chess,* and in the United Kingdom, the expression is *quick play*.

Rat Opening: The king's fianchetto opening (1. g3). See also *fianchetto*.

rating: A numerical representation of the strength of a chess player based upon his results in games against other graded players. In the United Kingdom, the term *grading* is used in place of rating.

recording a game: The process of writing down all the moves of a game, generally after each move is played.

refute: To prove that a previously accepted move, line, or opening is deficient even when best play is pursued by both sides.

repetition of position: A player may claim a draw if she can demonstrate that a threefold repetition of the position has occurred, with the same player having the move each time.

resign: To admit defeat of a game before being checkmated. The resigning player commonly tips over his king to signal resignation or says, "I resign" to the opponent. Resignation immediately ends the game.

retrograde analysis: To analyze a position to deduce previous moves or to explain how the position was reached.

round robin: A tournament where each contestant plays one game with every other contestant. See also *double round robin*.

royal game: A commonly used description for the game of chess.

Ruy Lopez: 1. e4 e5, 2. Nf3 Nc6, 3. Bb5. One of the oldest chess openings, Ruy Lopez analyzed it in his 1561 book *Libro del Ajedrez.* Also known as the *Spanish Game.*

sacrifice: To deliberately give up material to achieve an advantage. The advantage gained may be an attack, a gain in tempo, greater board control, the creation of an outpost, and so on. Chapter 8 has more about sacrifices.

scholar's mate: A four-move checkmate: 1. e4 e5, 2. Bc4 Bc5, 3. Qh5 Nf6, 4. Qxf7 mate. See also *fool's mate*.

score: (a) A written record of a game containing all the moves; (b) a player's result in a game, match, or tournament.

score sheet: The paper on which a chess score is recorded.

second: A term for someone who assists a chess player, generally providing advice on openings and assisting with analysis. The assistance may be in preparation for a match or tournament or may take place during a match or tournament (before an adjourned game is resumed, for example), or both.

seesaw: A term to describe a series of alternating direct and discovered checks.

semi-closed game: Any game that begins with a black response to 1.d4 other than 1. ... d5. See also *closed game.*

semi-open game: Any game that begins with 1.e4 and any reply other than 1. ... e5. See also *open game.*

sham sacrifice: A move that appears to be a sacrifice but if accepted quickly yields the player offering the piece a gain in material or a strong positional advantage.

sharp: A descriptive term applied to a move or a series of moves that could be considered risky.

short castling: Castling on the kingside. See also *castling*.

shot: A colloquial term for a very strong and unexpected move.

simplify: To exchange material in order to reduce the possibility of an opponent's attack. The player with the better position is more likely to simplify than the player with the worse position.

simultaneous display: An event where a single player (commonly a strong player) plays a number of people all at the same time. Numerous boards are set up in a circle or rectangle, and the single player stands inside this area, moving from board to board, usually playing a single move at a time. Also known as *simultaneous exhibition* or *simul*.

skewer: An attack on a piece that results in the win of another, less valuable piece that is on the same rank, file, or diagonal after the attacked piece is moved.

skittles: Informal or casual chess games, often played quickly.

smothered mate: A form of checkmate by a knight against an enemy king that is unable to move because chessmen occupy all the squares around him. See also *checkmate*.

Spanish Game: See *Ruy Lopez*.

speculative: A description of a move or series of moves when the outcome can't be known.

spite check: A check by a player facing a certain loss that doesn't prevent the loss but only delays it. See also *check*.

stalemate: A situation where a player on the move isn't in check but can't make a legal move. For more than 100 years, stalemate has been deemed a draw. Before that, people in different places treated stalemate differently. For example, people have considered stalemate to be a win, a loss, and illegal, among other verdicts. See Chapter 4 for information on stalemate.

Staunton chessmen: Chessmen designed in 1835 by Nathaniel Cook, who convinced Howard Staunton in 1852 that they should be designated Staunton chessmen. They're the design that FIDE requires. See also *FIDE*.

strategy: The overall, long-range plan for a chess game. Chapter 12 provides information on chess strategy.

swindle: A combination that converts a player's position into a win or draw. Such a combination is generally considered to be either avoidable by the opponent or the result of luck.

Swiss system: A method of pairing players at a tournament, developed in Switzerland in the 19th century by Dr. Julius Muller and first employed in 1895. The three fundamental rules of the Swiss system are as follows: No player meets the same opponent twice; pairings should match players with scores that are as similar as possible; and the number of games as white and as black for each player should be kept as close as possible to equal throughout the tournament.

symmetrical pawn structure: A position where the pawns of one side mirror the position of the pawns of the other side.

symmetry: A position where the chessmen of one side mirror the position of the chessmen of the other side.

tactic: A move or moves that are expected to yield benefits in the short term. Chapter 7 covers chess tactics.

tempo: Italian for *time*. Generally, to lose a tempo is disadvantageous, and a general rule of thumb is that the loss of three tempi is equivalent to the loss of a pawn.

text move: In annotations, a reference to the move actually played or the main line being analyzed.

thematic move: A move that is consistent with the overall strategy pursued by the player. See also *strategy*.

theoretical novelty: A new move in an established opening. See also *opening*.

theory: A term to refer to the general body of accepted chess knowledge.

threat: A move that contains an implied or expressed attack on a piece or pawn or the position of the opponent.

tiebreaking system: A method used to determine a single winner when tournament play produces a tie. One tiebreaker is the playoff, but due to the time it takes to play additional games, a playoff often isn't feasible. Ties are sometimes resolved in favor of the player who won the most games, the player who won the individual game between the tied players, or the player who had black if the individual game between the players was drawn.

time limit: The amount of time allocated to each player in which a prescribed number of moves must be made. Failure to make all the moves within the time allotted results in a loss (or a draw in a small number of situations).

time trouble: A situation where a player has a small amount of time to make a large number of moves.

top board: In a team match, the player who competes against the strongest opponents. Sometimes referred to as *first board*.

touch-move: A chess rule that requires a player who touches a piece to actually move that piece (if it is his own) or take that piece (if it belongs to the opponent). If the player can't legally move or capture the touched piece, then he may make any move. A player may touch a piece and not be compelled to move or capture it if he first announces "*J'adoube*" or "I adjust." See also *adjust* and *J'adoube*.

tournament: A contest among more than two chess players. See Chapter 16 for an introduction to tournament play and etiquette.

tournament book: A collection of all the games of a tournament (or selected games if the tournament is very large). Generally, a tournament book also includes some or all of the following: crosstables, complete or partial results, annotations of interesting or important games, background information on players or the tournament, and photographs.

trap: A move whose natural reply results in a disadvantage to the replying player.

triangulation: A process whereby a king is moved twice to reach a square that it could attain in a single move. The beginning square and the two squares to which it is moved form a triangle. Triangulation is generally employed only in endings. See also *endgame*.

tripled pawns: Three pawns of the same color on a single file.

under-promotion: The promotion of a pawn to a piece other than a queen. See also *promotion*.

undoubling: To move one of a set of doubled pawns onto an adjacent file that contains no pawns of its own color, via a capture. See *doubled pawns*.

unit: A term that refers to both pieces and pawns. See also *piece* and *chessman*.

United States Chess Federation: The official governing body for chess in the United States. Often referred to by its abbreviation, USCF.

vacating sacrifice: A sacrifice intended to clear a square for another piece. See also *sacrifice*.

weak square: An important square that a player can't easily defend.

wing: See *flank*.

winning move: A move that creates a position in which the player can or does win.

winning the Exchange: Giving up a knight or a bishop for a rook. See also *Exchange*.

woodpusher: A derogatory term for a player who shows no understanding for chess but rather appears to simply push her pieces around the board.

World Chess Federation: See *FIDE*.

Zugzwang: The situation where a player's position is weakened by the mere fact that he is compelled to make a move.

Zwischenzug: German for *intermediate move,* which is a move that is made in between an apparently forced sequence of moves, improving the position of the player making the move.

Appendix B

Chess Resources

Some people are serious tournament competitors, while others enjoy the game more casually. This wide spectrum of chess players needs a range of chess information. Fortunately, an amazing array of resources of every kind exists.

Chess Books for Beginners

Chess players like to brag about their chess libraries. And libraries aren't tough to build — some say that more books have been written about chess than any other game. Hundreds of books are worth recommending, but it's best to start out modestly and purchase (or borrow) only what you need and what you will read. Here are some of my favorites:

- ✔ *Comprehensive Chess Course:* The multivolume *Comprehensive Chess Course* by three-time U.S. Chess Champion Grandmaster Lev Alburt (published by the Chess Information and Research Center) gets my highest recommendation. Its goal is to make it possible to progress from beginner to rated Expert in one set of books in the shortest time possible, covering all aspects of the game. You may contact GM Alburt by calling 212-794-8706.

- ✔ *Let's Play Chess: A Step by Step Guide for New Players:* Bruce Pandolfini is perhaps the best-known chess teacher in the world — in fact, he was played by Oscar-winning actor Ben Kingsley in the movie *Searching for Bobby Fischer.* (The movie never "found" Bobby — nor did it solve the mystery of why Kingsley gave Pandolfini, a Jewish-Italian American, an Irish accent!) In *Let's Play Chess,* published by Russell Enterprises, Pandolfini explains chess step by step — from the basic moves to what to expect at tournaments — in 800 short, numbered statements.

- ✔ *Logical Chess: Move By Move: Every Move Explained, New Algebraic Edition:* Written by Irving Chernev in 1957, this book has taught generations to play by explaining each and every move of 33 instructive games. Updated to algebraic notation by Batsford Chess Books in 2003, it continues to get rave reviews for its clarity and helpfulness.

✔ ***The U.S. Chess Federation's Official Rules of Chess, Fifth Edition:***
The official book of the United States Chess Federation, edited by Tim
Just and Daniel B. Burg and published by Random House, gives you all
the rules, both U.S. and international, as well as information on many
other chess-related topics, like how to organize and run an official
tournament.

Chess Equipment

The one thing players of all levels need is a chess set and board. In casual,
club, and even tournament play, many dedicated players use a vinyl roll-up
board and an inexpensive plastic set — of official Staunton design, of course
(see Chapter 1 for details). But the more you play, the more you'll appreciate
the look and feel of wooden sets and boards. If you want to play in tournaments, you should also buy a chess clock, required in official competitions.
Both analog and digital chess clocks are available, but the digital ones have
become the standard. The following resources offer large inventories and
reliable service:

✔ www.chesscafe.com carries thousands of products for the player,
including sets, boards, clocks, chess computers, and software, as well as
books and articles on all aspects of the game.

✔ www.chesshouse.com is another site that offers a comprehensive line
of chess equipment.

✔ www.chessusa.com specializes in chess equipment but also carries
other games.

✔ www.uschess.org, the website of the United States Chess Federation,
offers a wide variety of sets, boards, and clocks (as well as books). This
site also offers great articles and videos on chess events.

Informative Internet Resources

One of the best things about the Internet for a chess enthusiast is the sheer
number of useful websites dedicated to some aspect of the game. Following is
a list of chess sites that I visit on a regular basis or especially admire (check
out additional online resources in Chapter 17):

✔ **About Chess:** About.com has an excellent site to help you learn more
about chess: chess.about.com. It also features a lively discussion
board on a variety of chess-related topics.

- **Chess TV:** At www.chesstv.eu, a very professional and entertaining video webcast is offered in both Swedish and English, covering the latest and most important events in chess around the world. The show offers chess puzzles, chess history, and chess instruction. Episodes are about 30 minutes long, and more than 100 previous episodes are available in English.

- **ChessBase:** This site at www.chessbase.com is the home of some of the most sophisticated chess software available and is also a great site for news.

- **Chess.FM:** A service affiliated with The Internet Chess Club, this webcast (found at www.chessclub.com/chessfm) offers "The Game of the Week," plus podcasts on specific openings, general improvement, and a lot more, all by best-known GMs and teachers.

- **The Week in Chess (TWIC):** One of the most up-to-date and comprehensive informational sites is TWIC. You'll find the latest news, games, and tournament results, along with informed book reviews, updated weekly. You can check out the site at www.chess.co.uk/twic.

The Internet is designed to be surfed, so don't limit yourself to what you see here. Because the Internet changes daily, I recommend that you develop your own list of favorites and keep exploring every now and then to see whether any new sites have cropped up.

U.S. Places to See and Games to Play

If you get the chance, you can visit a number of places of special interest to chess lovers in the United States. You'll find a rich atmosphere and historic photos, as well as people who share your interest in the game. (But don't forget that there are hundreds of local chess clubs throughout the U.S., too. See Chapter 16 for details.)

- **Chess Club and Scholastic Center of Saint Louis:** Located at 4657 Maryland Avenue in the popular Central West End of St. Louis, Missouri, this relatively new club, outfitted with beautiful rooms and high-tech, big-screen electronic displays, has become, under the direction of philanthropist Rex Sinquefield, the center of chess in the U.S. It has hosted repeated U.S. Championships and other important events. Visitors are welcome. Its phone number is 314-361-CHESS (2437). Visit it online at www.saintlouischessclub.org.

- **The John G. White Collection:** Located on the third floor of the Cleveland, Ohio, main library at 325 Superior Avenue N.E., the John G. White Collection is the chess world's largest research and reference library. It includes some of the rarest books and materials available in the United States. The main library's website is www.cpl.org, and its phone number is 216-623-2800.

- **Marshall Chess Club:** Located in Manhattan's Greenwich Village, New York, since 1931, the Marshall Chess Club was co-founded in 1915 by Frank Marshall, the longest-reigning U.S. Champion of all time. The club has a rich tradition, lots of memorabilia, and plenty of action — from offhand blitz games to serious tournaments. Anyone can visit or play in many of the tournaments held there. It's located at 23 W. 10th St., New York, NY; you can reach the club by phone at 212-477-3716. Also check out its website at www.marshallchessclub.org.

- **Mechanics' Institute Chess Room:** Founded in 1854 and located on the fourth floor at 57 Post Street in San Francisco, the Mechanics' Institute Chess Room is the oldest chess club in continuous existence. Anyone can visit, but you have to be a member to participate in its events. Contact the club by phone at 415-421-2258 or visit the website at www.chessclub.org.

- **World Chess Hall of Fame & Sidney Samole Chess Museum:** The World Chess Hall of Fame & Sidney Samole Chess Museum is dedicated to telling the stories of the greatest players in history. It also has some wonderfully rare material. It has recently been moved from Miami to 4652 Maryland Plaza, across the street from the Chess Club and Scholastic Center of Saint Louis (see the preceding bullet). (So now you can get two of the most important chess sites in the world in one photo!) Find out about upcoming events at the museum and other pertinent info by calling 314-361-CHESS (2437) or by visiting the club's website at www.worldchesshof.org.

Index

Apple & Macs

iPad For Dummies
978-0-470-58027-1

iPhone For Dummies,
4th Edition
978-0-470-87870-5

MacBook For Dummies, 3rd
Edition
978-0-470-76918-8

Mac OS X Snow Leopard For
Dummies
978-0-470-43543-4

Business

Bookkeeping For Dummies
978-0-7645-9848-7

Job Interviews
For Dummies,
3rd Edition
978-0-470-17748-8

Resumes For Dummies,
5th Edition
978-0-470-08037-5

Starting an
Online Business
For Dummies,
6th Edition
978-0-470-60210-2

Stock Investing
For Dummies,
3rd Edition
978-0-470-40114-9

Successful
Time Management
For Dummies
978-0-470-29034-7

Computer Hardware

BlackBerry
For Dummies,
4th Edition
978-0-470-60700-8

Computers For Seniors
For Dummies,
2nd Edition
978-0-470-53483-0

PCs For Dummies,
Windows
7 Edition
978-0-470-46542-4

Laptops For Dummies,
4th Edition
978-0-470-57829-2

Cooking & Entertaining

Cooking Basics
For Dummies,
3rd Edition
978-0-7645-7206-7

Wine For Dummies,
4th Edition
978-0-470-04579-4

Diet & Nutrition

Dieting For Dummies,
2nd Edition
978-0-7645-4149-0

Nutrition For Dummies,
4th Edition
978-0-471-79868-2

Weight Training
For Dummies,
3rd Edition
978-0-471-76845-6

Digital Photography

Digital SLR Cameras &
Photography For Dummies,
3rd Edition
978-0-470-46606-3

Photoshop Elements 8
For Dummies
978-0-470-52967-6

Gardening

Gardening Basics
For Dummies
978-0-470-03749-2

Organic Gardening
For Dummies,
2nd Edition
978-0-470-43067-5

Green/Sustainable

Raising Chickens
For Dummies
978-0-470-46544-8

Green Cleaning
For Dummies
978-0-470-39106-8

Health

Diabetes For Dummies,
3rd Edition
978-0-470-27086-8

Food Allergies
For Dummies
978-0-470-09584-3

Living Gluten-Free
For Dummies,
2nd Edition
978-0-470-58589-4

Hobbies/General

Chess For Dummies,
2nd Edition
978-0-7645-8404-6

Drawing
Cartoons & Comics
For Dummies
978-0-470-42683-8

Knitting For Dummies,
2nd Edition
978-0-470-28747-7

Organizing
For Dummies
978-0-7645-5300-4

Su Doku For Dummies
978-0-470-01892-7

Home Improvement

Home Maintenance
For Dummies,
2nd Edition
978-0-470-43063-7

Home Theater
For Dummies,
3rd Edition
978-0-470-41189-6

Living the
Country Lifestyle
All-in-One
For Dummies
978-0-470-43061-3

Solar Power Your Home
For Dummies,
2nd Edition
978-0-470-59678-4

Internet

Blogging For Dummies,
3rd Edition
978-0-470-61996-4

eBay For Dummies,
6th Edition
978-0-470-49741-8

Facebook For Dummies,
3rd Edition
978-0-470-87804-0

Web Marketing
For Dummies,
2nd Edition
978-0-470-37181-7

WordPress
For Dummies,
3rd Edition
978-0-470-59274-8

Language & Foreign Language

French For Dummies
978-0-7645-5193-2

Italian Phrases
For Dummies
978-0-7645-7203-6

Spanish For Dummies,
2nd Edition
978-0-470-87855-2

Spanish
For Dummies,
Audio Set
978-0-470-09585-0

Math & Science

Algebra I
For Dummies,
2nd Edition
978-0-470-55964-2

Biology For Dummies,
2nd Edition
978-0-470-59875-7

Calculus For Dummies
978-0-7645-2498-1

Chemistry For Dummies
978-0-7645-5430-8

Microsoft Office

Excel 2010 For Dummies
978-0-470-48953-6

Office 2010 All-in-One
For Dummies
978-0-470-49748-7

Office 2010 For Dummies,
Book + DVD Bundle
978-0-470-62698-6

Word 2010 For Dummies
978-0-470-48772-3

Music

Guitar For Dummies,
2nd Edition
978-0-7645-9904-0

iPod & iTunes For
Dummies, 8th Edition
978-0-470-87871-2

Piano Exercises
For Dummies
978-0-470-38765-8

Parenting & Education

Parenting For Dummies,
2nd Edition
978-0-7645-5418-6

Type 1 Diabetes
For Dummies
978-0-470-17811-9

Pets

Cats For Dummies,
2nd Edition
978-0-7645-5275-5

Dog Training For Dummies,
3rd Edition
978-0-470-60029-0

Puppies For Dummies,
2nd Edition
978-0-470-03717-1

Religion & Inspiration

The Bible For Dummies
978-0-7645-5296-0

Catholicism For Dummies
978-0-7645-5391-2

Women in the Bible
For Dummies
978-0-7645-8475-6

Self-Help & Relationship

Anger Management
For Dummies
978-0-470-03715-7

Overcoming Anxiety
For Dummies,
2nd Edition
978-0-470-57441-6

Sports

Baseball
For Dummies,
3rd Edition
978-0-7645-7537-2

Basketball
For Dummies,
2nd Edition
978-0-7645-5248-9

Golf For Dummies,
3rd Edition
978-0-471-76871-5

Web Development

Web Design
All-in-One
For Dummies
978-0-470-41796-6

Web Sites
Do-It-Yourself
For Dummies,
2nd Edition
978-0-470-56520-9

Windows 7

Windows 7
For Dummies
978-0-470-49743-2

Windows 7
For Dummies,
Book + DVD Bundle
978-0-470-52398-8

Windows 7 All-in-One
For Dummies
978-0-470-48763-1

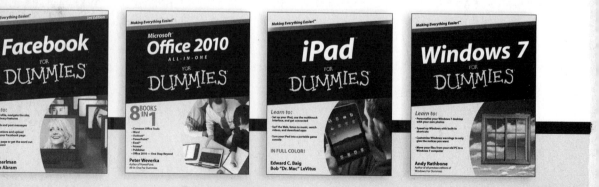

Available wherever books are sold. For more information or to order direct: U.S. customers visit www.dummies.com or call 1-877-762-2974.
U.K. customers visit www.wileyeurope.com or call (0) 1243 843291. Canadian customers visit www.wiley.ca or call 1-800-567-4797.